I0813010

IMAGES
of America

AROUND ORANGE

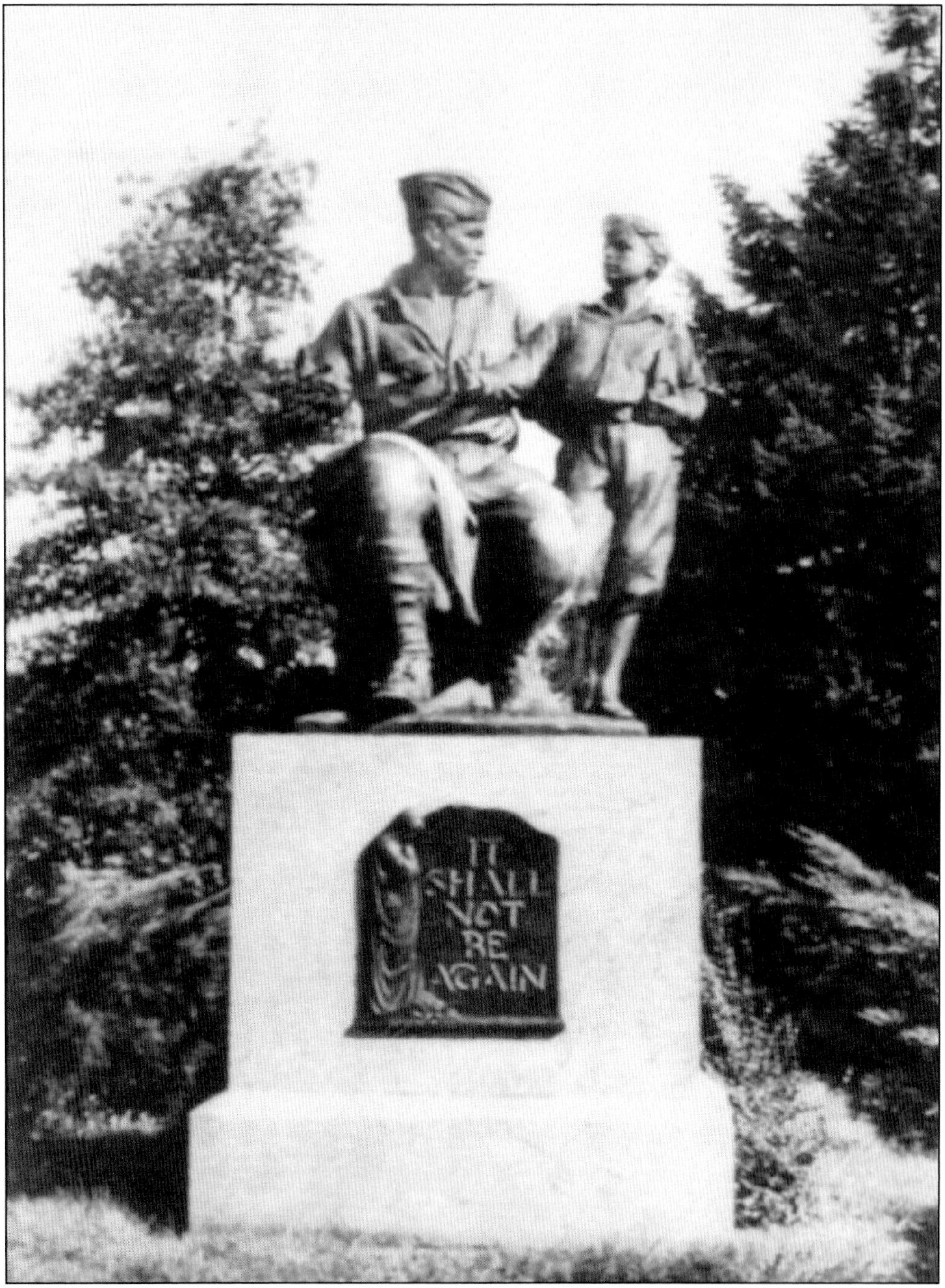

Joseph Pollia of New York sculpted the statue that stands in Memorial Park. It was dedicated on Memorial Day, 1934. Referring to World War I, the statue declares, "It Shall Not Be Again." (Collotype.)

On the cover: Postal employees are shown standing in front of the post office in 1910. At that time the post office was located at 16 East Main Street. Interestingly, the Orange post office has been located on North, East, West, and now, on South Main Streets. (Author's collection.)

IMAGES
of America

AROUND ORANGE

Robert J. Tuholski, Ph.D.

ARCADIA
PUBLISHING

Copyright © 2006 by Robert J. Tuholski, Ph.D.
ISBN 978-0-7385-4920-0

Published by Arcadia Publishing
Charleston, South Carolina

Printed in the United States of America

Library of Congress Catalog Card Number: 2006930236

For all general information contact Arcadia Publishing at:
Telephone 843-853-2070
Fax 843-853-0044
E-mail sales@arcadiapublishing.com
For customer service and orders:
Toll-Free 1-888-313-2665

Visit us on the Internet at www.arcadiapublishing.com

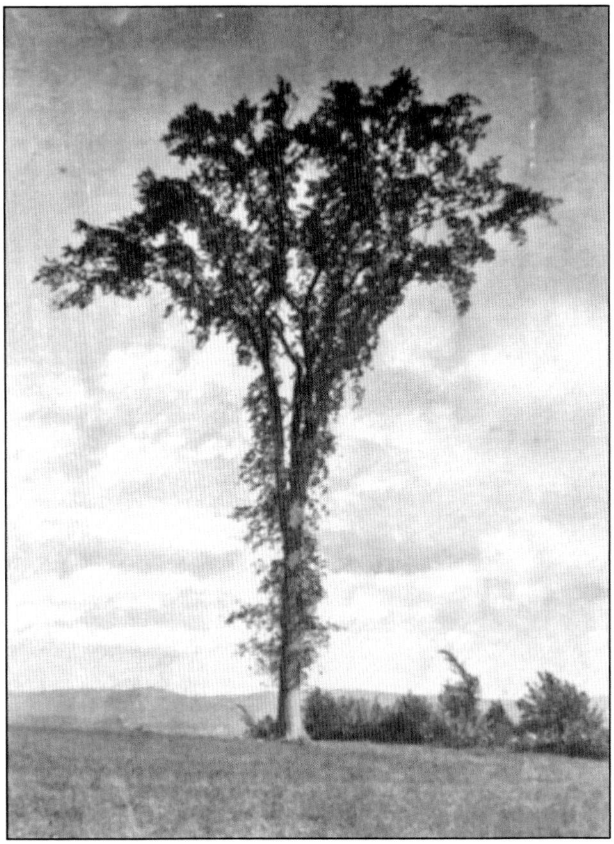

Native Americans and early settlers used the sentinel elm as a tower from which a danger signal could be displayed. Standing 93 feet tall and perched atop one of the highest hills in the area, the tree could be seen for miles. The tree stood to the west of North Orange Road alongside Sentinel Elm Road. It could be seen from Warwick; Wendell; Petersham; New Salem; Erving; Richmond, New Hampshire; and Tully. It was lost to high winds in October 1931. (C. E. Ingalls.)

Contents

Acknowledgments		6
Introduction		7
1.	Buildings and Businesses	9
2.	Residences, Streets, and Scenes	41
3.	Orange's Centennial Celebration	71
4.	Disaster	91
5.	North Orange and Tully	99
6.	Athol	107
7.	Erving and Wendell	113
8.	New Salem and Warwick	121
Bibliography		127

ACKNOWLEDGMENTS

The author would like to express special thanks to Rosamond E. Malatesta, M. Ed., of the Tewksbury, Massachusetts, public schools, for her encouragement, suggestions, research, and editorial assistance. Thanks are also extended to all those who added facts, figures, and recollections to supplement the images shown herein. Without their help the book would not have been possible.

Rather than a definitive history of the town of Orange, this work presents photographic illustrations of Orange and its environs in the years surrounding the turn of the 20th century. It is not all-inclusive; a historical work of that nature would need to be far more comprehensive. Selected images are used to provide a broad view of life in and around Orange during that period. The images are used solely from the collection of the author. When known, the originator of each image is shown in parentheses after the caption.

INTRODUCTION

Orange is located in the northeastern corner of Franklin County. It is bordered to the northeast by Royalston, to the east by Athol, to the south and southwest by New Salem, to the west by Erving, and to the northwest and north by Warwick. It was created as the district of Orange in 1783 and was composed of parts of Athol, Royalston, Warwick, and Erving. The inhabitants of that area petitioned to build a meetinghouse, citing hardship of travel to the distant centers of Athol, Royalston, and Warwick to attend Sabbath day services. Attendance was mandatory and strictly enforced. The present day North Orange Universalist Church became the first meeting house in Orange. The district was named in honor of Prince William of Orange who became King of England. The district of Orange stretched south to the north banks of the river named "Baygwage" by the Nipmuck Indians who traveled and inhabited the area before the settlers. Baygwage is now called the Millers River. The present day center of Orange was known as South Orange.

The district of Orange was primarily an agrarian society with a scattering of gristmill and sawmill operations. The creation of two bridges across the Millers River and a dam harnessing its waterpower provided the impetus for the development of the area earlier known as South Orange.

Orange was incorporated as a town in 1810. Furthermore, in 1837, the town of Orange was enlarged through the annexation of land south of the Millers River belonging to New Salem. This addition included the area southward and surrounding Lake Mattawa, earlier known as North Pond.

Because of the abundant waterpower of the Millers River, South Orange became the center of Orange and of industrialization. Internationally known manufacturers of machine, sewing machines, and foodstuffs came into existence in the mid- to late 19th and early 20th centuries. Around 1900, the first factory dedicated to the manufacture of automobiles in the United States, the Grout Automobile Company, was established in Orange. The Rodney Hunt Company, the New Home Sewing Machine Company, and the Minute Tapioca Company were the major manufacturers in the town.

The towns surrounding Orange found their roots in a similar fashion. While Warwick, Royalston, and New Salem remained primarily agrarian with smaller mills dotting the landscape, Erving and Athol became manufacturing based and remain so today in the papermaking and metalworking industries respectively.

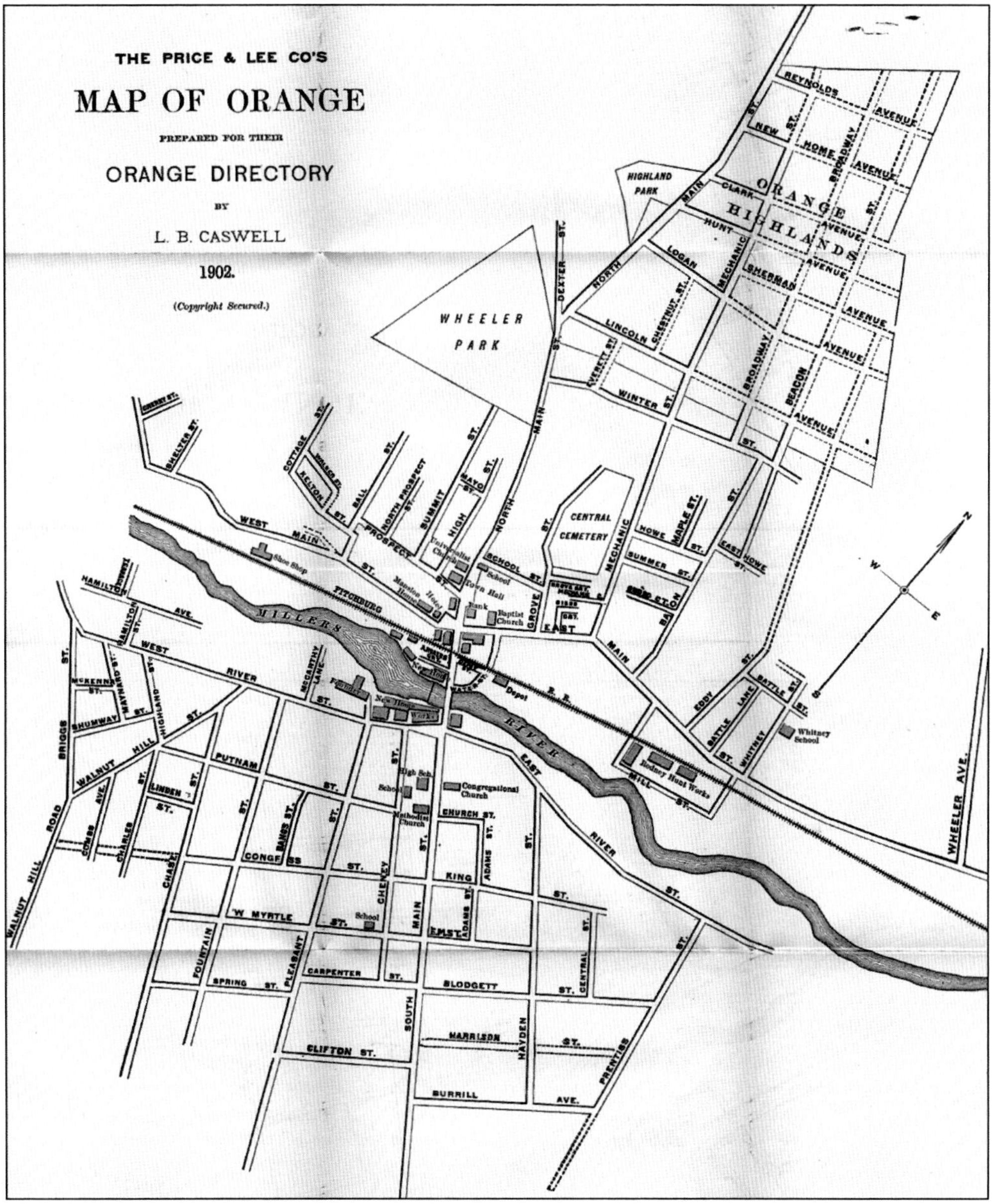

Orange is seen is this map by L. B. Caswell as it appeared in 1902 in the Price and Lee Company *Athol-Orange Directory, 1902.*

One

BUILDINGS AND BUSINESSES

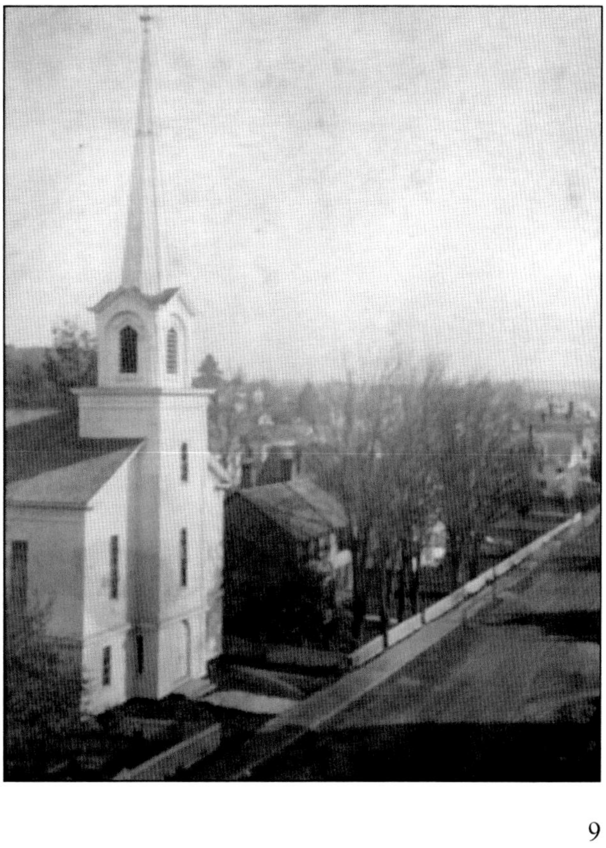

The Baptist Church is prominently displayed in this mid-1870s view of East Main Street looking east. The church building was dedicated in 1874. It still stands, minus the steeple, and has been considerably altered over the years. Today, Cumberland Farms convenience store is immediately to the right of the church. (C. H. Wells.)

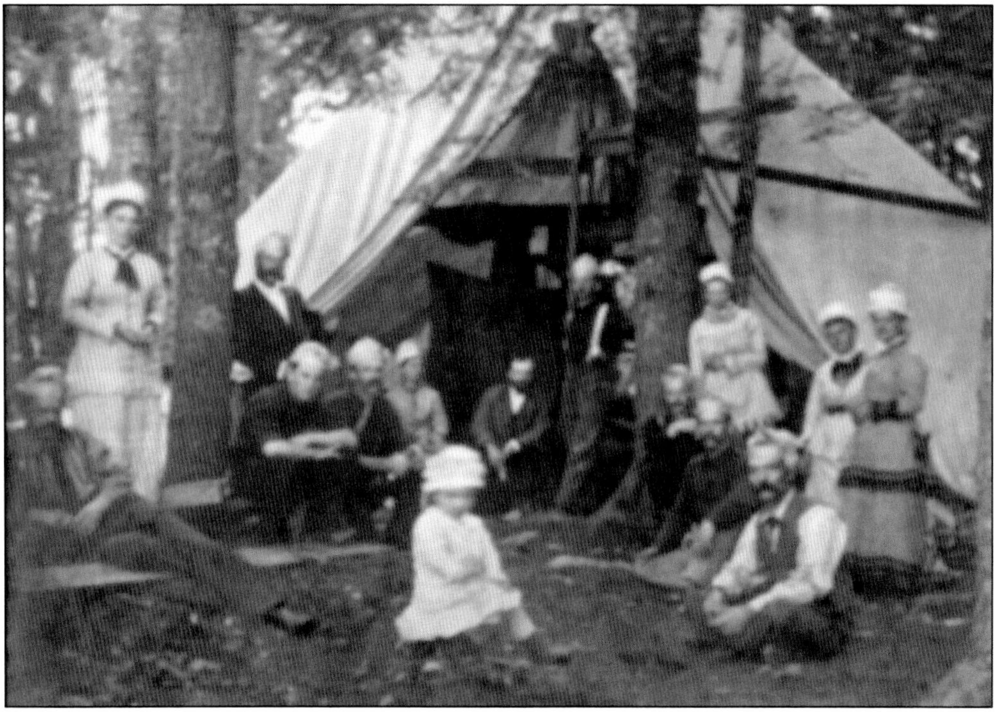

Members of the Orange Baptist Church choir are shown enjoying an outing at Spofford Lake in New Hampshire in this 1879 image.

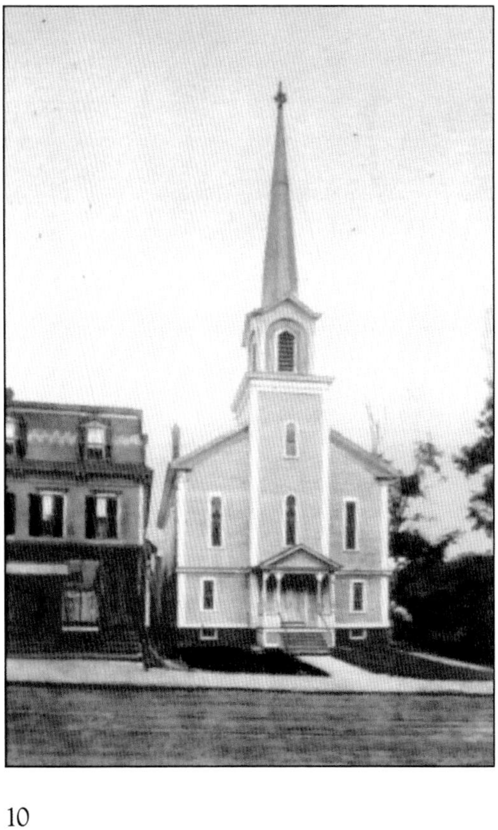

A more recent picture of the Baptist Church, from about 1920, shows the block to the left that still stands today.

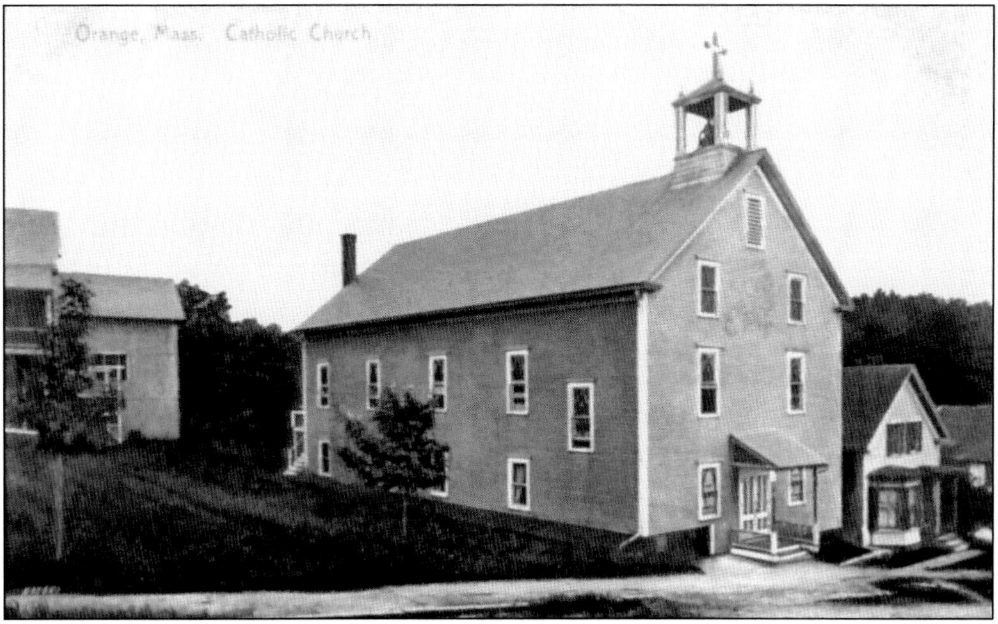

Saint Mary's Catholic Church was housed in this building on School Street from 1904 to 1954. This church was closed when the congregation moved to a new building at West Myrtle and Cheney Streets. (Leighton.)

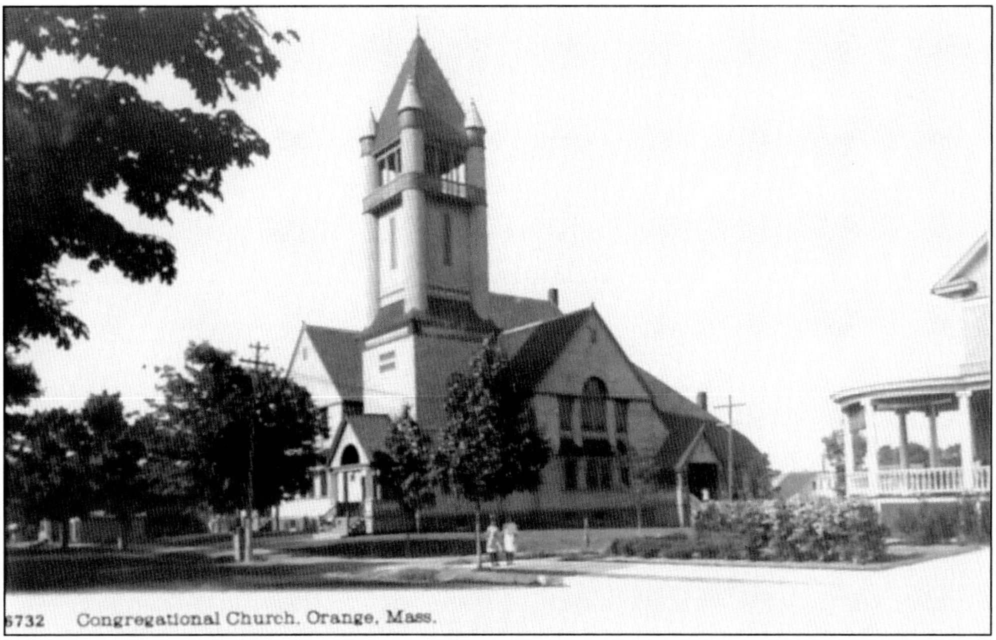

The Central Congregational Church on South Main Street replaced the Congregational Church that was lost to fire in 1891. It was built in 1893 and incorporated as the Central Congregational Church in 1889. It is shown here around 1915. (Underwood.)

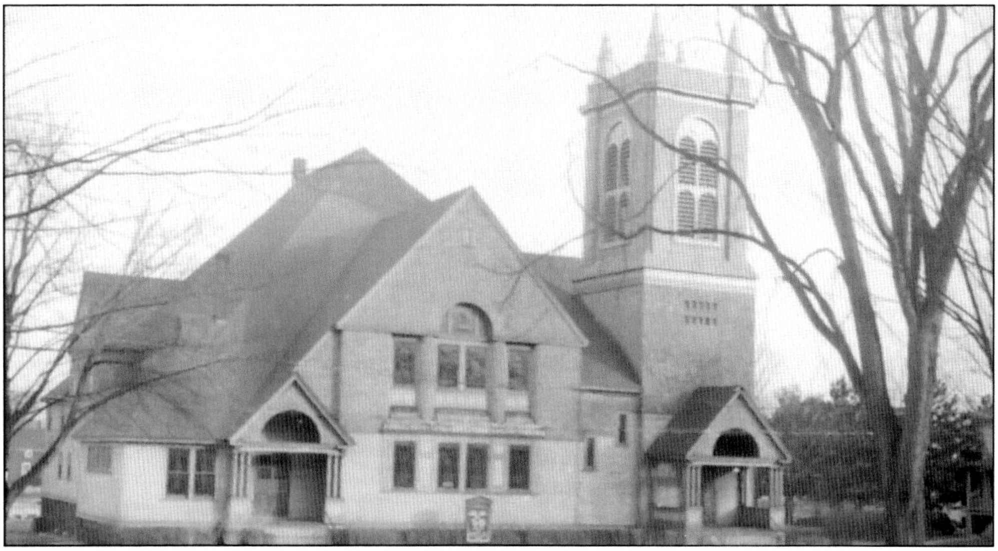

The Central Congregational Church is shown here around 1940, looking much as it does today, minus the steeple that was lost to the hurricane of 1938.

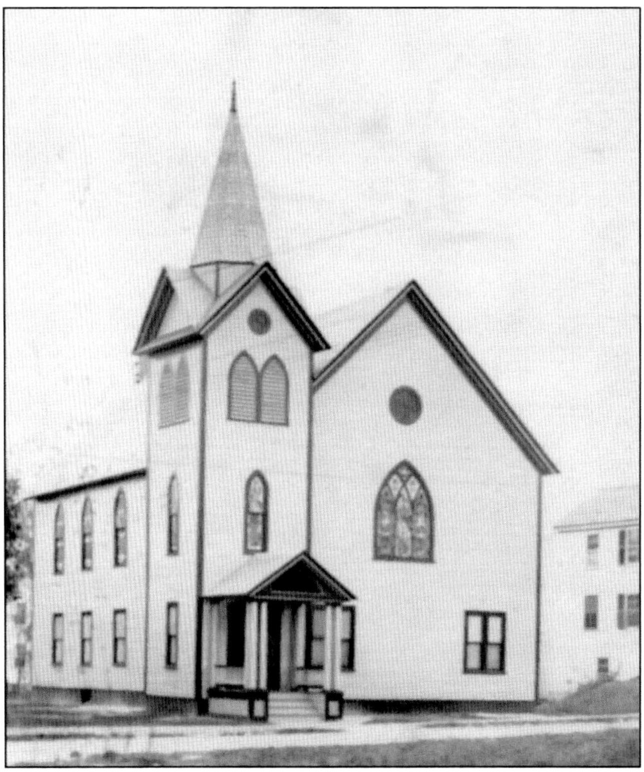

The Swedish Congregational Church at the corner of Pleasant and Putnam Streets is shown around 1912. It was dedicated in 1891 and today is the Mission Covenant Church.

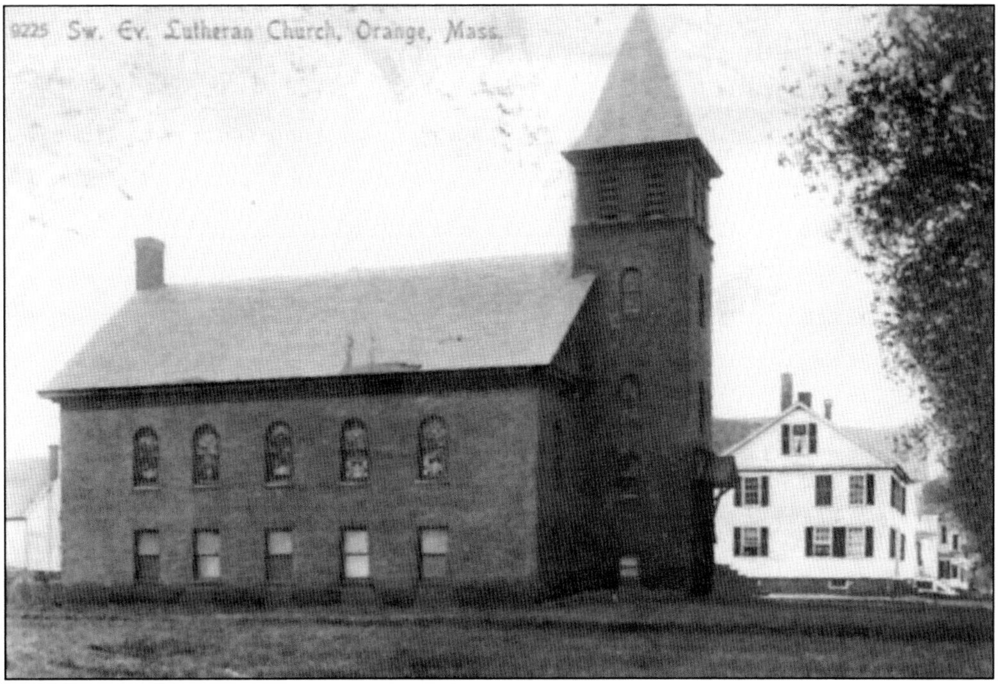

The Swedish Evangelical Lutheran Church on Cheney Street is shown in this *c.* 1905 image. It was built and dedicated in 1896. Today it is the Bethany Evangelical Lutheran Church. (A. F. Lundborg.)

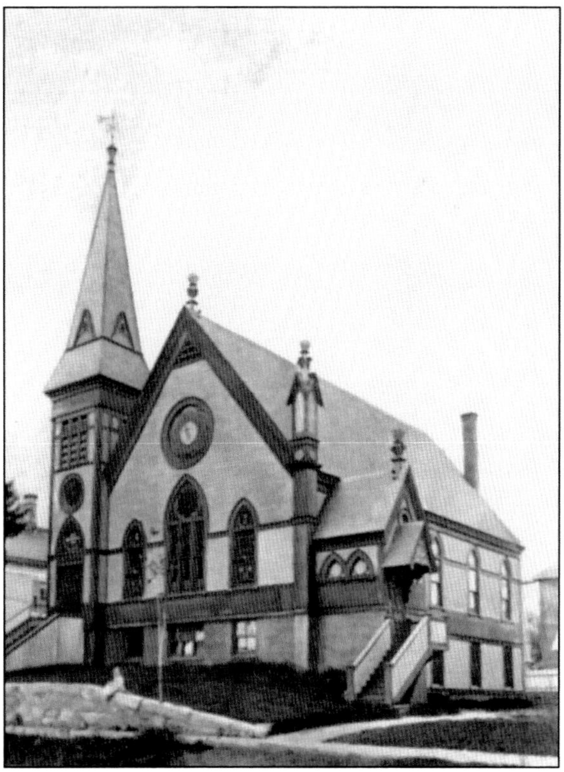

The Methodist Episcopal Church on South Main Street is shown here about 1907. The church was organized in 1875.

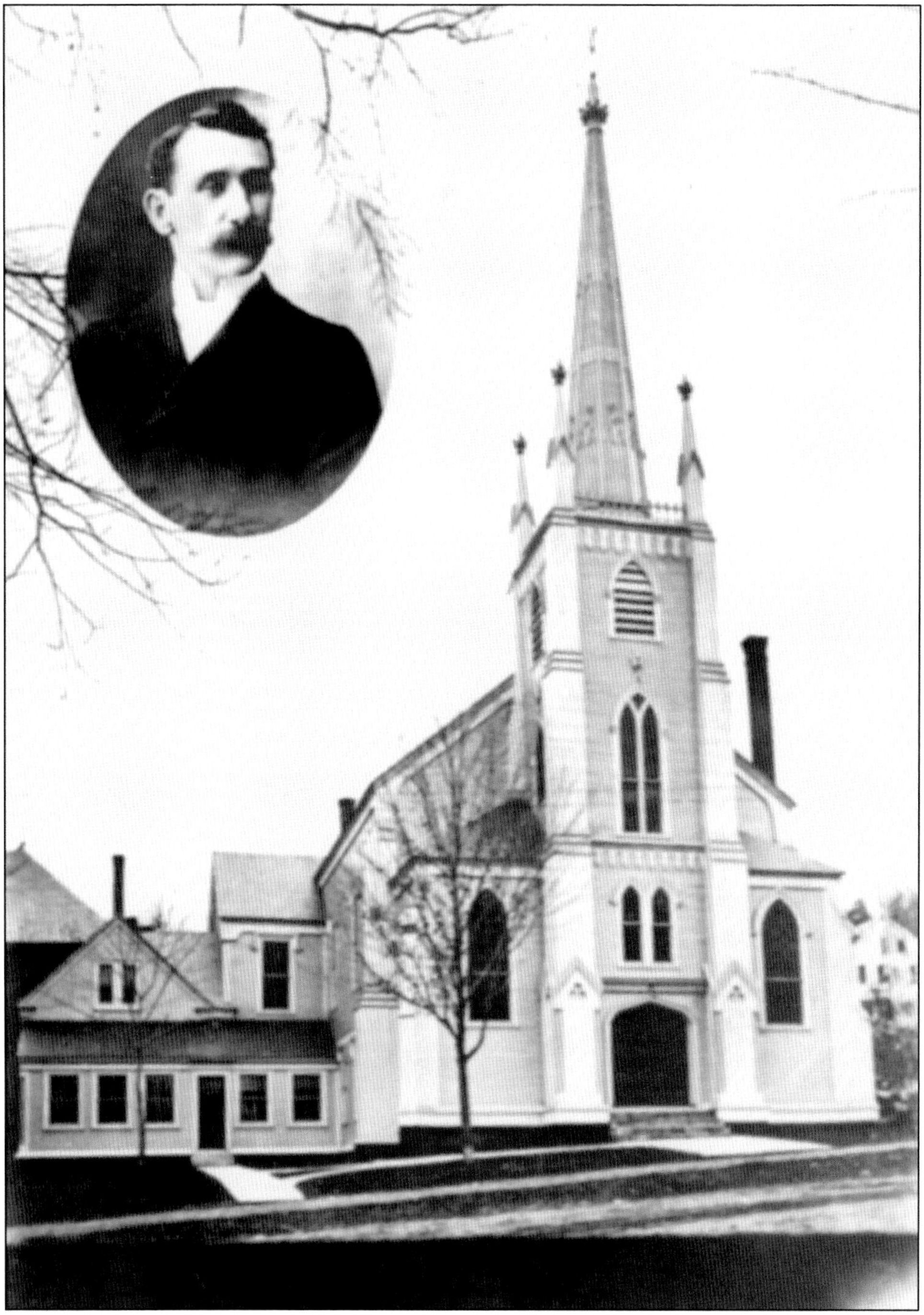

The Universalist Church on North Main Street is shown in this image, with the new minister, around 1909. The new minister is identified on the reverse as Mr. Crandall. The First Universalist Church was organized in 1853. In 1856, the Universalists purchased a meeting house shared by Baptists, Congregationalists, and the Universalists that was located on the east side of North Main Street. They then moved the building to the present location on the west side of the street where they modified it and eventually added lower floor amenities.

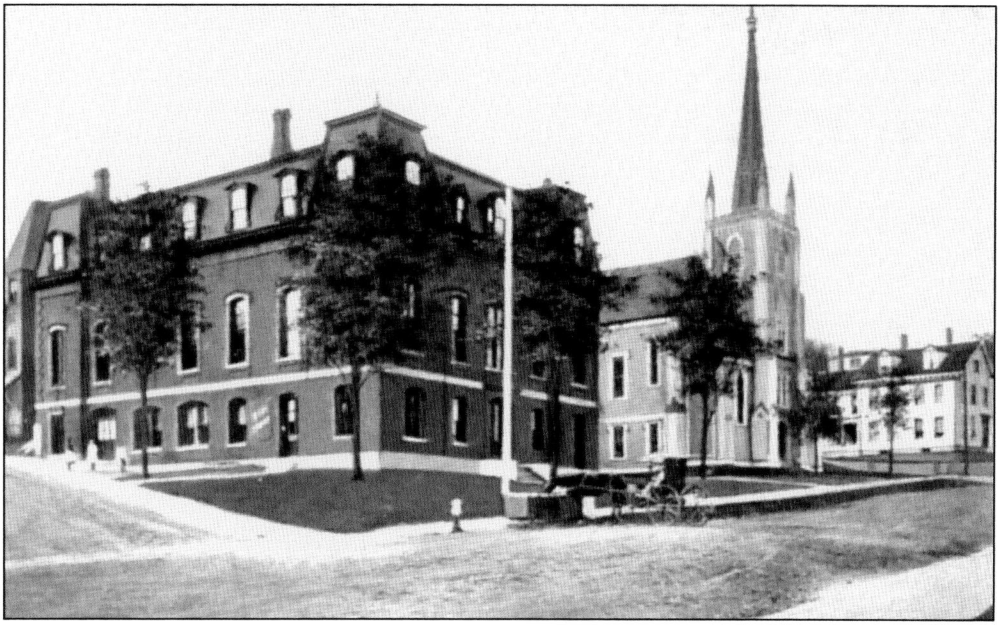

Shown prior to 1913 when it was remodeled, the Orange Town Hall on the west side of North Main Street was built in 1868. Prospect Street is to the left with the Universalist Church and the Stephen French home to the right. (Leighton.)

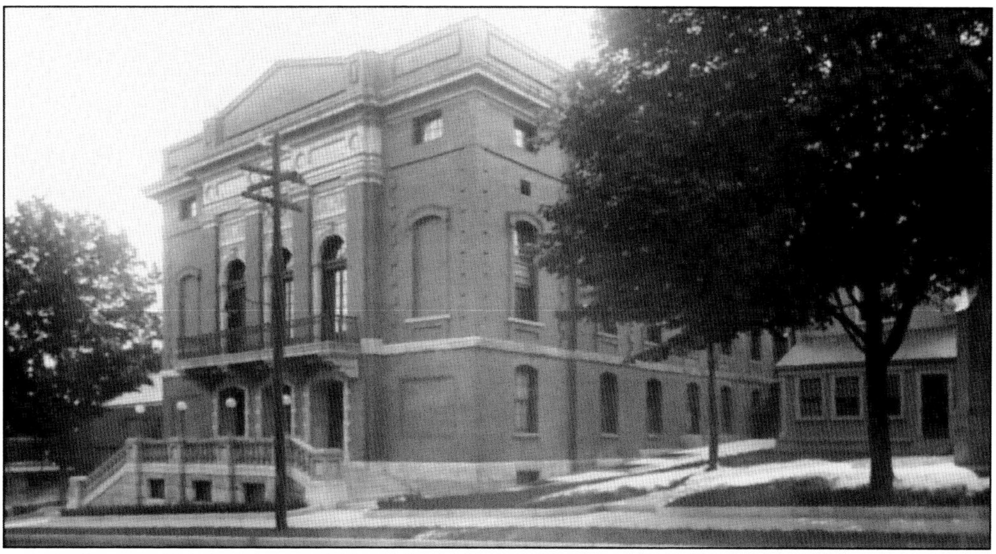

Pictured around 1913 is the newly remodeled Orange Town Hall with a portion of the Universalist Church visible at the right. For many years this building served as home for the Orange Police Department. (Underwood.)

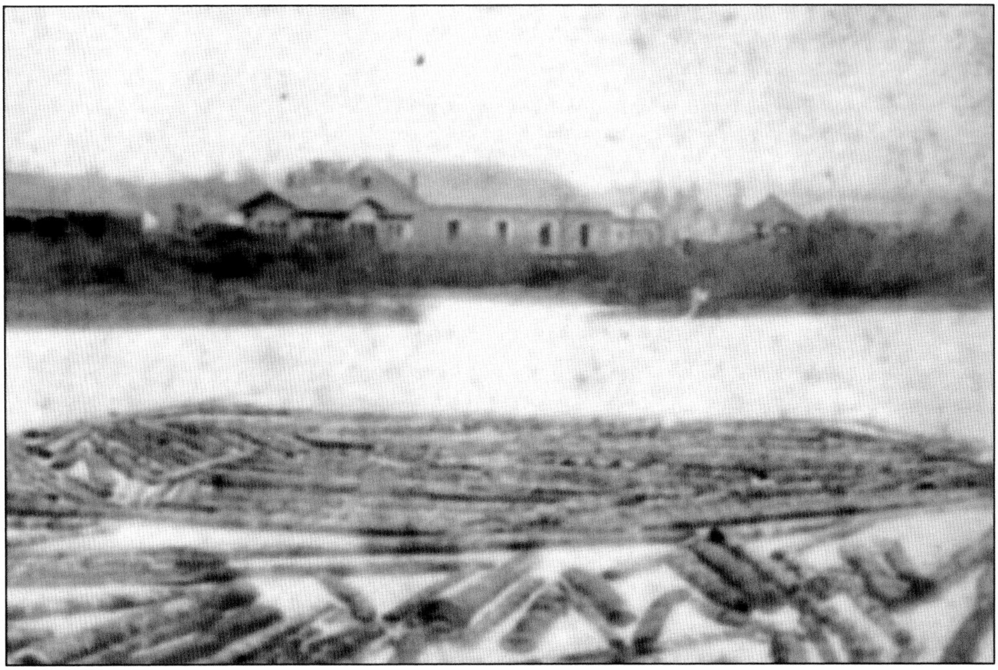

Viewed from the south side of the Millers River looking north is the Orange Railroad Station. It was located east of the present day fire station. Note the logs in the river. Floating logs was a typical means of transporting forestry materials. (Union View.)

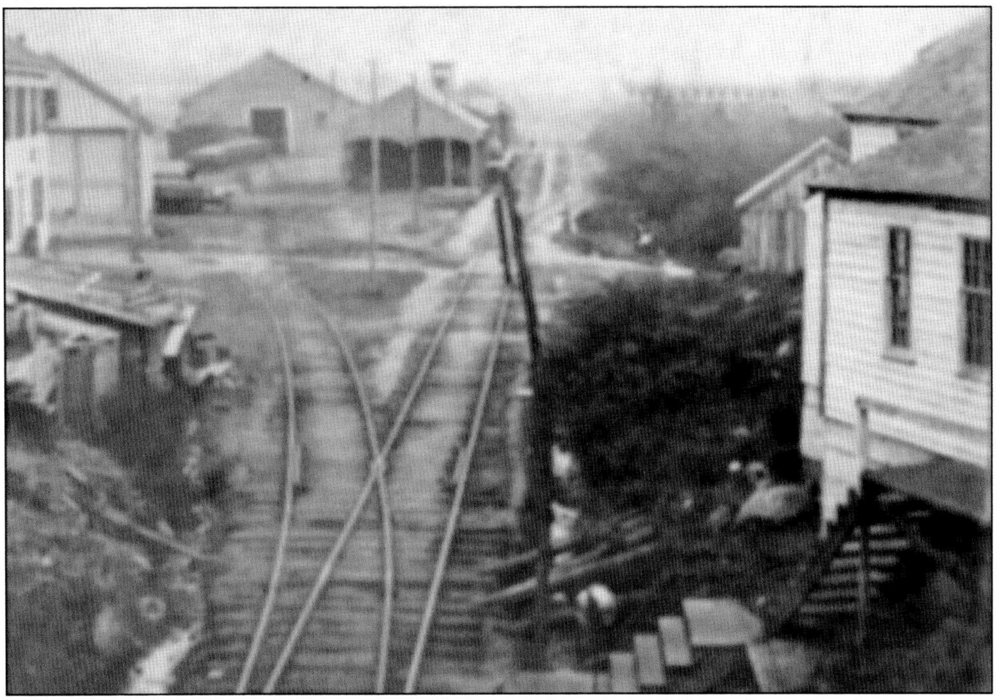

The Orange Railroad Station is shown around 1870 as viewed from the railroad overpass on South Main Street looking west toward Athol. In the distance at the upper right is the H. H. Whitney furniture shop. (Lesure.)

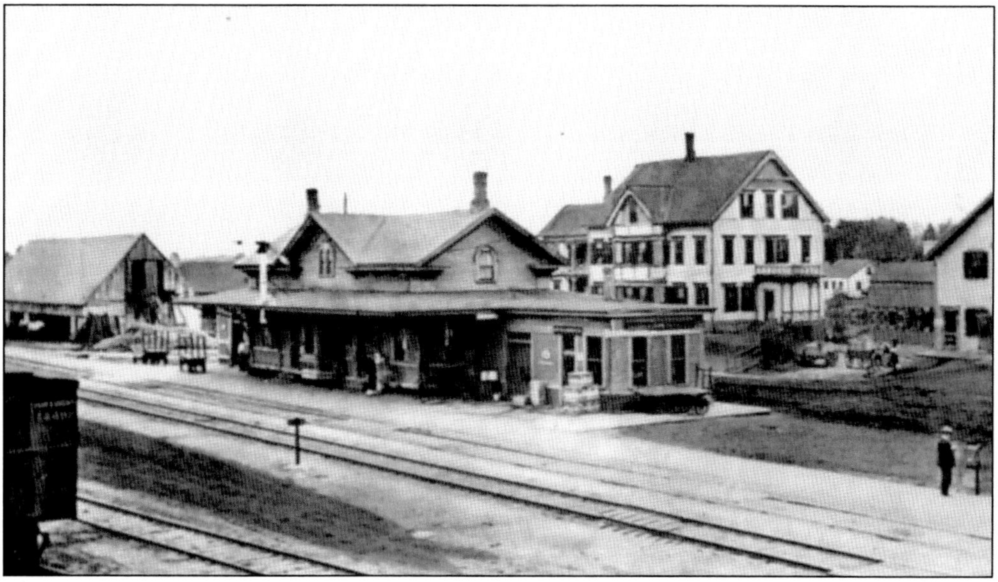

The new Orange Railroad Station appears here looking from the present day Orange District Court parking lot.

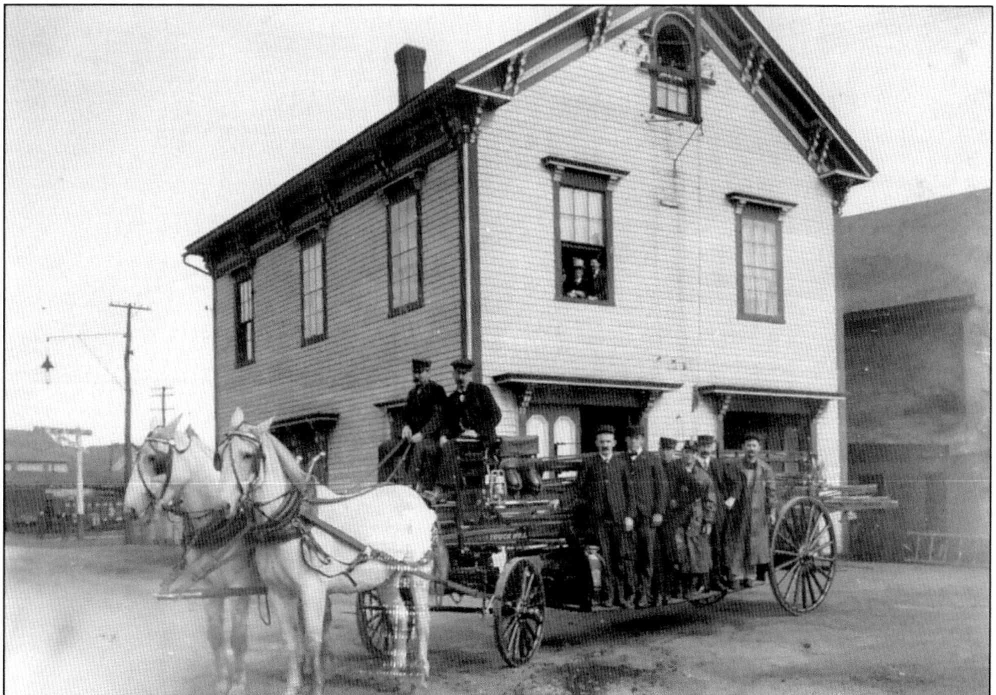

Volunteer firefighters of the Orange Fire Department are shown here around 1900. This fire station was built in 1896 and was located on Water Street, then named Depot Street, on the site of the present day station. (Carter.)

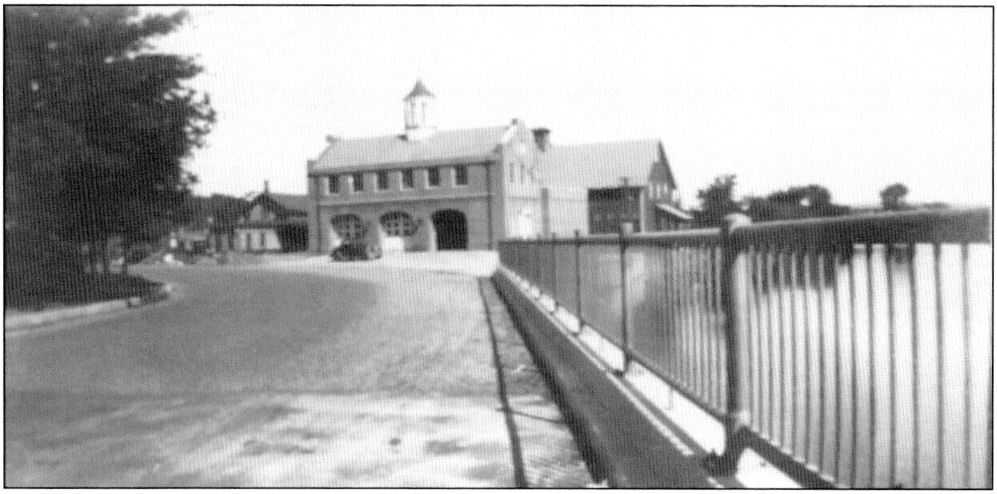

The present day fire station, built in 1936, is shown here with the Orange Railroad Station visible to the left. In the previous photograph of the 1896 station, the doors opened toward the river. The new station doors open facing Water Street. (Kingsbury.)

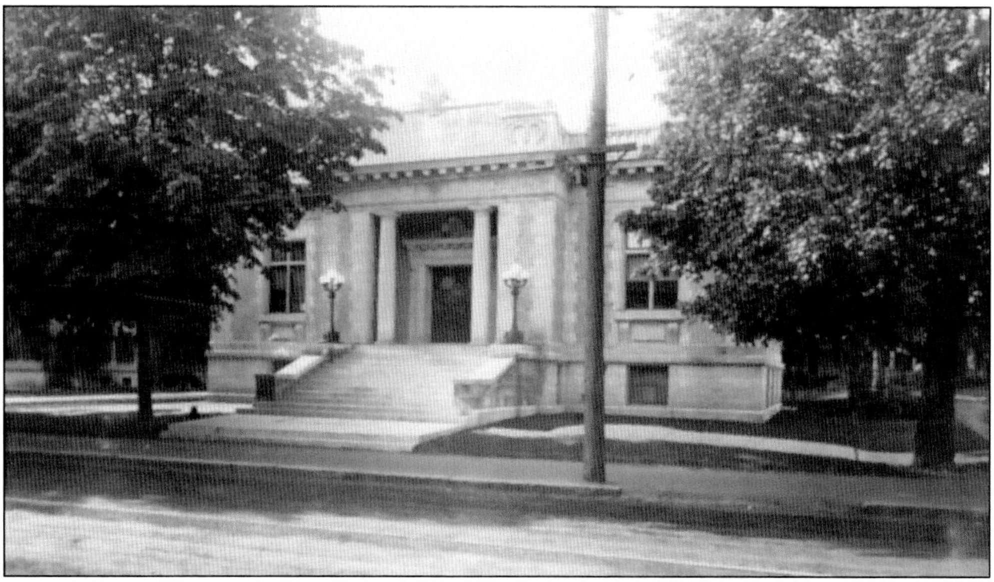

The Wheeler Memorial Library at the corner of East Main and Grove Streets was built on the site of the former home of Dr. I. T. Johnson. It was given to the town by Alvira Wheeler Thompson in memory of her late husband John W. Wheeler who was president and treasurer of the New Home Sewing Machine Company. The library was dedicated in 1914. (Underwood.)

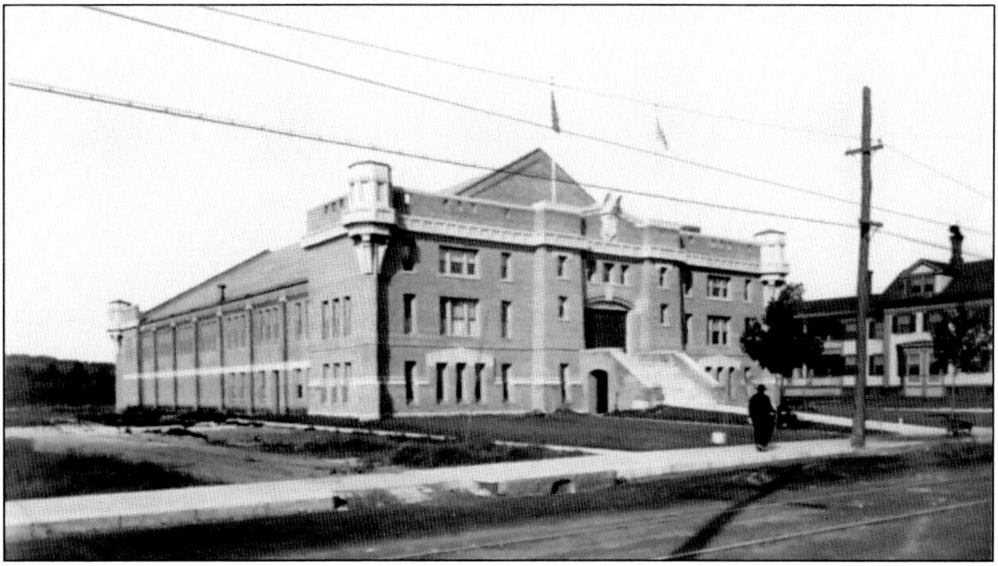

The stone and brick Orange Armory was built at 135 East Main Street at a cost of $60,000. Construction began on May 15, 1912, with dedication on November 14, 1913. Prior to construction of the armory, Company E, 2nd Regiment Massachusetts Volunteer Militia (MVM) had been housed on the upper level of the old town hall.

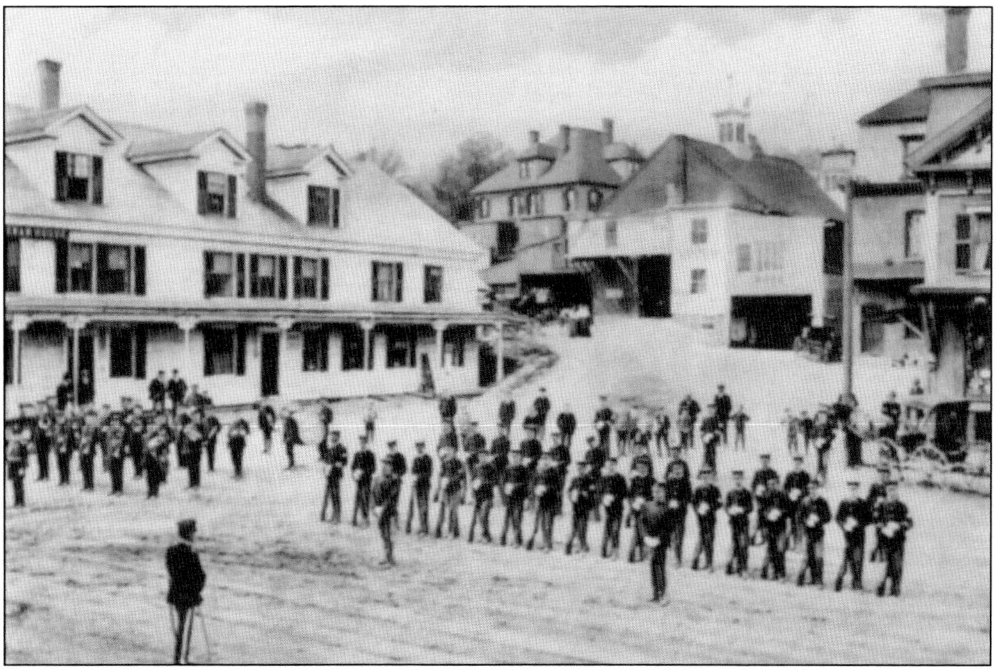

Shown in this image is Company E in full military regalia assembling beside the Putnam House on West Main Street. The unit was transferred from Shelburne Falls to Orange in 1885 and mustered as Company E. (Carter.)

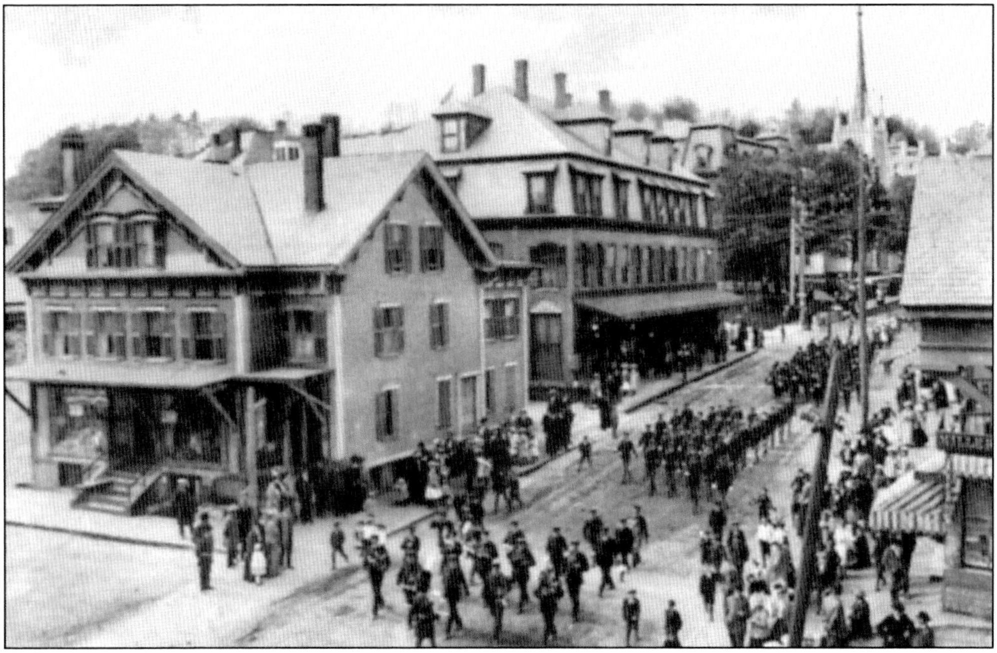

Company E, 2nd Regiment Massachusetts Volunteer Militia, is shown marching down North Main Street on Memorial Day, May 30, 1907. The Harlow Block at the corner of North and West Main Streets is at the left. Next is Abraham's Temple that was built by Abraham Putnam. The town hall and Universalist Church are visible behind the trees. (Carter.)

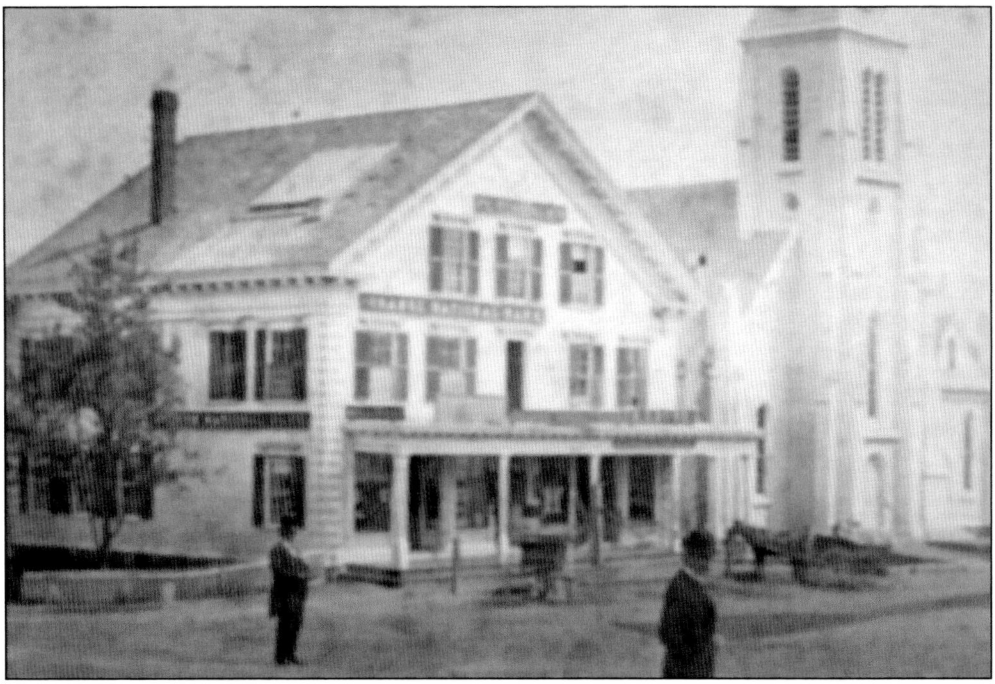

The Bank Block and Congregational Church at the intersection of East and South Main Streets are shown in this mid-1870s image. The Bank Block housed both the Orange National Bank and the Orange Savings Bank. (Wells.)

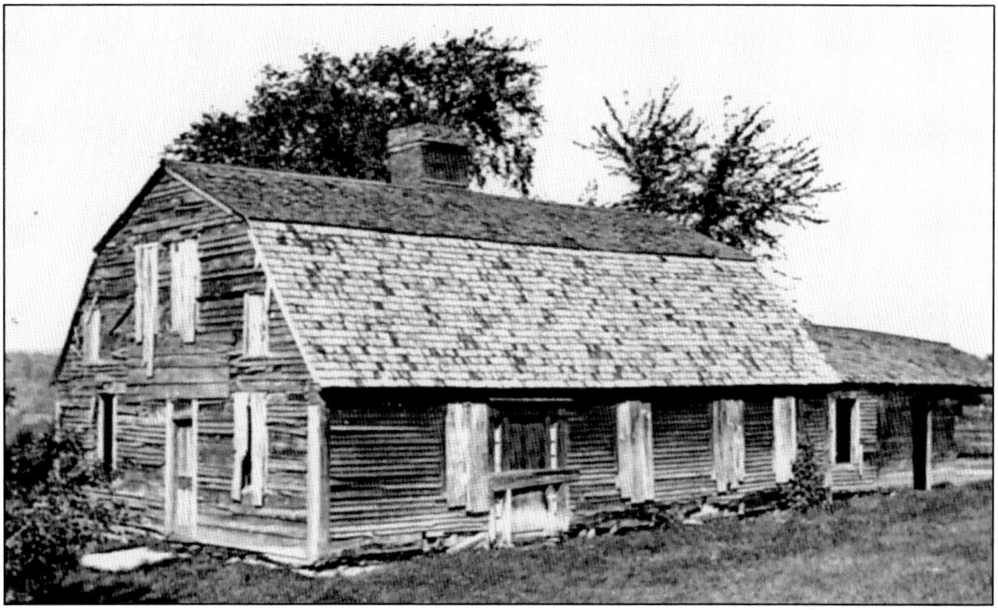

The first home of masonry in western Massachusetts was built in 1750 on Old Walnut Hill Road. At that time the area surrounding the home was part of New Salem.

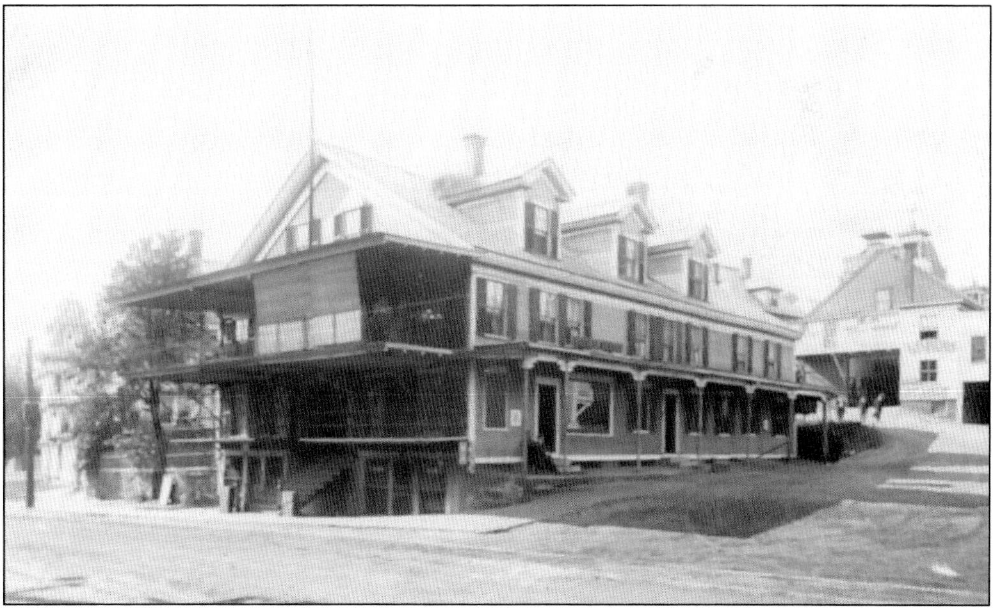

The Putnam House that was located on West Main Street where a vacant gas station now stands is shown in this *c.* 1915 picture. Originally the tavern of Ahaz Thayer, built in 1801, the Putnam House was rebuilt many times over its long and prosperous history under generations of the Putnam family. It was razed in 1933. (Underwood.)

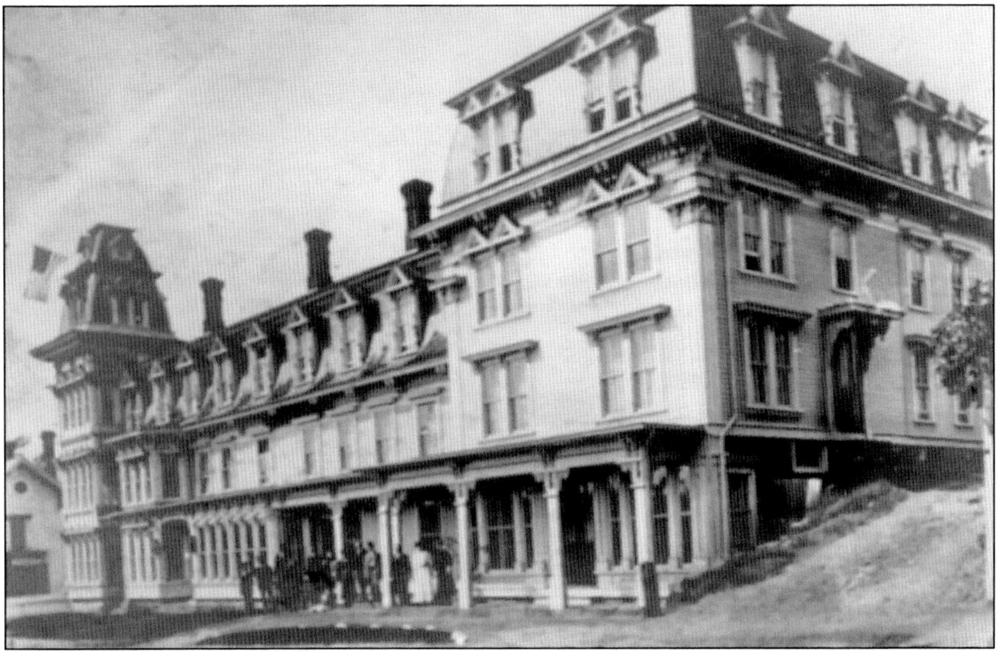

The Mansion House, shown here around 1900, evolved from a house and carriage business built by John Ramsey in 1837 at 22 West Main Street. Ramsey remodeled the property into a hotel when he gave up the carriage making business. In the 1890s the Mansion House was at its zenith. It was demolished in 1973.

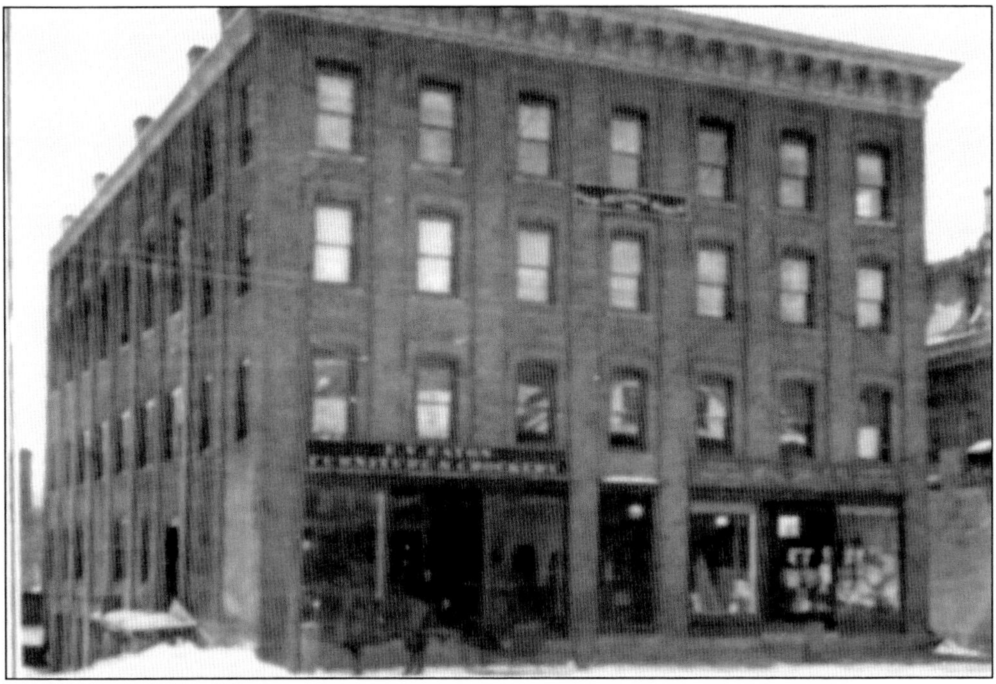

The "new" Odd Fellows Building at 7½ West Main Street is shown here around 1906. Social Lodge 182, International Order of Odd Fellows (IOOF) had met in several locations prior to purchasing the old Putnam Opera House. It was refurbished and occupied by the Odd Fellows in 1905.

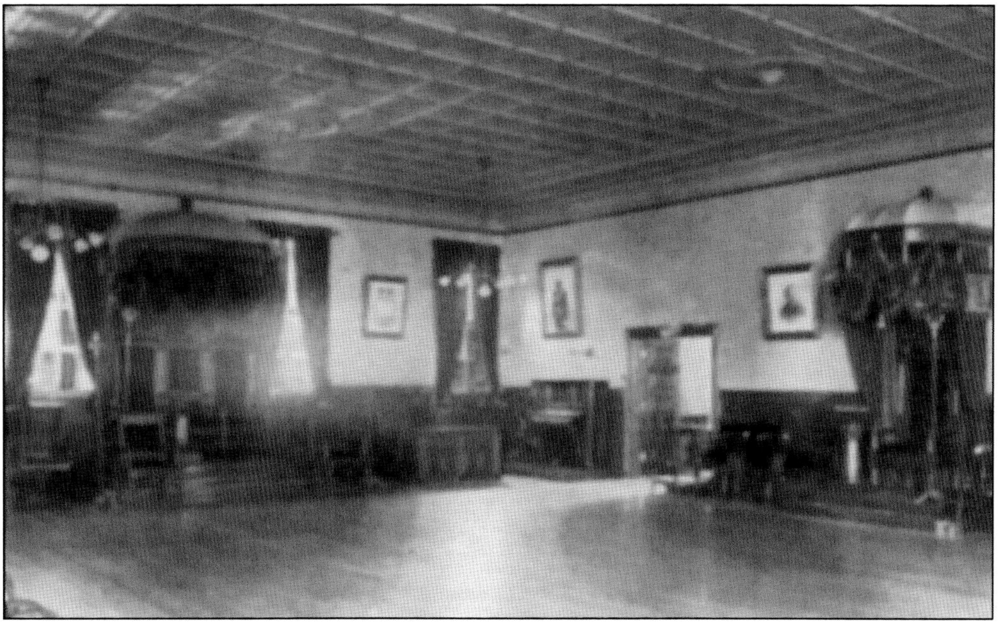

The lodge room of Social Lodge 182, IOOF, at 7½ West Main Street is shown in this image.

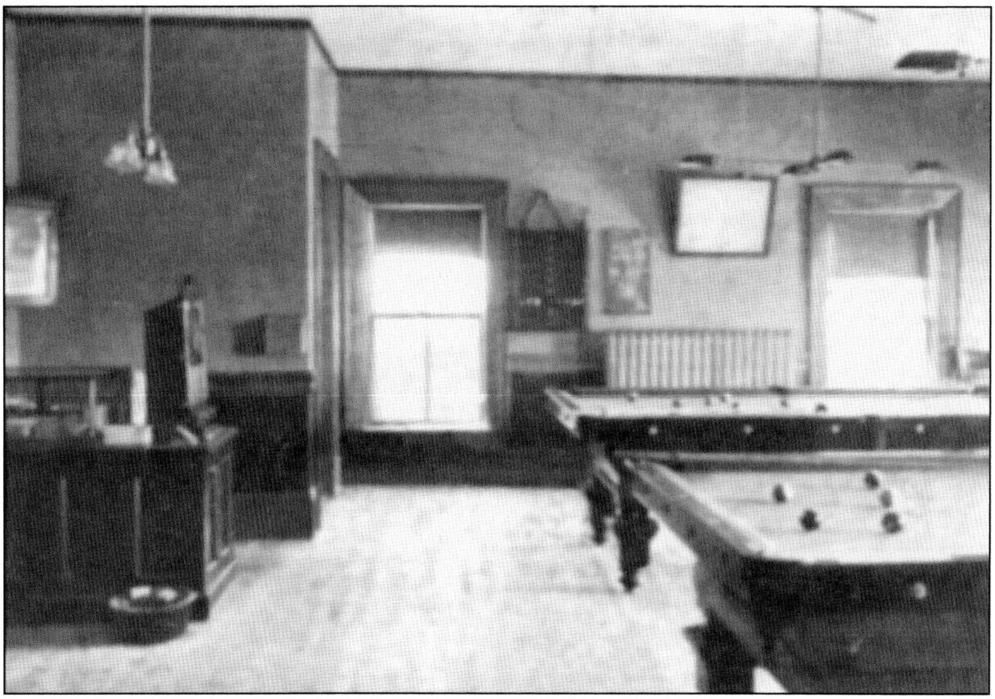

The poolroom of Social Lodge 182, IOOF at 7½ West Main Street is shown in this image.

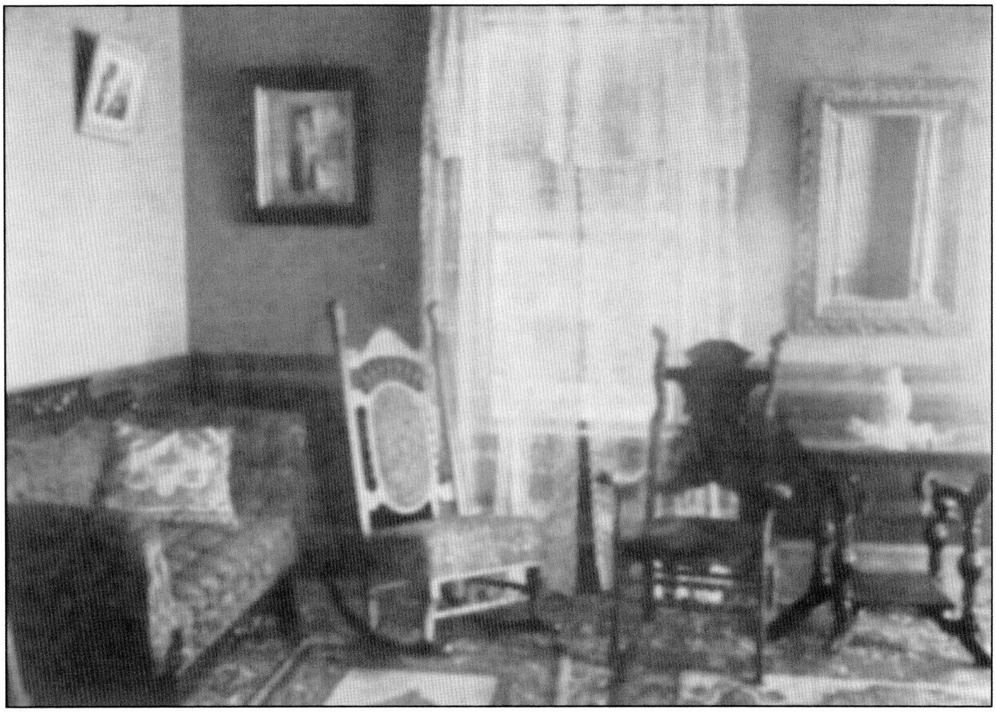

The ladies parlor of Social Lodge 182, International Order of Odd Fellows (IOOF), at 7½ West Main Street is shown in this image.

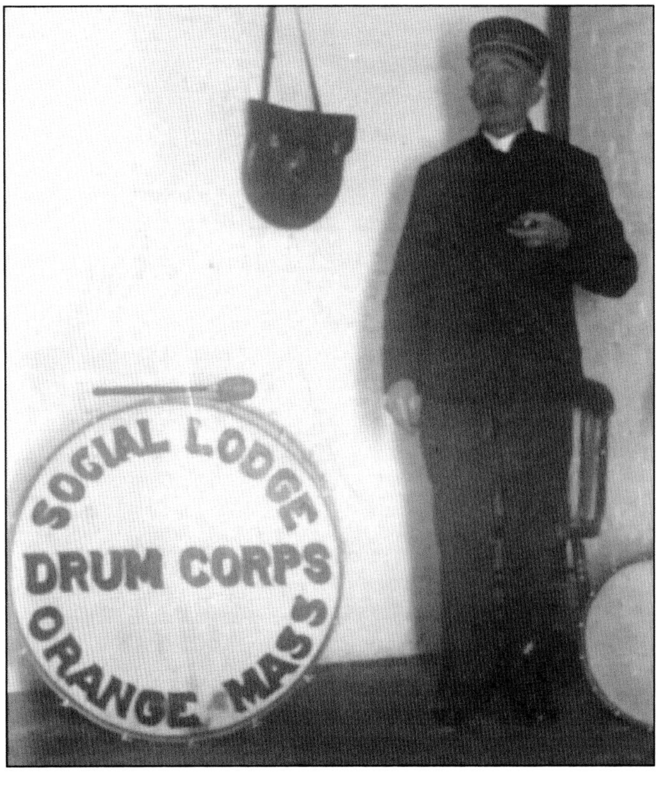

This sprightly gentleman, a member of Social Lodge 182, IOOF, proudly displays the wares of the lodge's drum corps around 1905.

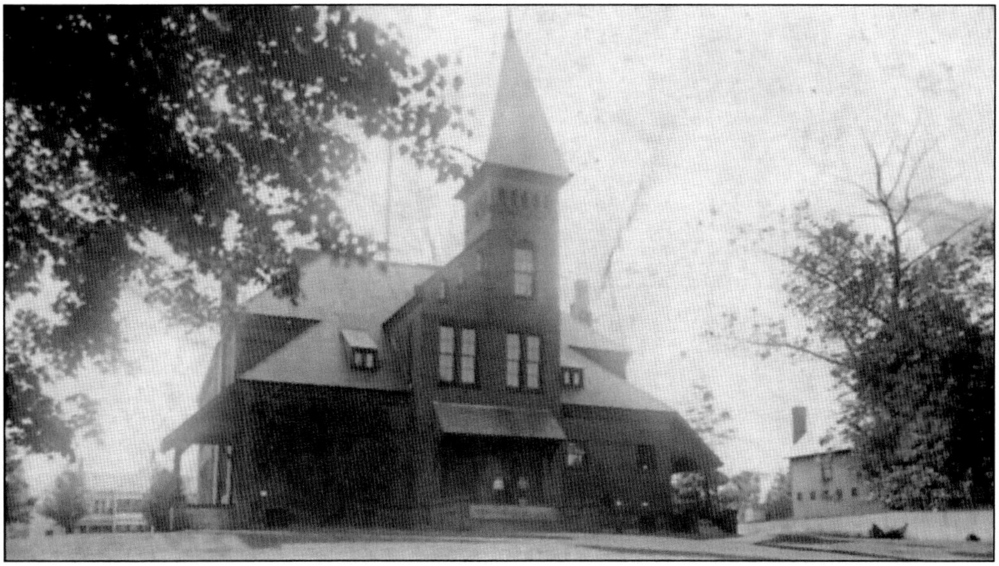

Orange High School, shown here around 1914, was completed in 1878 on South Main Street at the site of the present day Butterfield School. It cost the town of Orange $14,000 and was in service, with additions, in 1899 until 1927, when it was extensively remodeled. (Underwood.)

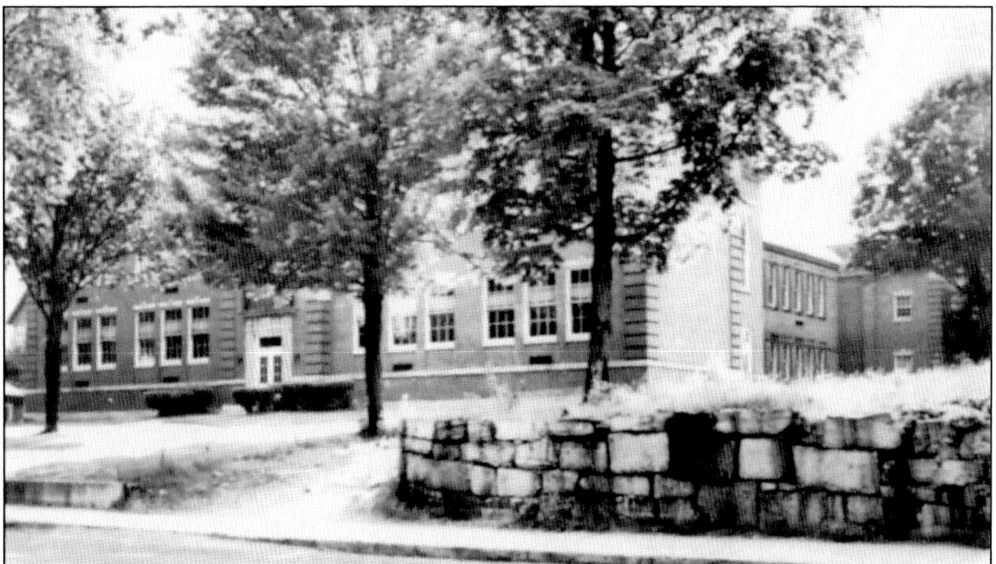

Orange High School is shown in this image after the extensive remodeling of 1927. It served as a high school until 1957 when the Mahar Regional High School was opened. It is now the Butterfield School. (Fairbanks.).

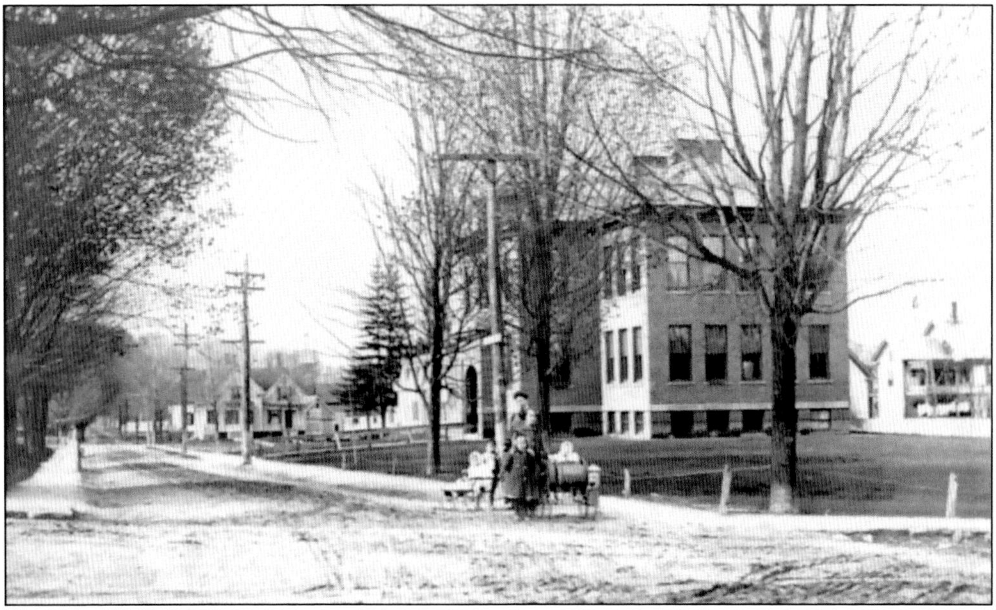

The South School at 107 Cheney Street is shown in this photograph. It was opened in 1908 and served as an elementary school until 1957 when the Butterfield School, formerly the high school, was opened as an elementary school. Also located on Cheney Street was the Cheney Street School at number 39. Both schools were razed.

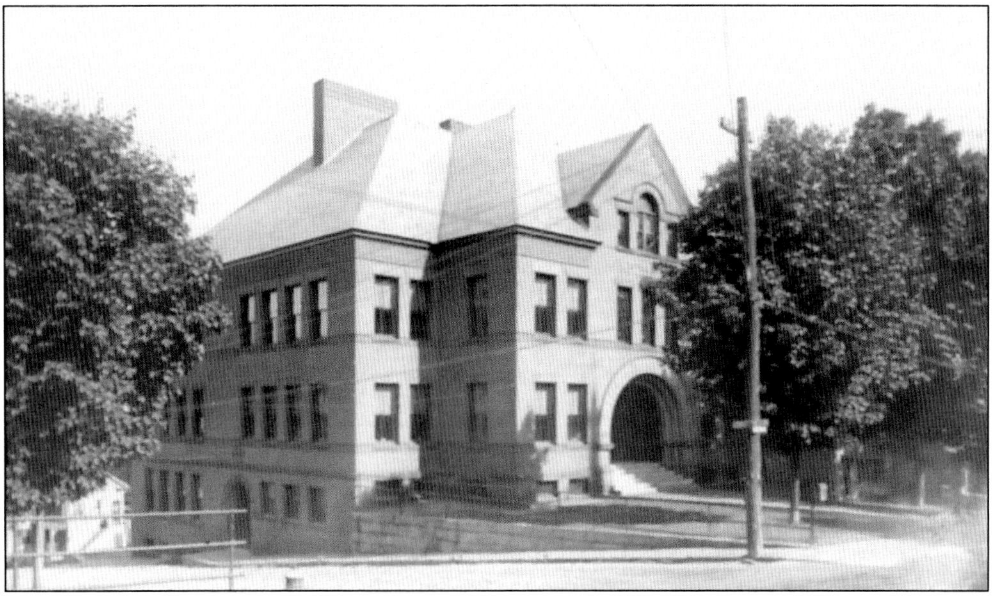

The Central School on North Main Street was opened in 1894. It served as an elementary school until 1957 when the students were transferred to the Butterfield School on South Main Street. It is still in use today but not as a public school. (Underwood.)

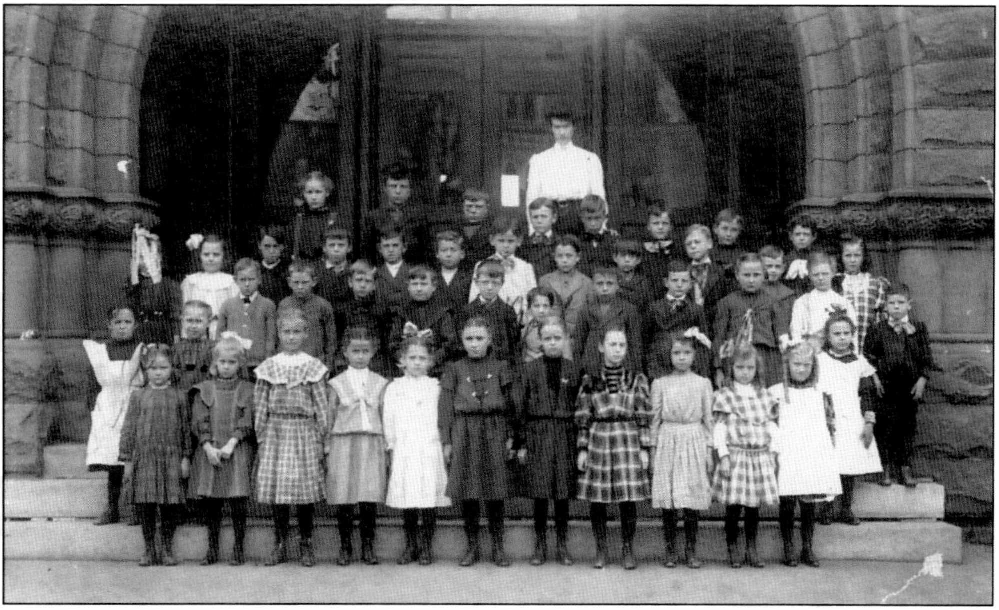

Though very neatly dressed and standing in a perfect pose, it is quite obvious that smiling was not the order of the day when this *c.* 1900 photograph was taken in front of the Central School.

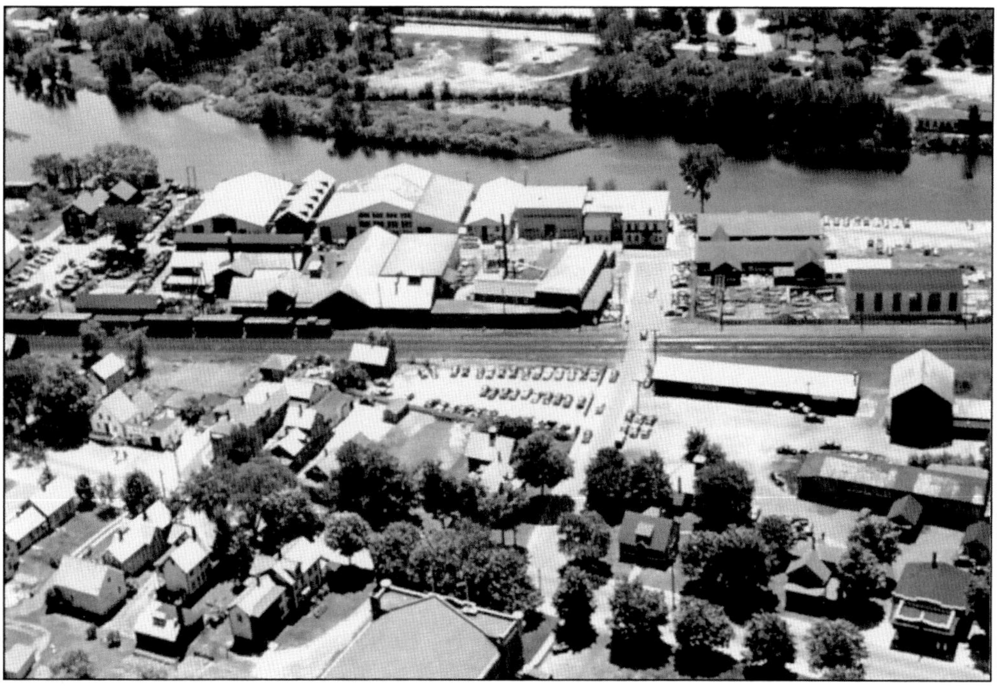

This aerial image from around 1950 shows the Rodney Hunt Company, makers of comprehensive gate and valve products. The company is located on Mill Street along the banks of the Millers River. It was founded in 1840 by Rodney Hunt and has been in continual operation ever since. Mill Street appears vertically across the railroad tracks with the Orange Armory on East Main Street in the bottom center of the photograph.

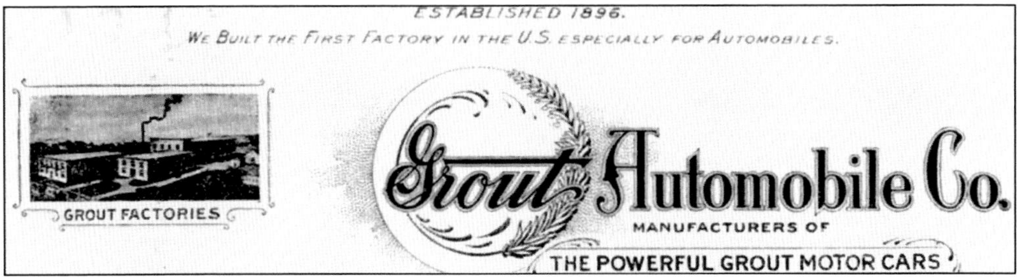

The Grout Automobile Company was the first factory in the United States built especially for the production of automobiles, as touted by the company letterhead shown here. The company, established in 1896, produced steam and gasoline-powered automobiles. It went out of business in 1913.

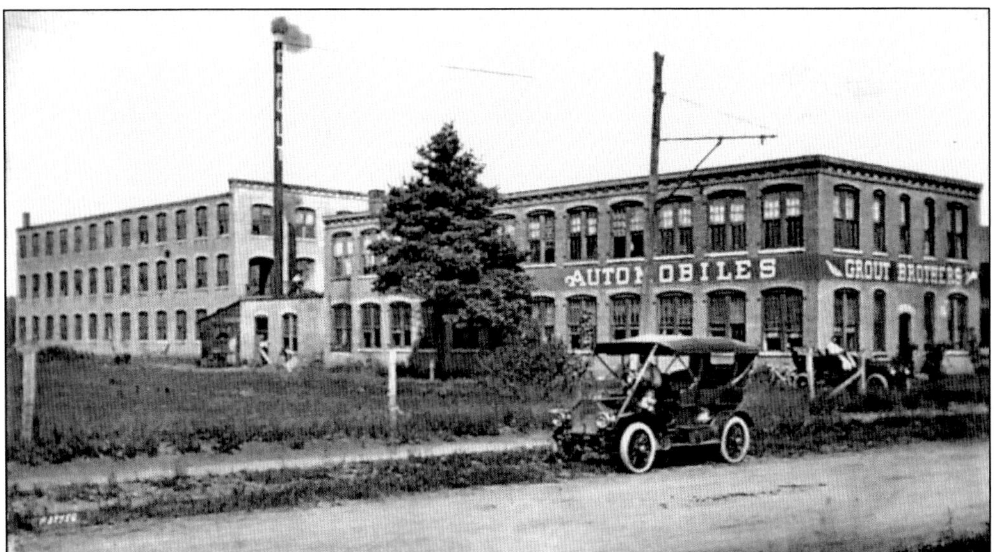

The Grout Automobile Company was located on East Main Street in the buildings now occupied by Pete's Tire Barn. This facility was also used by the Minute Tapioca Company and later to manufacture shoes. (Blanchard, Young.)

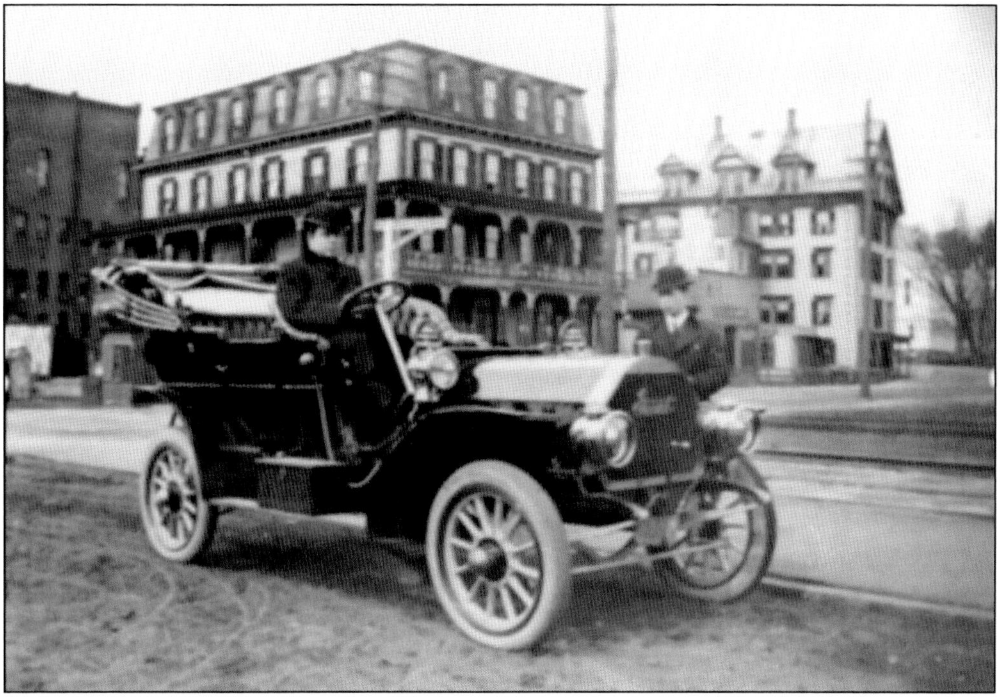

The Grout automobile pictured here is near the Waverly House in the background that stood in the present-day Orange District Court parking lot.

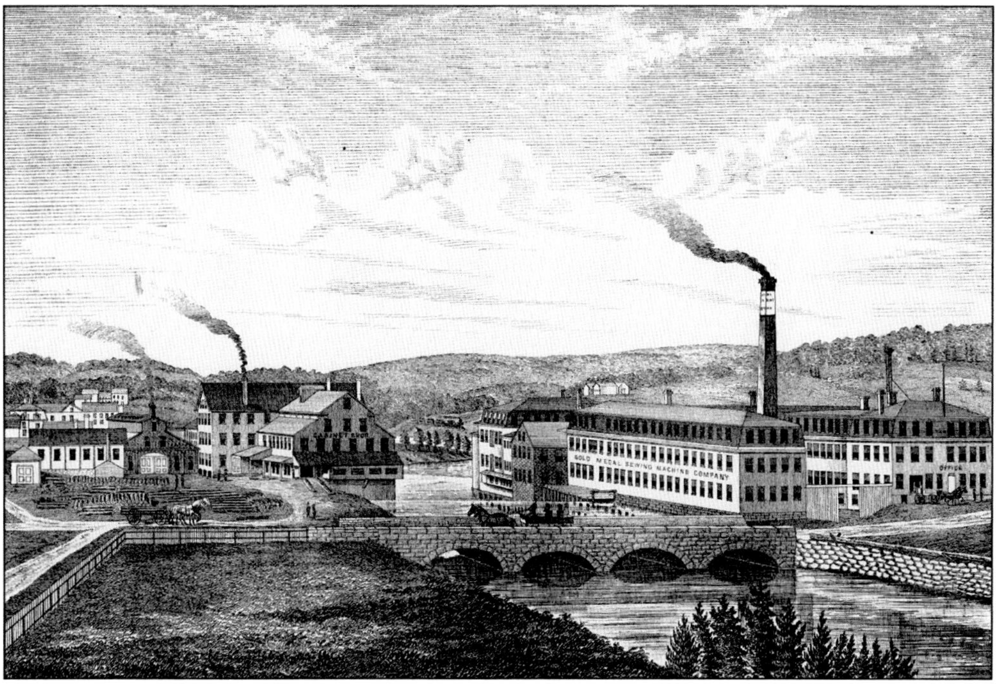

Illustrated is the Gold Medal Sewing Machine Company, predecessor of the New Home Sewing Machine Company. It was established in 1860. The illustration is looking west along the Millers River with the stone arched South Main Street bridge in the foreground.

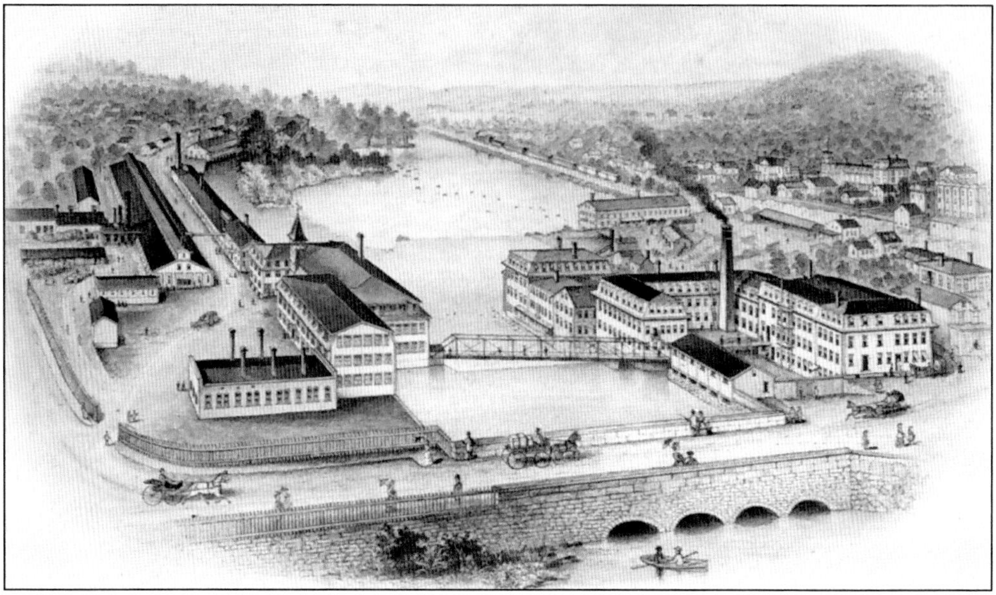

This illustration shows the New Home Sewing Machine Company around 1882 when the Gold Medal Sewing Machine Company was reorganized and re-named.

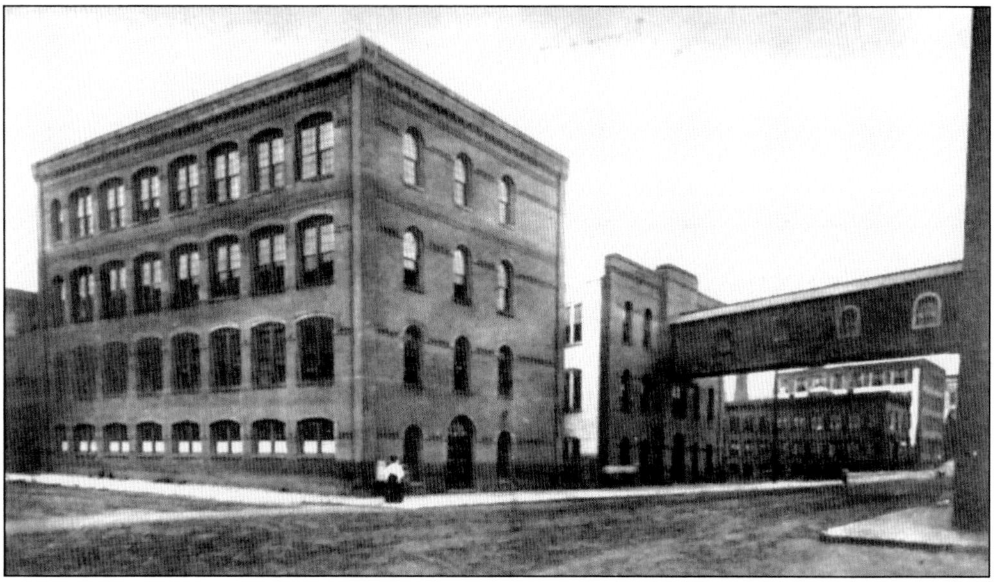

By the time of this image of the New Home Sewing Company, about 1908, the buildings had all been rebuilt with brick. To the left is West River Street. East River Street is to the right and in the center is South Main Street looking toward the square. (Metropolitan News.)

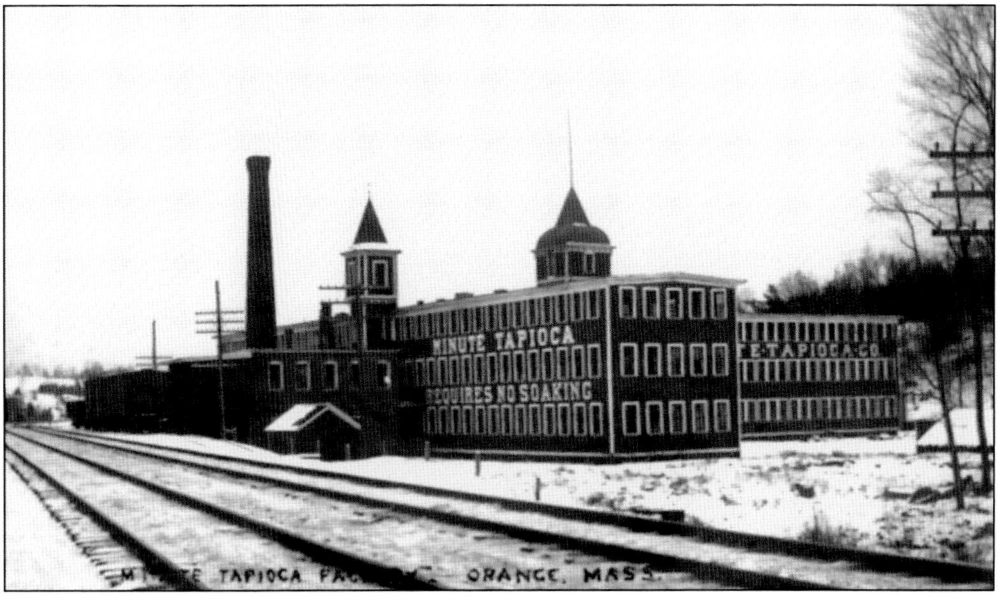

This view, looking northwest from the railroad tracks, is of the Minute Tapioca factory. West Main Street passes the building at the far right. The Minute Tapioca brand came into existence when it was manufactured by the Whitman Grocery Company, located on Water Street in 1895. The company purchased the shoe factory of J. B. Reynolds on West Main Street in 1902, shown here around 1910, and changed its name to the Minute Tapioca Company in 1908.

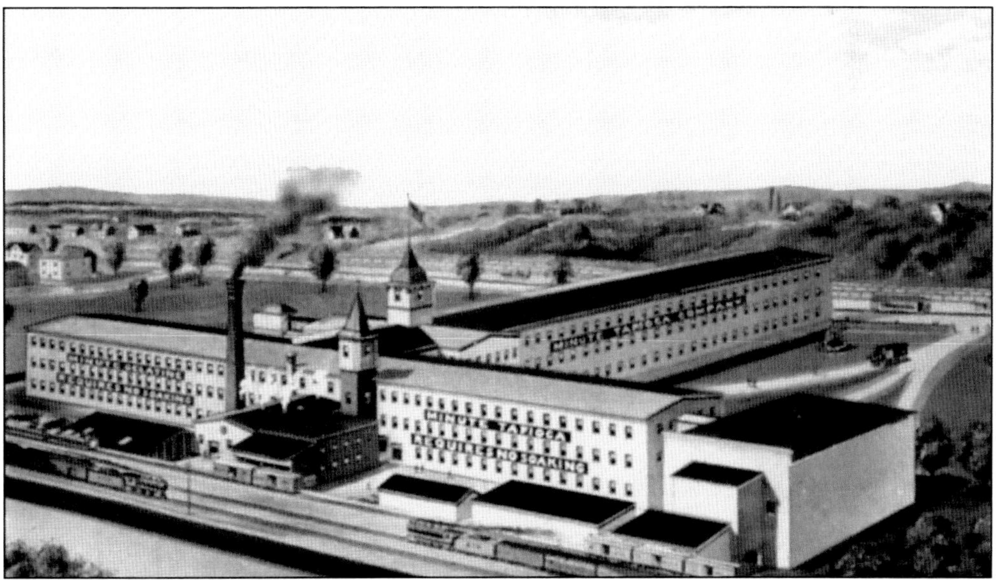

This c. 1925 view of the Minute Tapioca factory shows considerable expansion from the way it looked in the above image. The company thrived in Orange through the first half of the 20th century. It closed in 1967. (Hughes.)

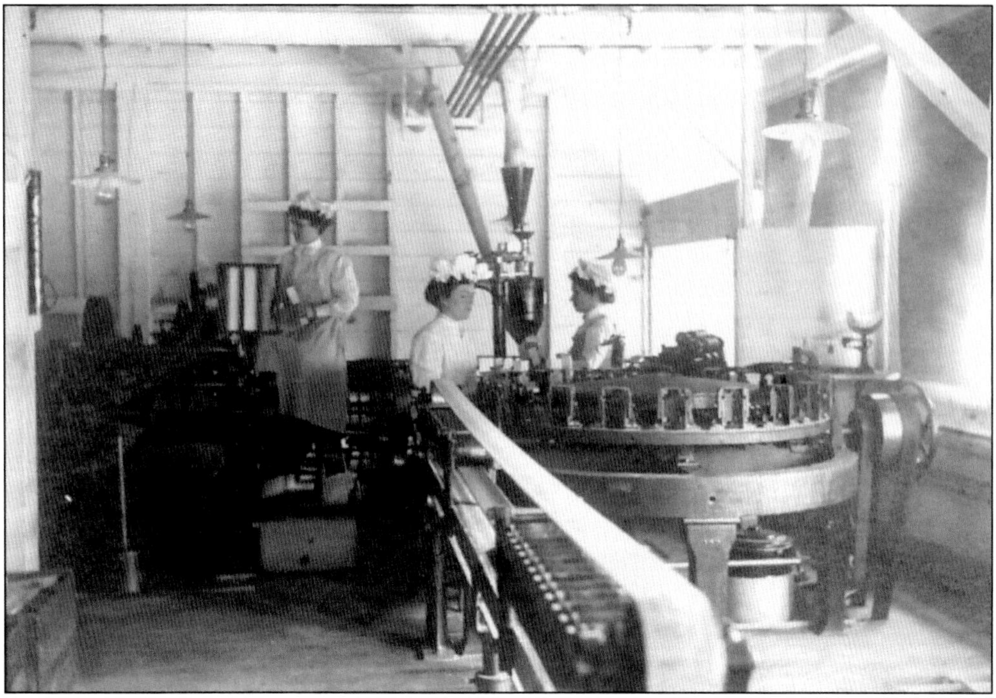

This interior view of the Minute Tapioca factory shows automated machinery used in filling boxes in the early 1900s. (Thompson.)

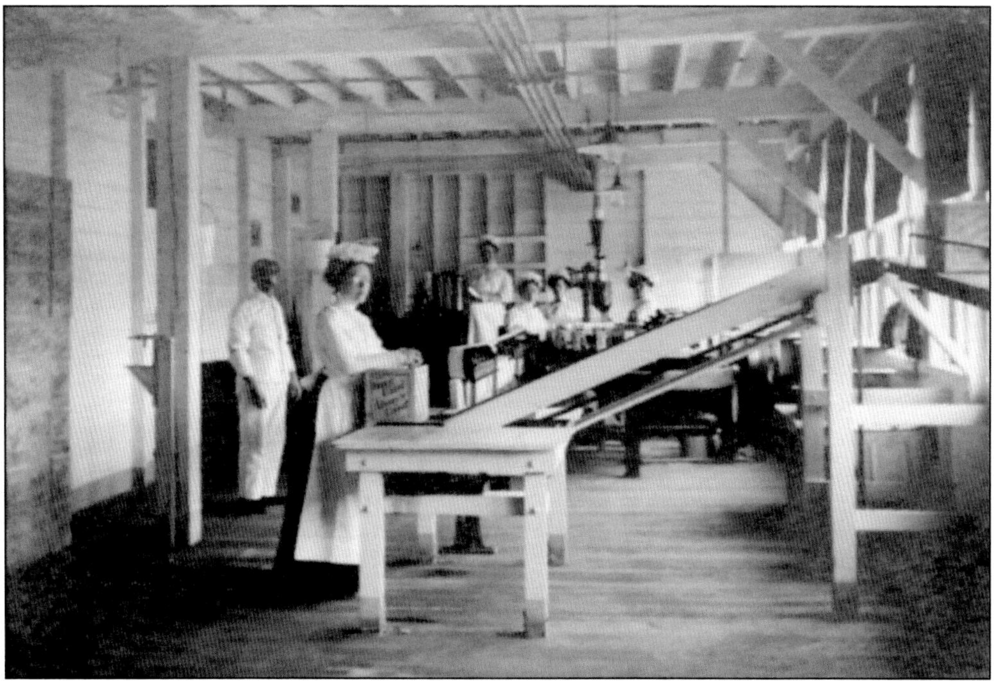

This early 1900s interior view of the Minute Tapioca factory shows the packing of boxes into cartons with the Minute Tapioca slogan, "Once Used, Always Used," prominently emblazoned on the cartons.

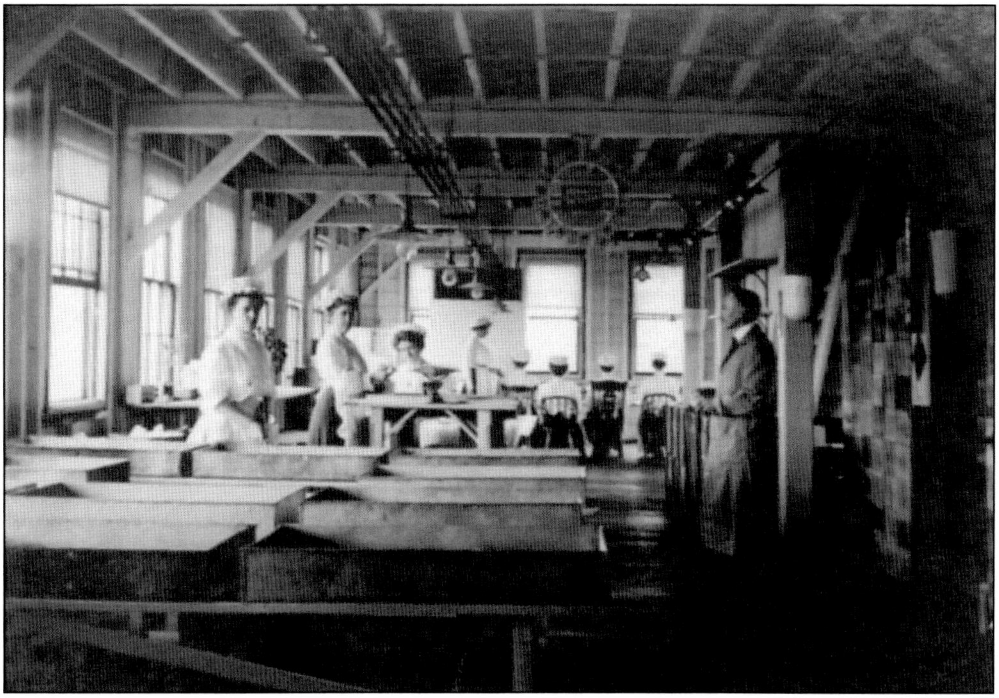

Production work at the Minute Tapioca factory is shown in this early 1900s view. Note that the production workers are all women with the male supervisor at the right.

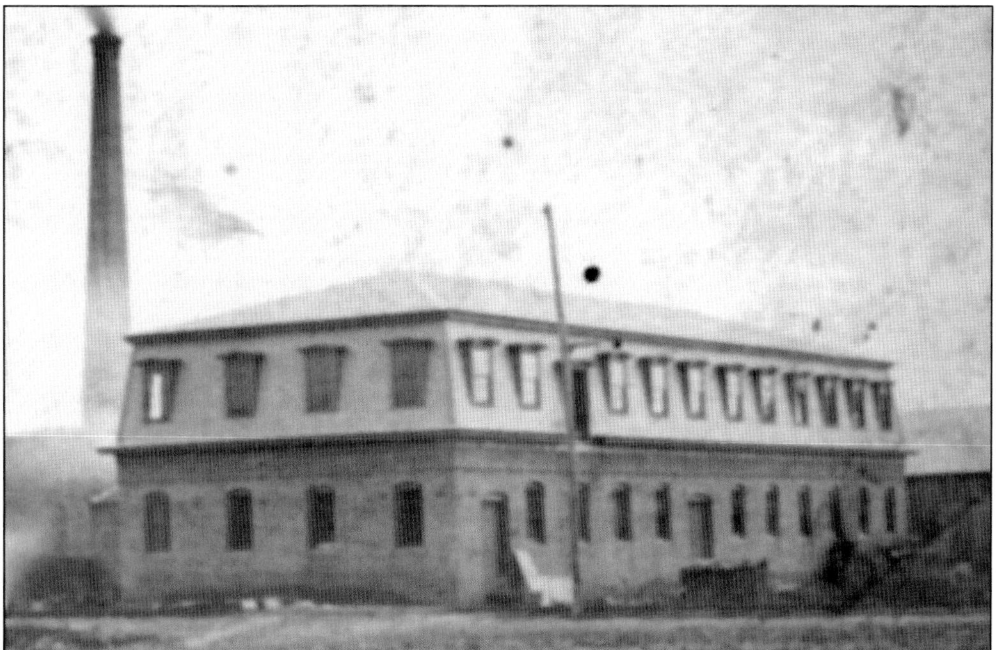

This view from the 1870s shows the H. H. Whitney Furniture shop that was located between the railroad tracks and the Millers River, east of the present day fire station at the end of what is now Mill Street.

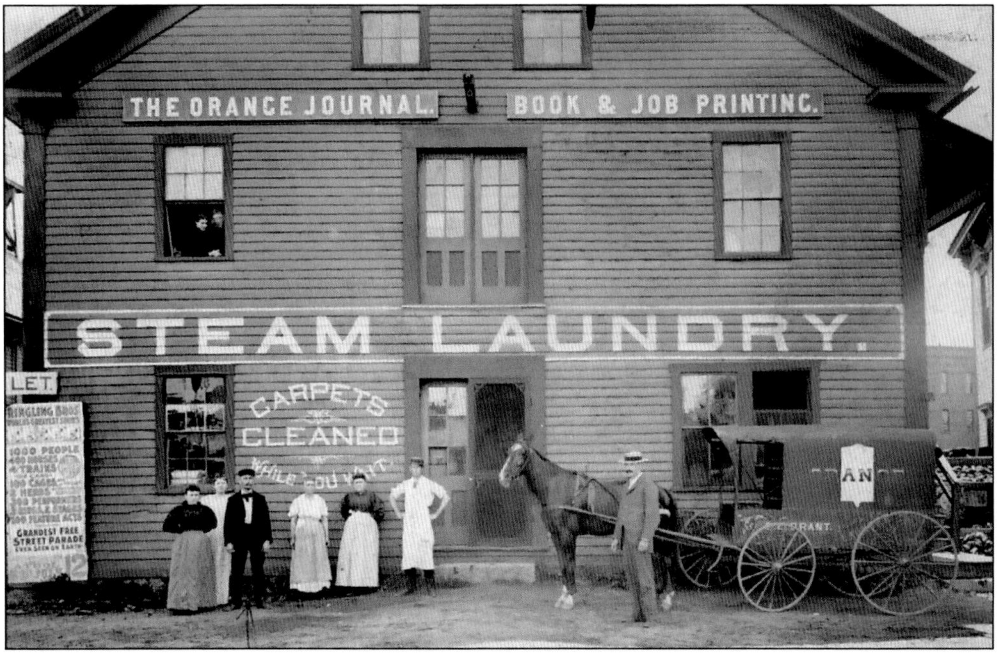

The Orange Steam Laundry was located opposite the railroad station and was the next building east of the fire station. The building also housed the *Orange Journal* that was founded in 1883 and purchased in 1899 by Dexter L. Crandall who owned the *Orange Enterprise* resulting in the *Enterprise and Journal*. The photograph is from around 1895.

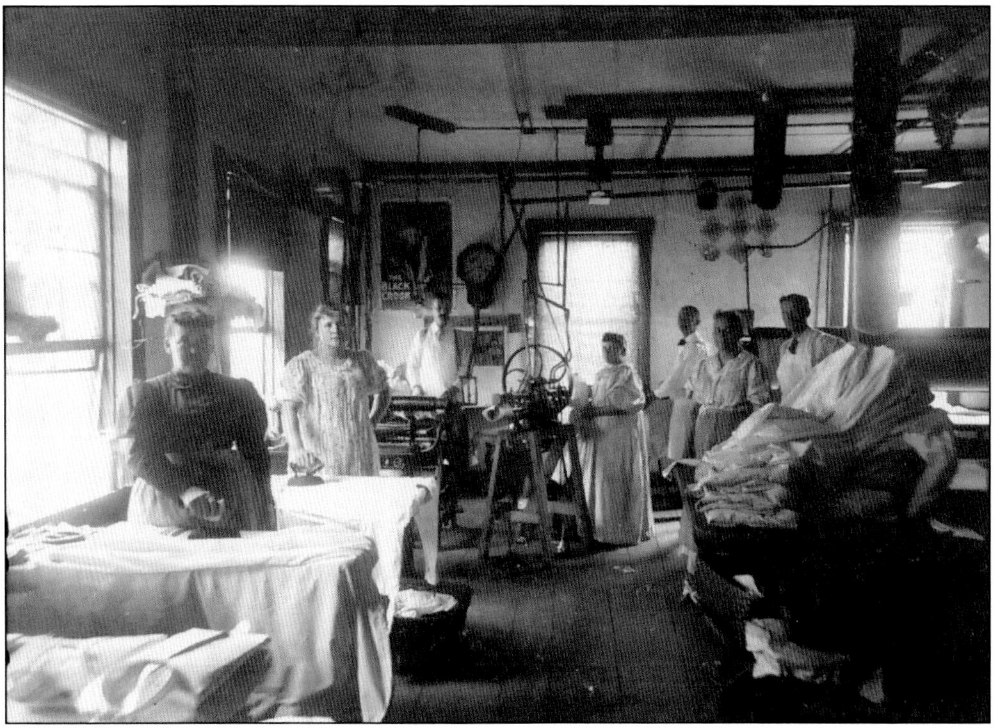

This image shows the interior of the Orange Steam Laundry about 1900.

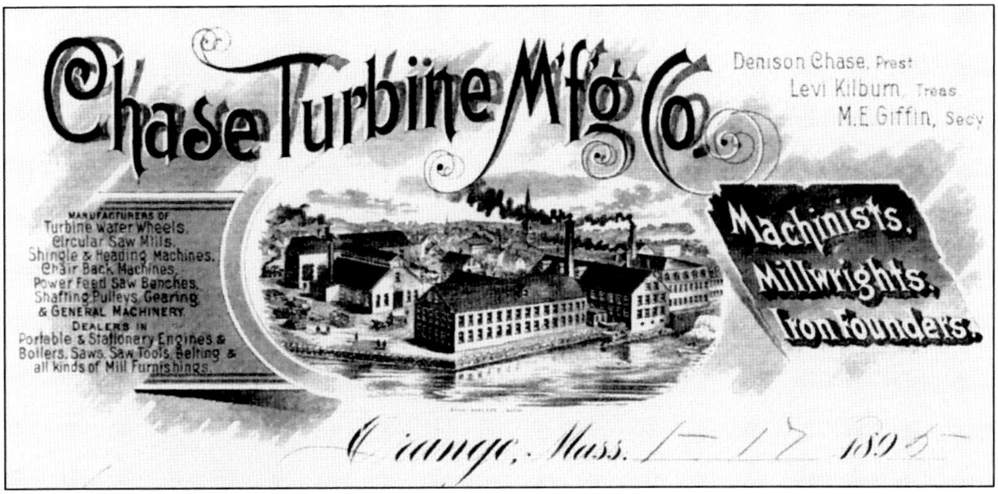

This company letterhead, dated 1895, shows an illustration of the Chase Turbine Manufacturing Company. The company was located at 18 Chase Court to the rear of the present day Riveto Manufacturing Company on South Main Street.

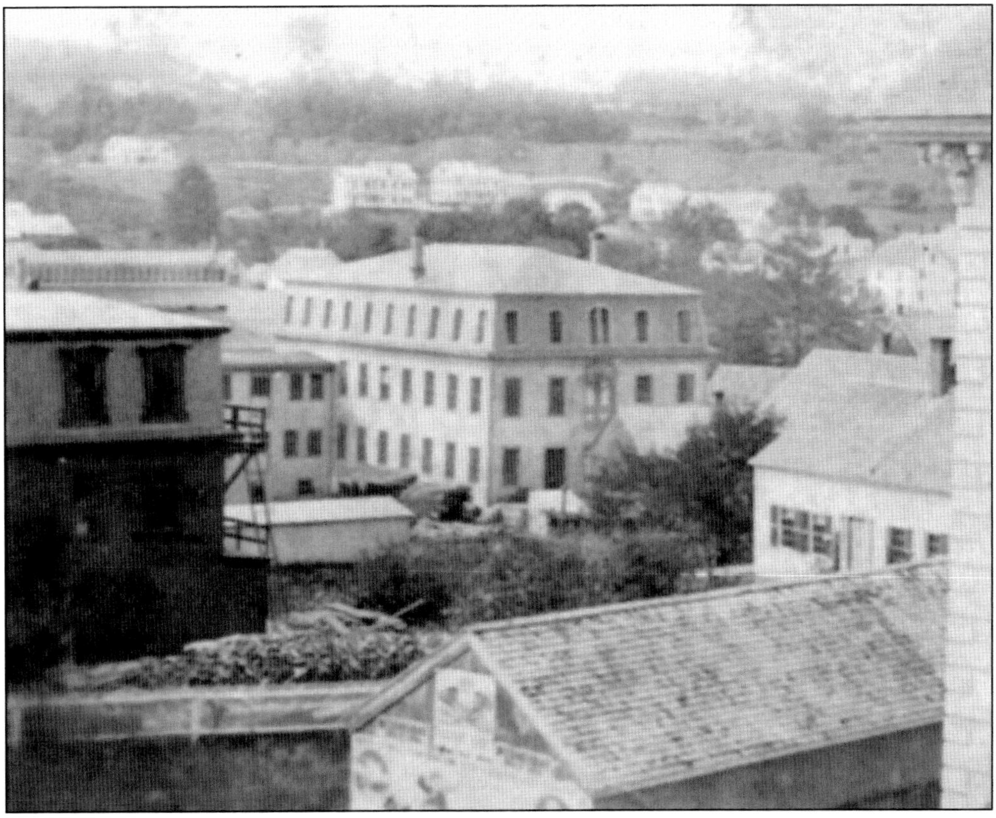

Shown in this view, from around 1874, is the L. Kilburn and Company Chair Factory that stood to the rear of the present day Riveto Manufacturing Company on South Main Street until it burned December 9, 1882.

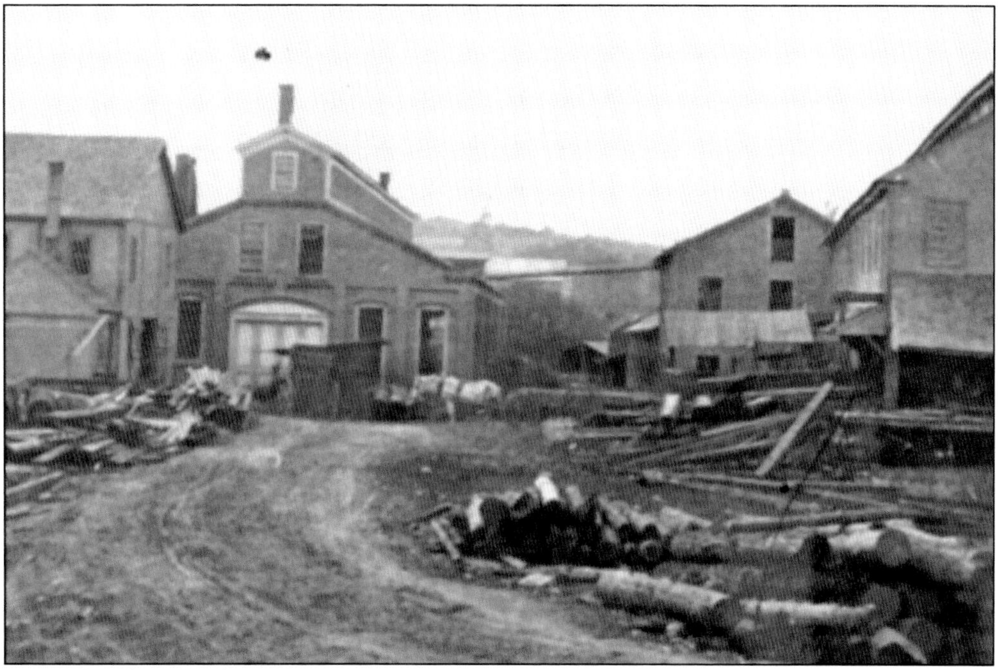

The old mill yard, cabinet, and toy shop at the corner of South Main and West River Streets is shown in this photograph from about 1870. The building at the right burned March 26, 1879. (Union View.)

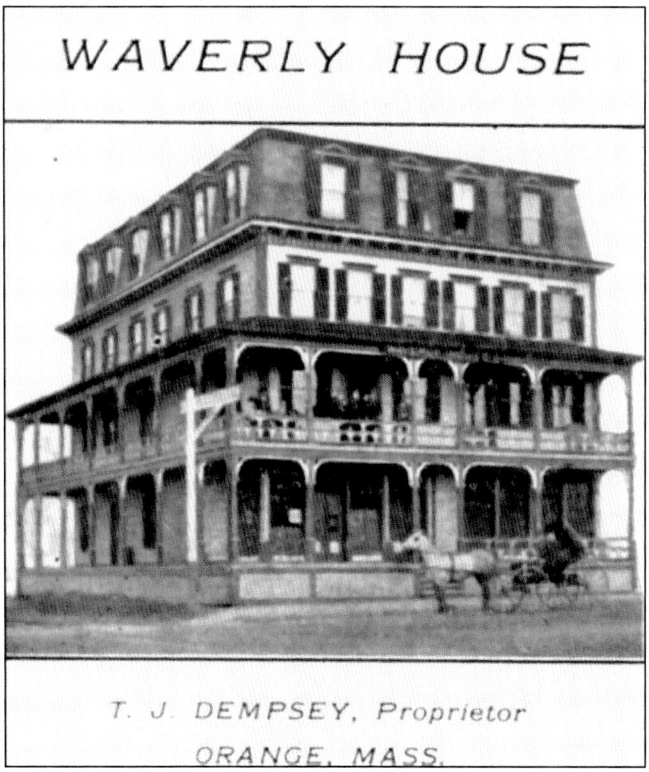

The Waverly House that stood in the present day Orange District Court parking lot is shown here, around 1905. As a two-story building named the American House, the building was extensively remodeled after the fire of 1891.

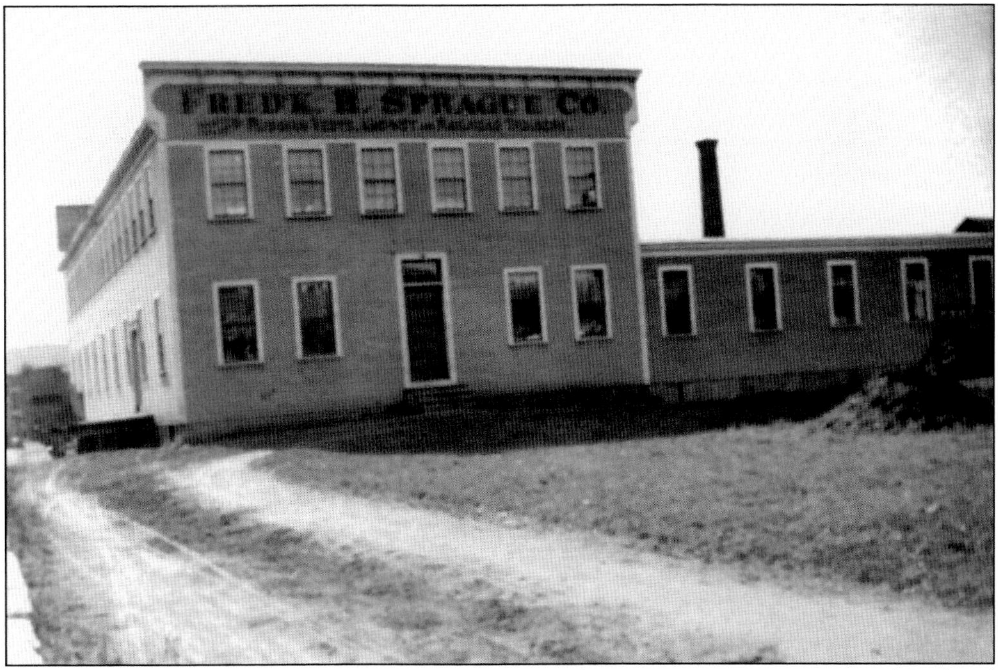

Frederick H. Sprague and Company, manufacturers of Russian Vests, Kno-wet, and Railroad Trousers was located at 108 East Main Street in this *c.* 1905 photograph.

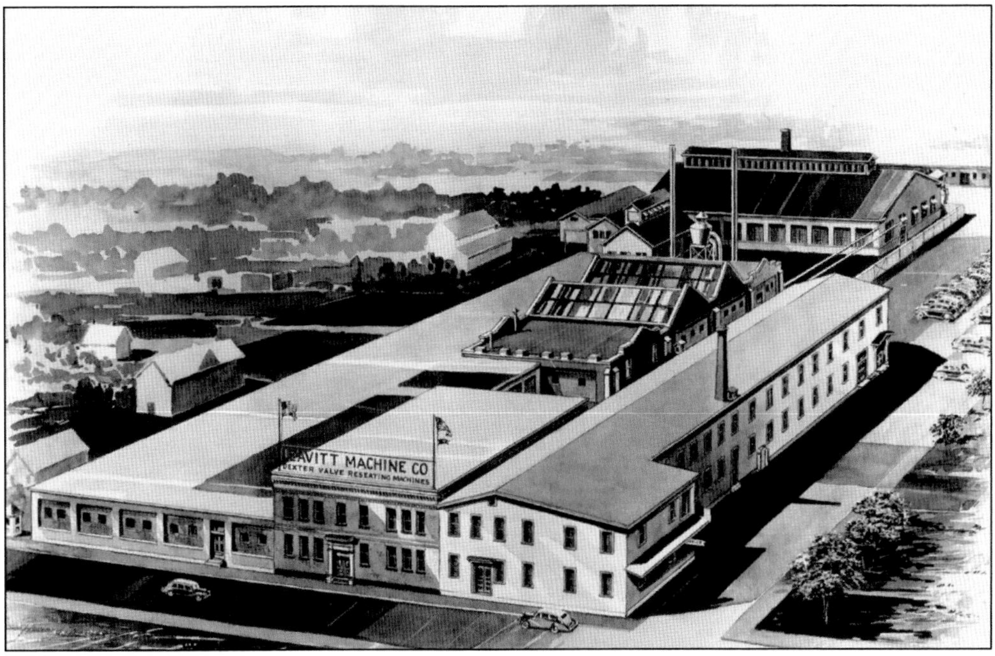

The Leavitt Machine Company, established in 1890, is shown in this illustration from the early 1950s. Located at 14 East River Street directly across South Main Street from the present day post office, the facility is currently unused and available.

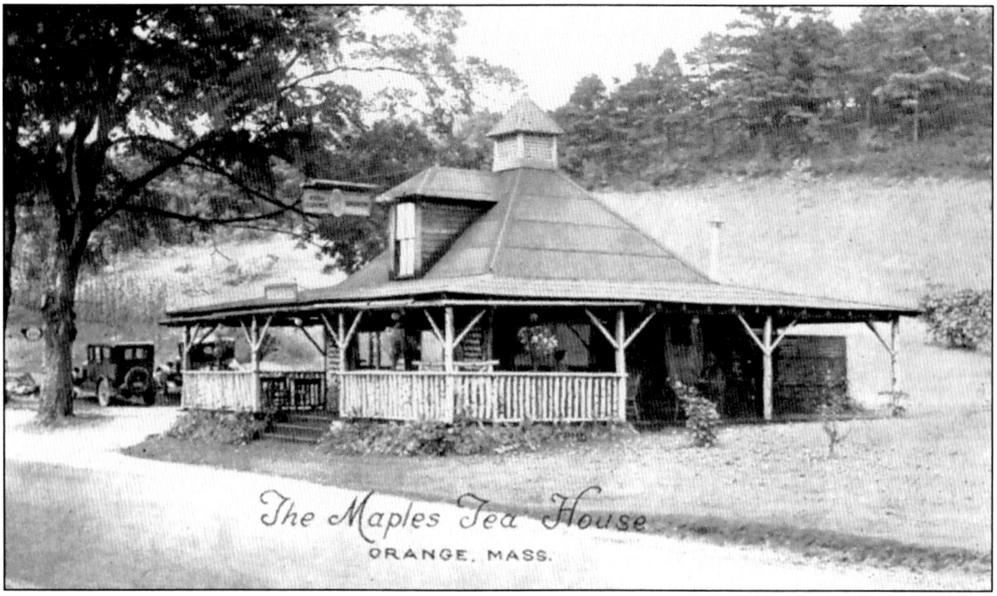

The Maples Tea Room was located on West Orange Road. Margaret P. Hamilton was the proprietor when this mid-1930s photograph was taken.

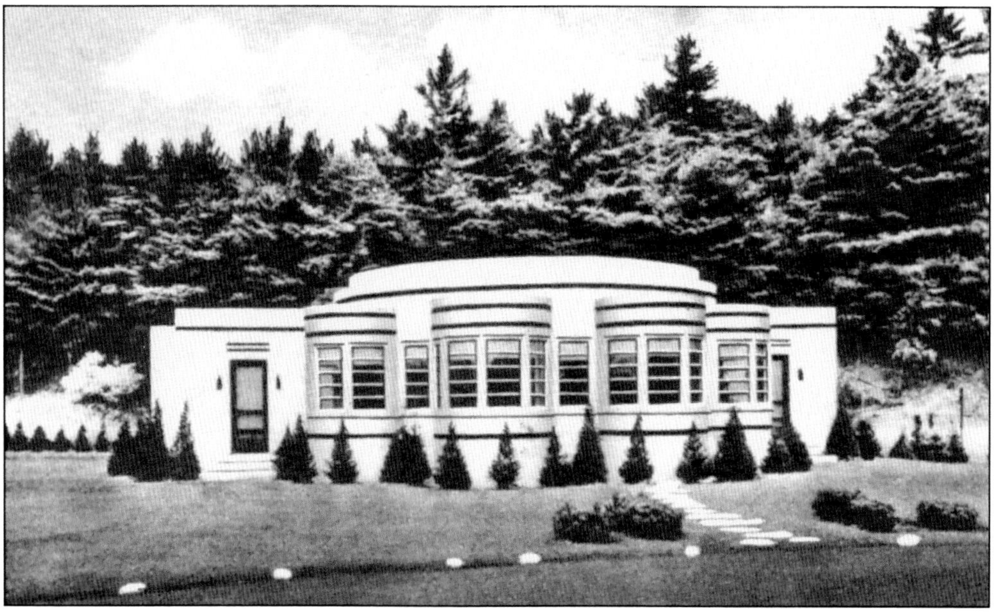
The White Drum restaurant and tea room was operated by Elizabeth L. Shovan in 1944. Located on West Orange Road at the Warwick Road intersection, it is currently the Oriental House restaurant.

Whipples store and block was located on North Main Street. An 1871 map of Orange shows that this was the only structure between West Main and Prospect Streets at the time of this 1870s photograph.

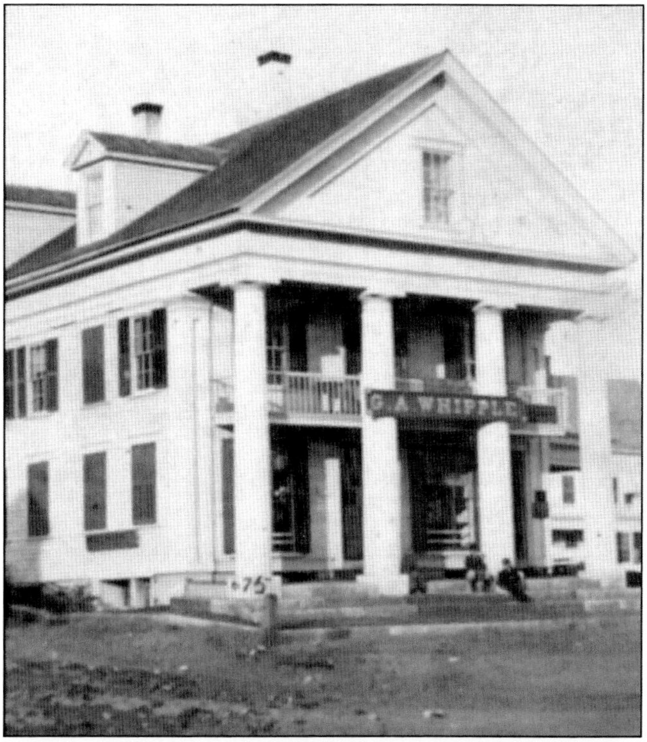

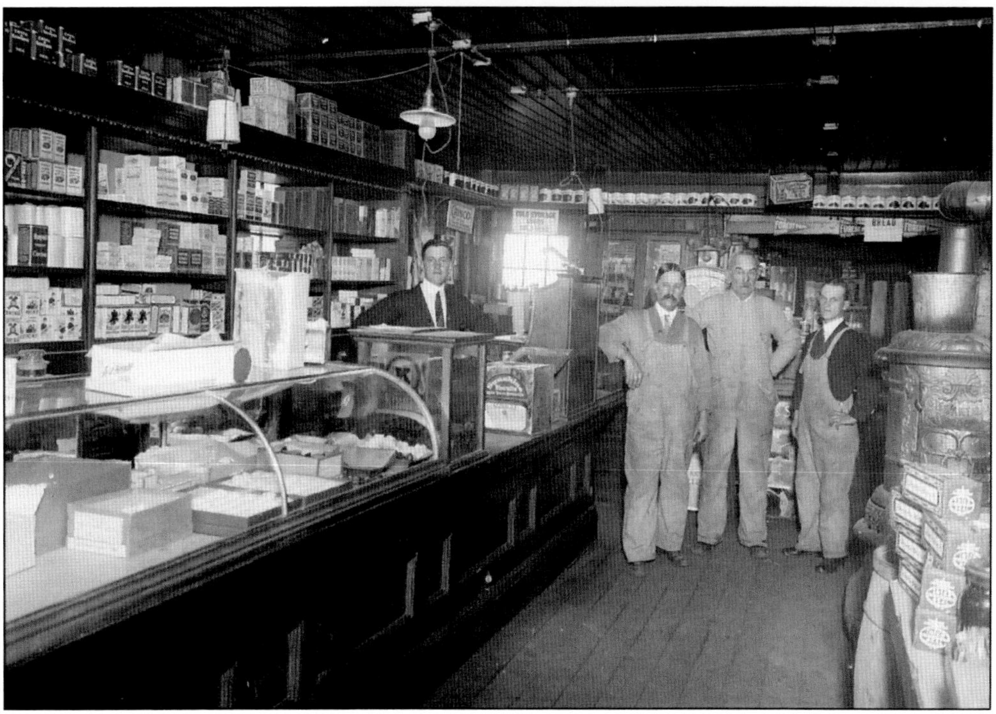

This c. 1895 photograph is of the interior of Frye and Burrill's store that was located on South Main Street at the corner of Railroad Street (now Depot Street). This location was in the area that is now Memorial Park.

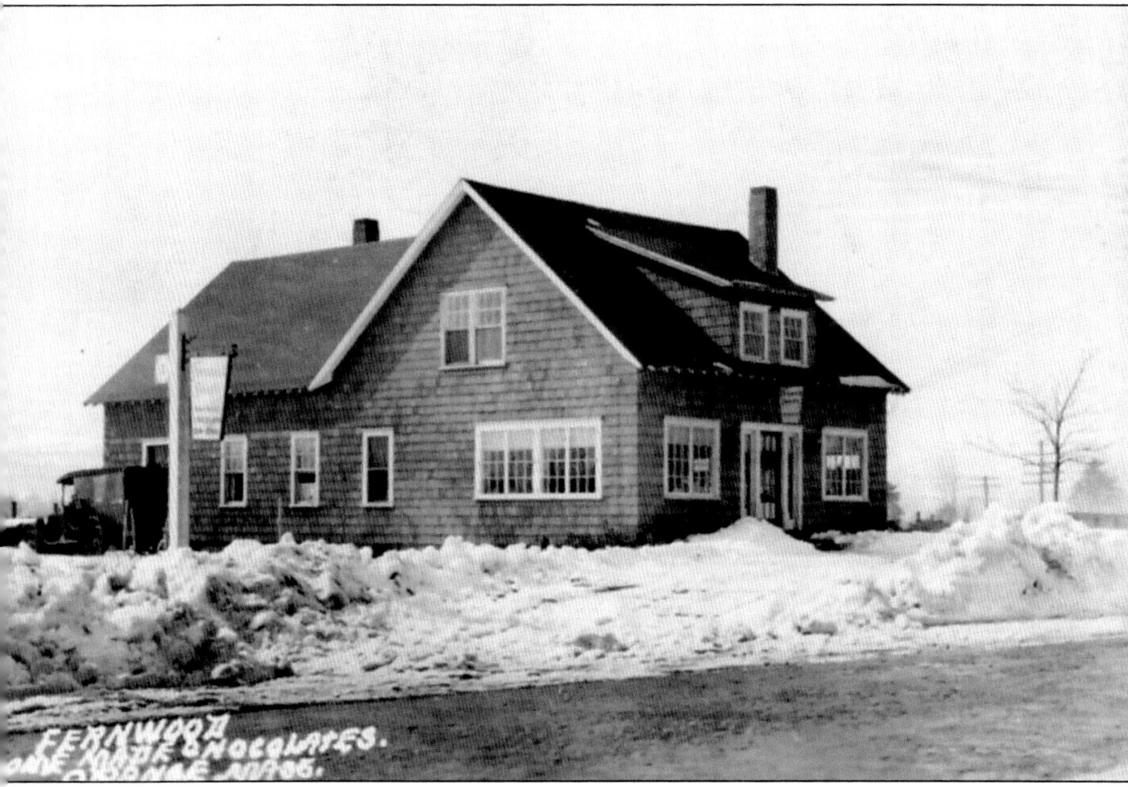

Chester Hunt was proprietor of Fernwood Sweets at 326 East Main Street in the 1930s when this photograph was taken. In later years, the Fernwood was a lounge and is now the Tea House restaurant.

Two

Residences, Streets, and Scenes

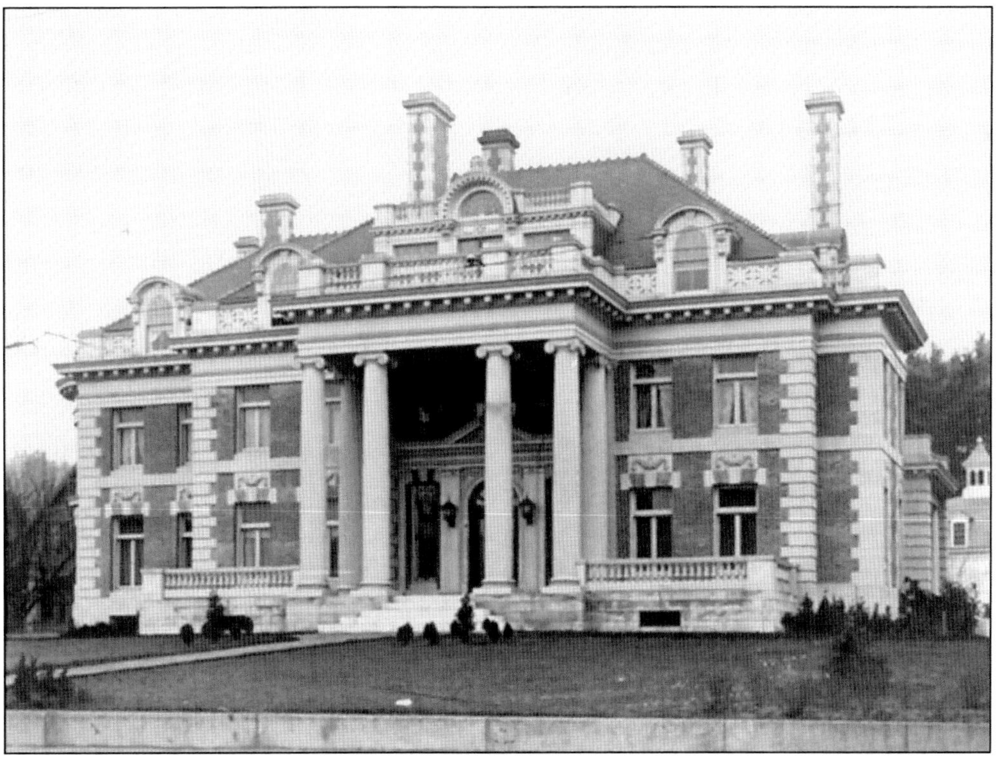

The John W. Wheeler residence on East Main Street is perhaps the most recognizable house in Orange. Wheeler was president and treasurer of the New Home Sewing Machine Company. The house is shown around 1903 when it was completed.

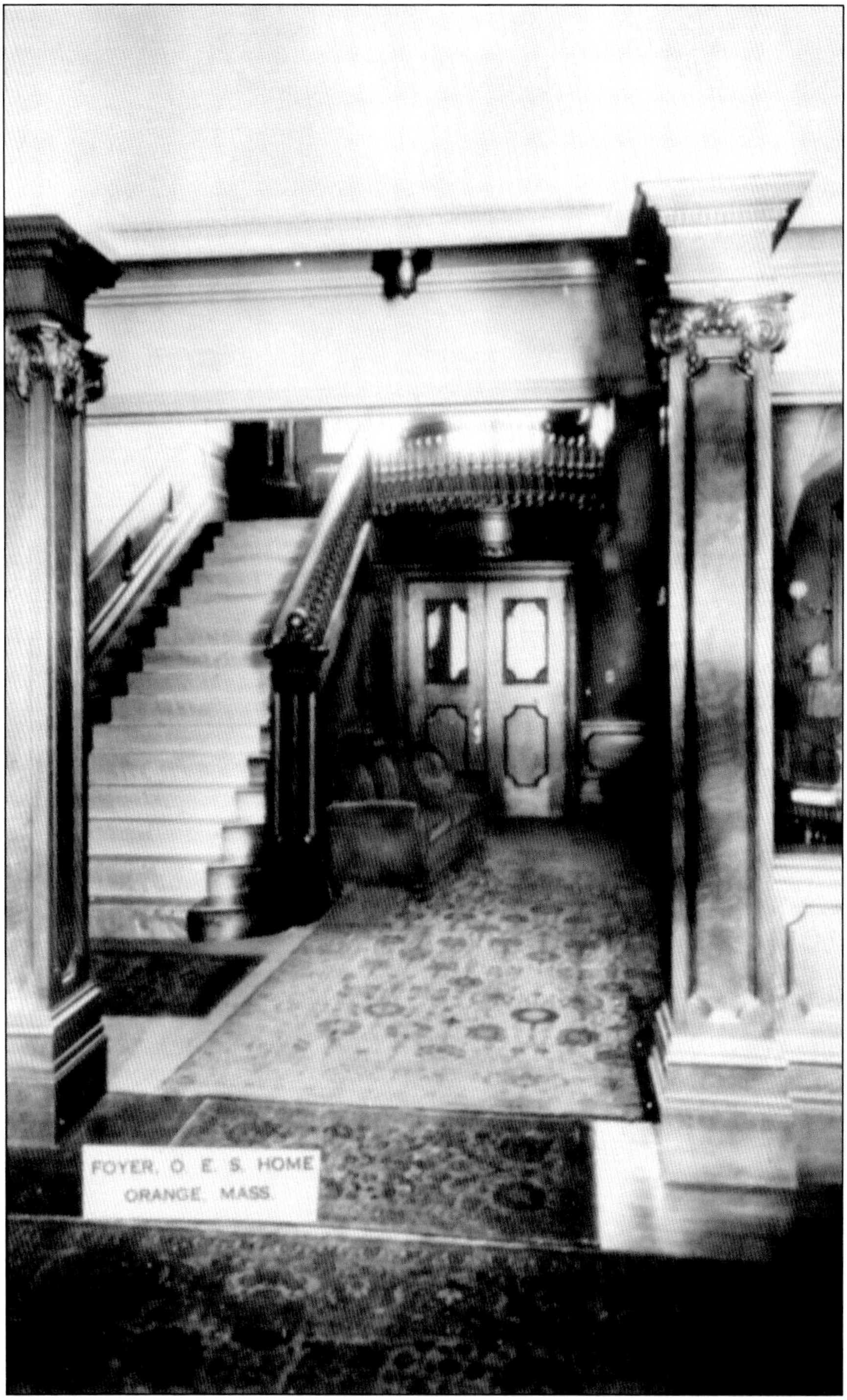

After the death of John W. Wheeler in 1910, the Wheeler Mansion was taken over by the Masonic Eastern Star Home of Massachusetts in 1925. It was remodeled to provide accommodations for Eastern Star Order residents. The foyer, pictured here around 1930, testifies to the elegance of the building.

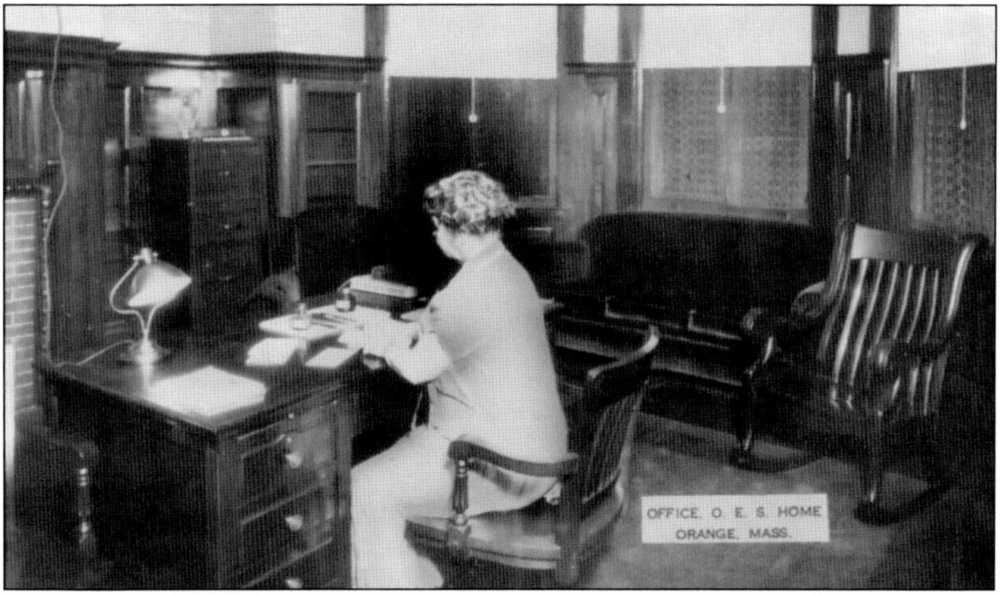

The office of the Eastern Star Home (above), and the matron's sitting room (below) are shown in these interior views of the former Wheeler Mansion.

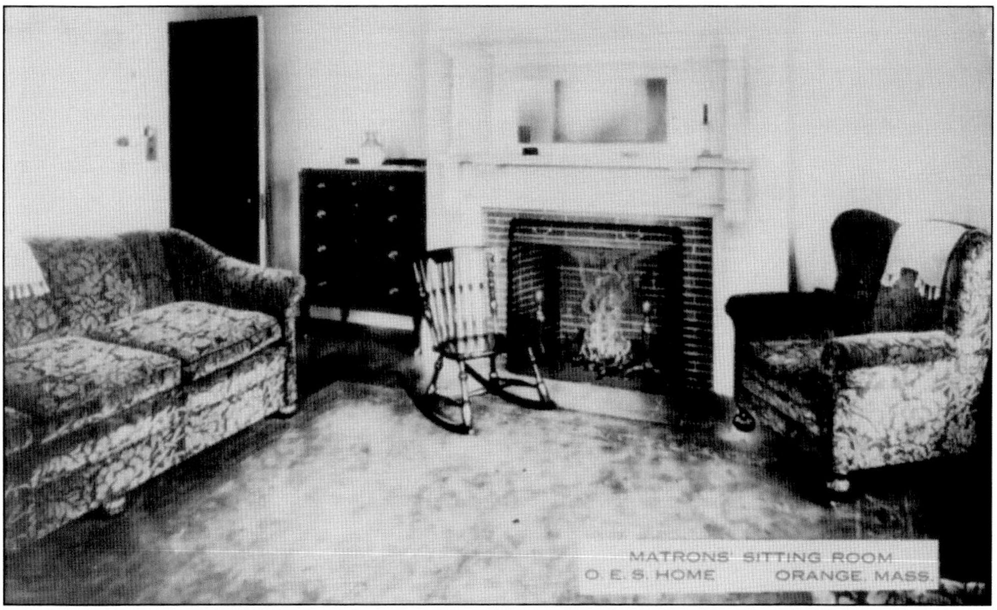

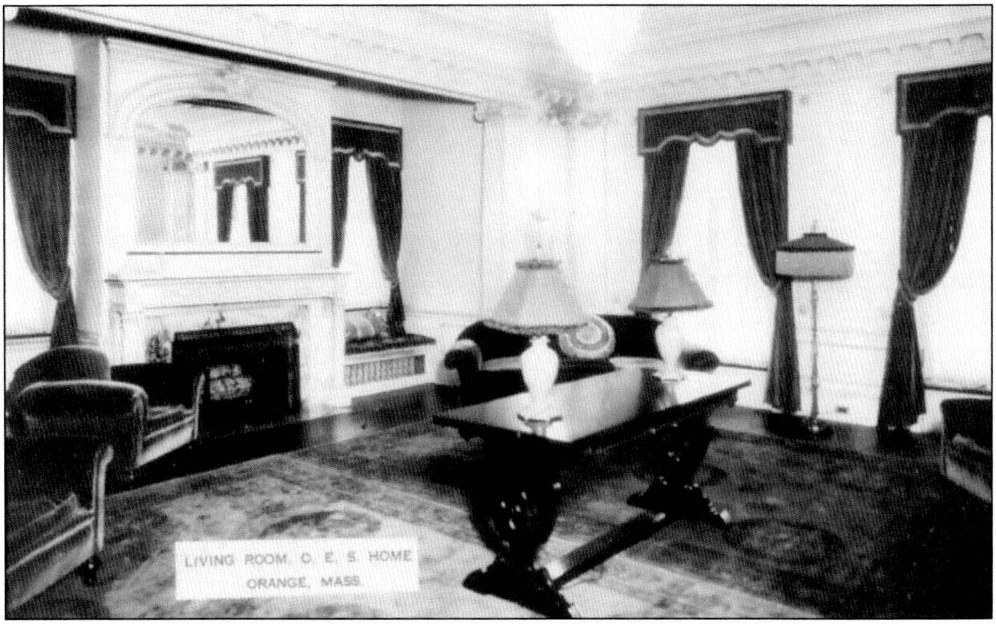

Further elegance of the former Wheeler Mansion is shown in these interior images of the Eastern Star Home showing the living room (above), and the library (below).

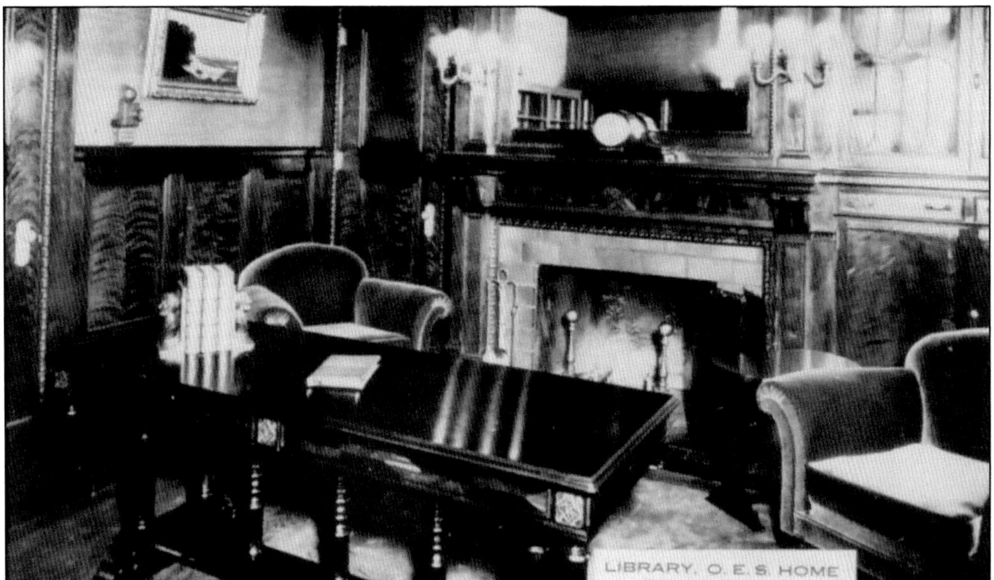

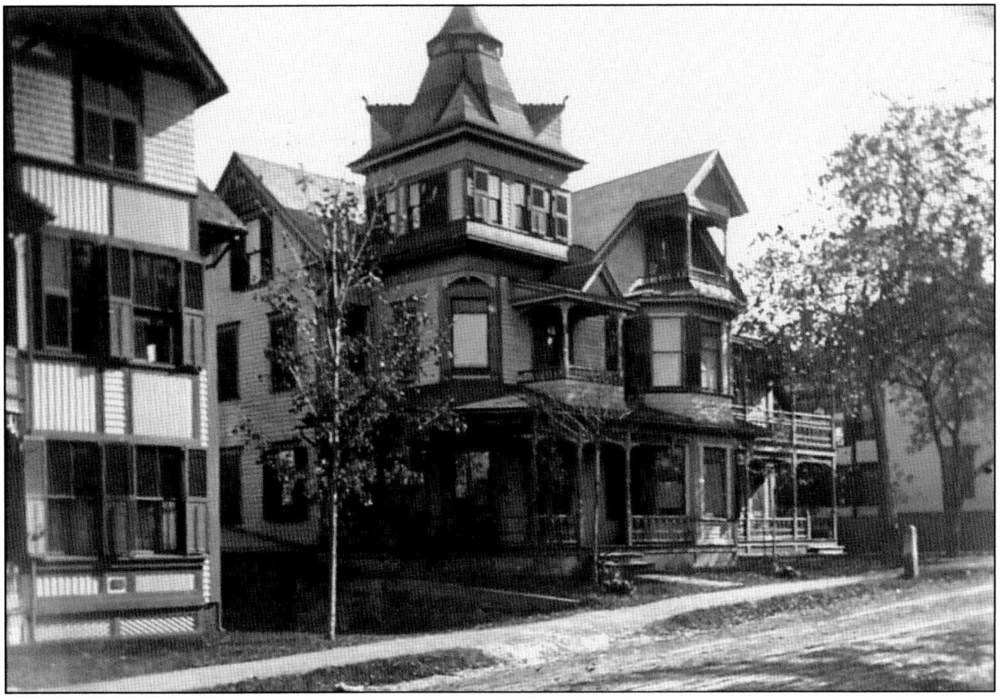

The home of Orin W. Wright at 77 Pleasant Street is shown about 1907. Wright was a lumber dealer.

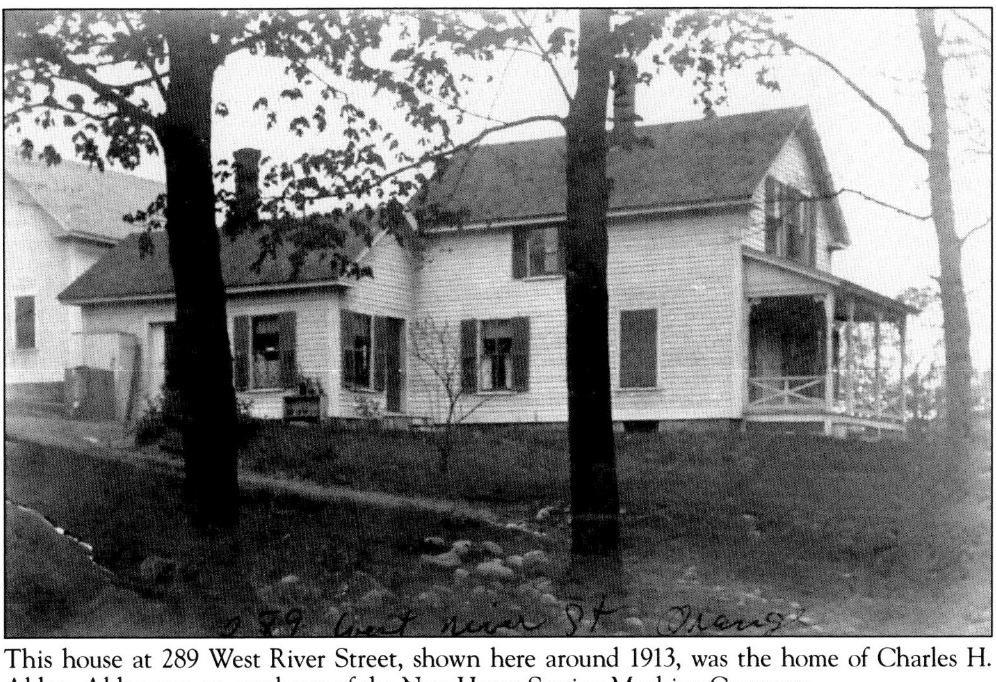

This house at 289 West River Street, shown here around 1913, was the home of Charles H. Alden. Alden was an employee of the New Home Sewing Machine Company.

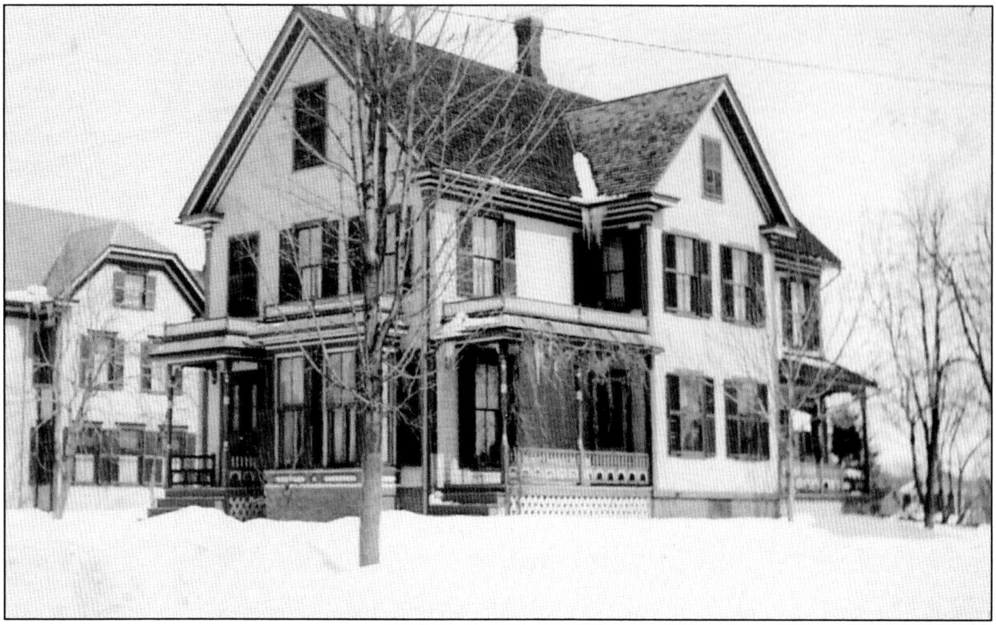

This *c.* 1913 image shows the home of Emma C. Coolidge at 133 South Main Street. She was the widow of Charles P. Coolidge who was employed at the Rodney Hunt Company.

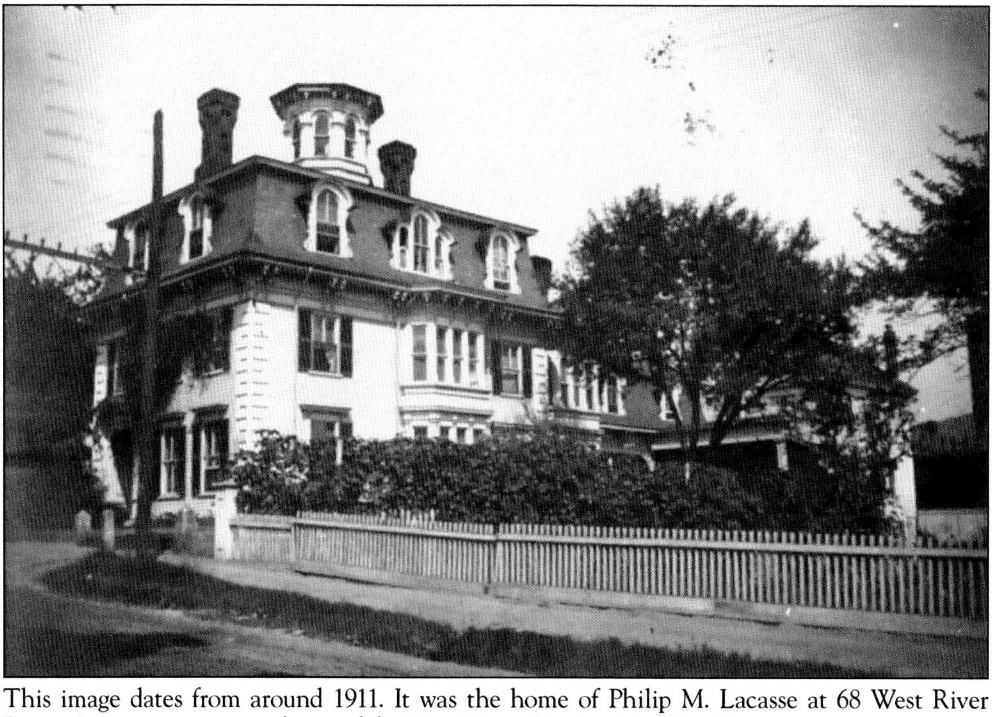

This image dates from around 1911. It was the home of Philip M. Lacasse at 68 West River Street. Lacasse was an employee of the New Home Sewing Machine Company.

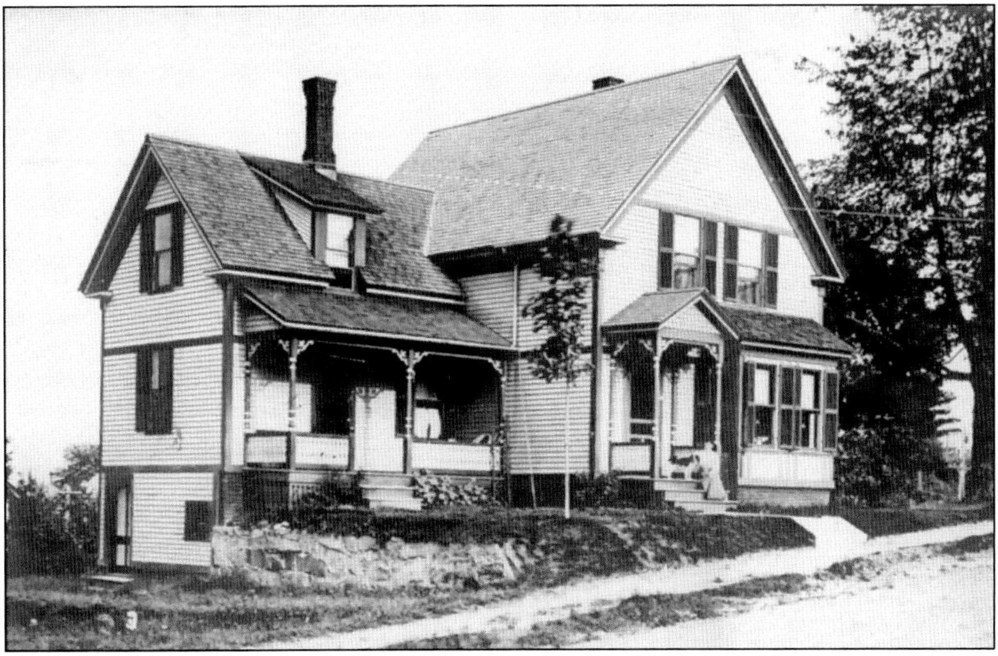

The home of William E. Ash, 33 Maynard Street, is shown in this picture from about 1907. Ash was employed at the New Home Sewing Machine Company.

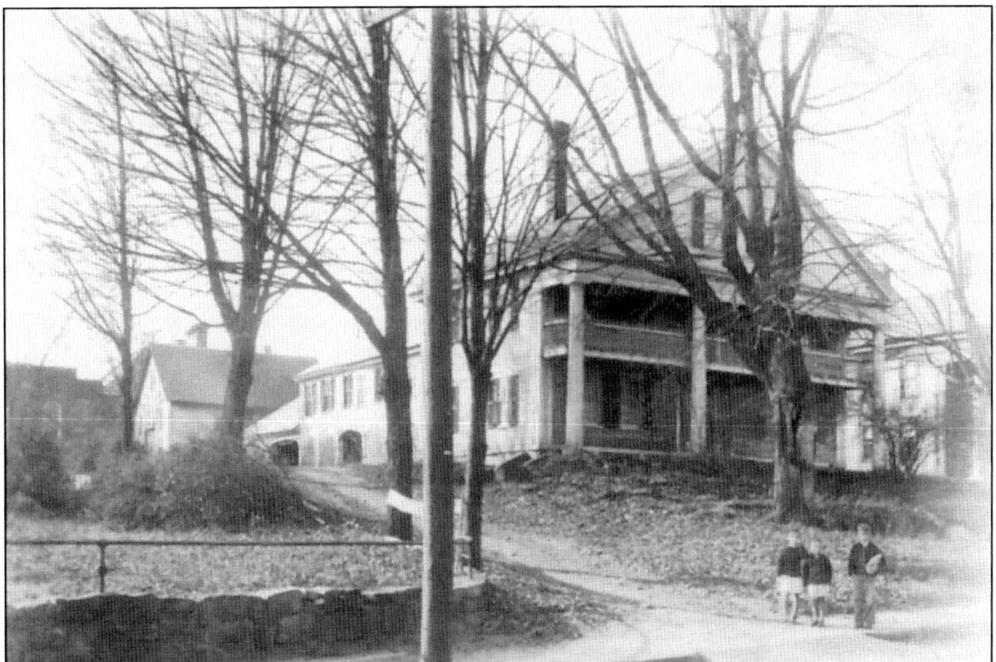

Shown in this photograph is the Butterfield house at the corner of South Main and West River Streets. It was built in 1825 and razed to build the current post office in 1937.

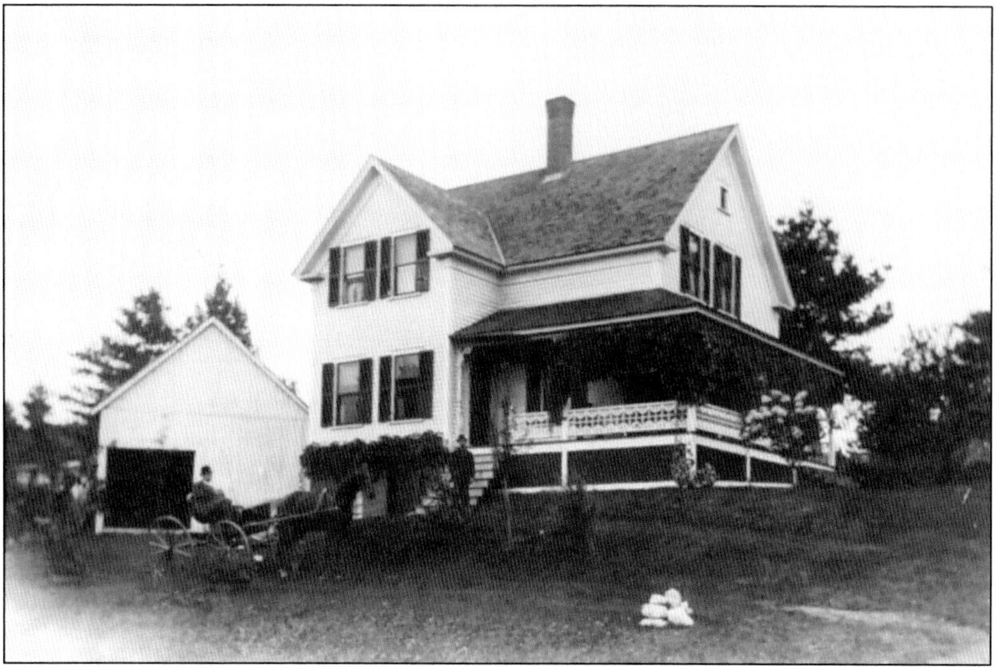

The home of Jesse Bigwood at 19 Clifton Street is shown in this image from around 1914. Bigwood was an employee of the New Home Sewing Machine Company.

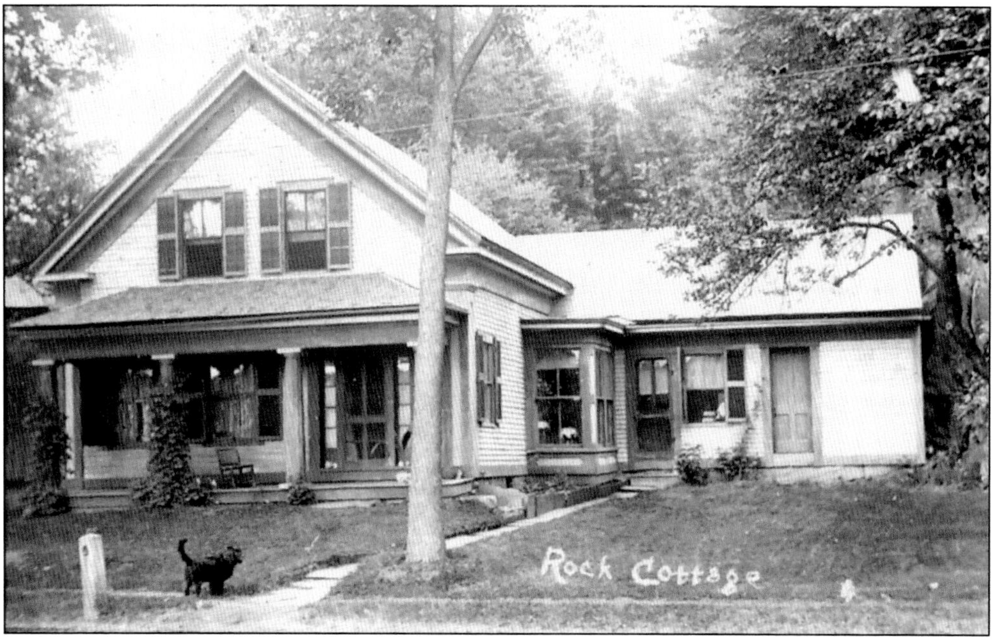

Pictured in this image is the home of Georgine Hastings, widow of George A. Hastings, at 176 West Main Street around 1914.

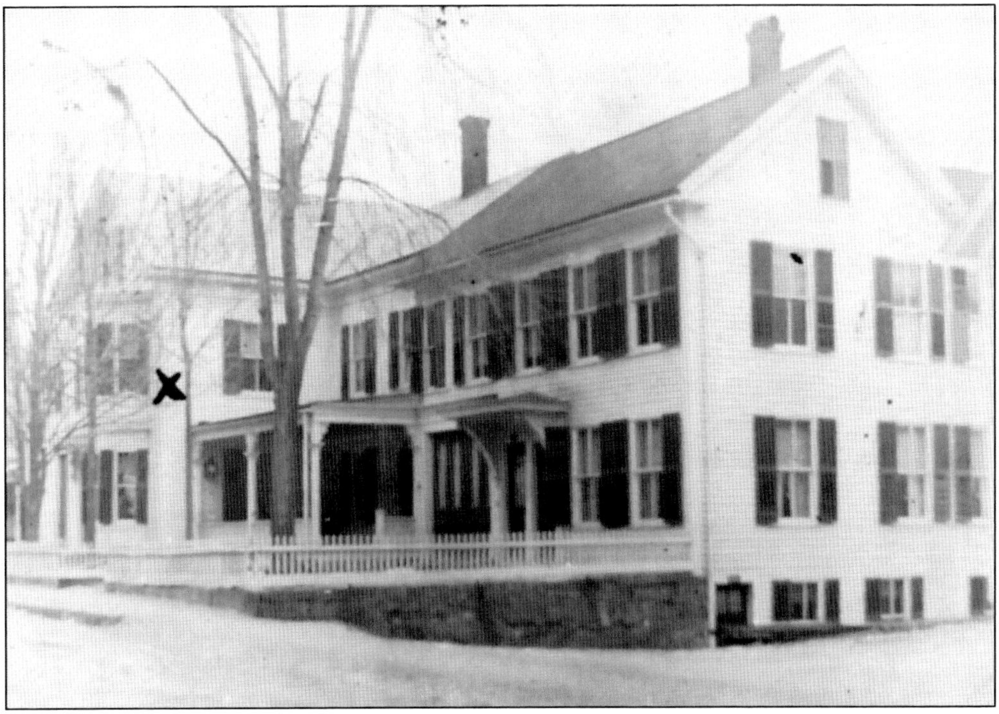

The residence of George M. Mayo at 120 North Main Street is shown here about 1907. Mayo was employed at the New Home Sewing Machine Company.

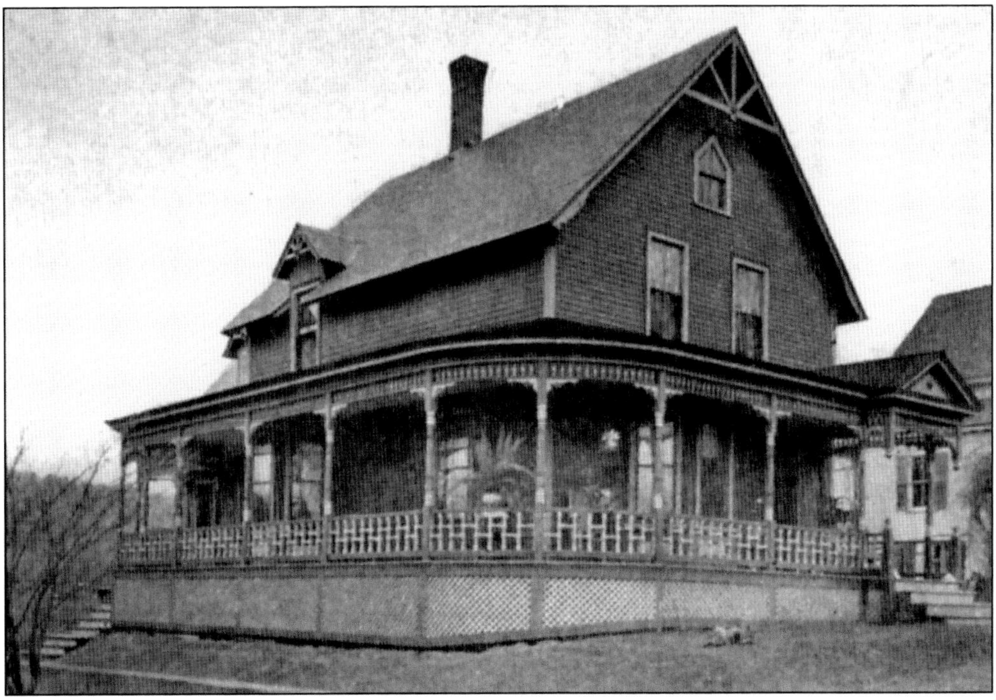

The residence of Edward F. Geckler at 229 North Main Street is shown here around 1905. Geckler was employed at the New Home Sewing Machine Company. His wife was employed as a dressmaker.

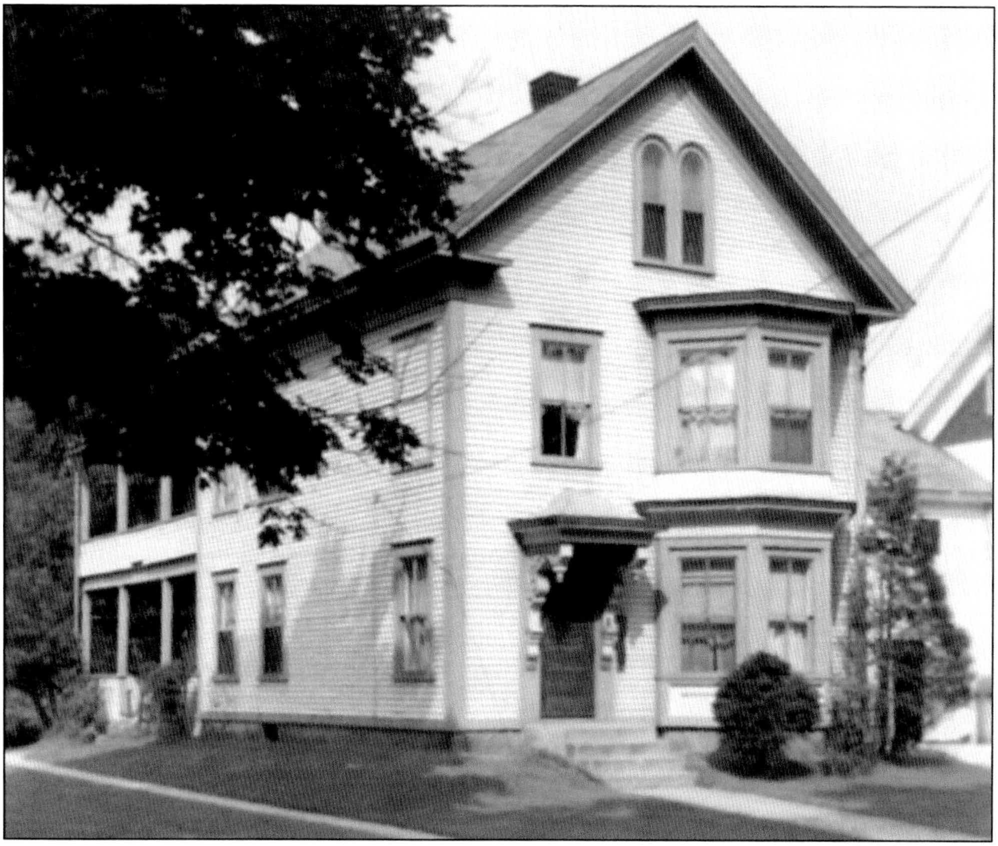

This postcard, dated September 30, 1948, announces the October 1 opening of the Specialty Shop at the 36 Cheney Street residence of Harry and Blanche Burnett.

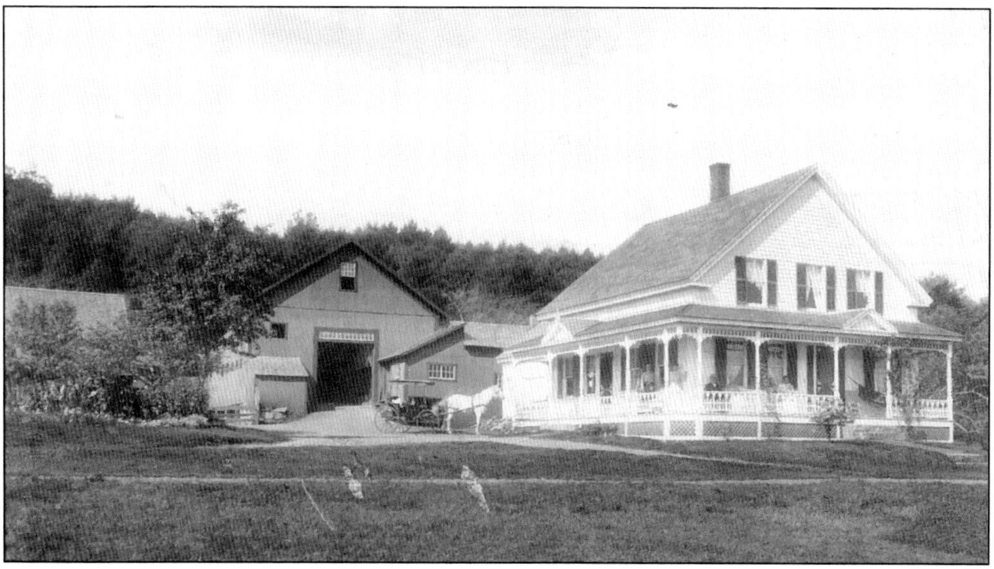

Located at 150 Holtshire Road, this photograph from the early 1900s shows the residence of Henry and Angela Coolidge. Coolidge was a farmer and lumber dealer.

This *c.* 1910 image shows the home of Catherine S. Putnam at 11 Prospect Street. She was the widow of Abraham P. Putnam, proprietor of the Putnam House. (Stratton.)

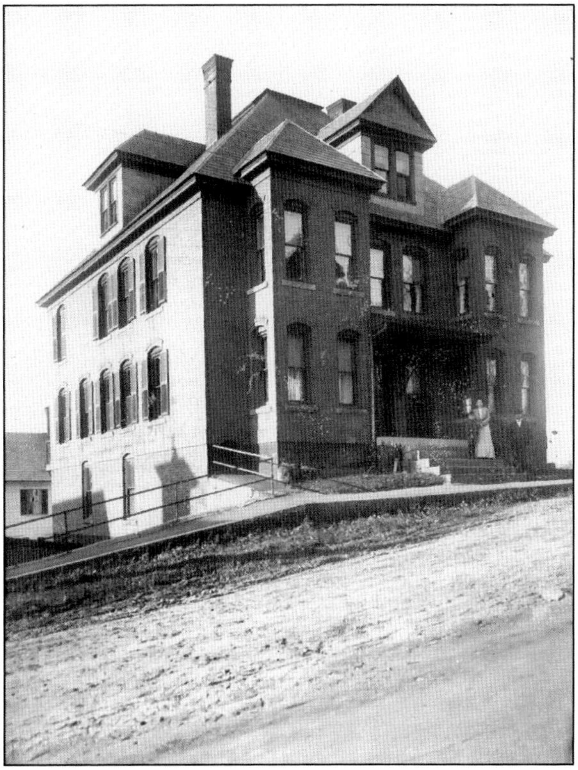

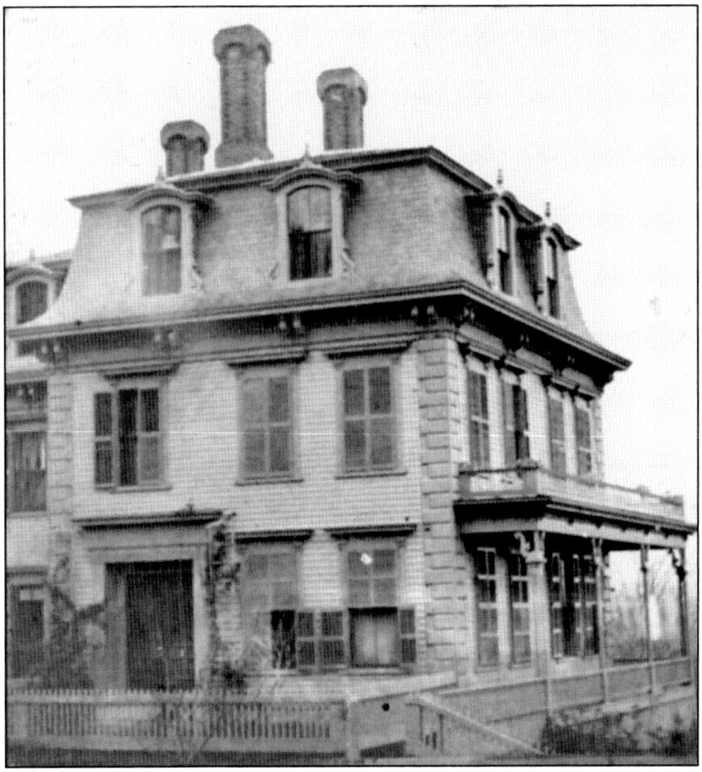

The residence of Levi Kilburn at 32 High Street is shown here about 1880. Kilburn was treasurer of the Chase Turbine Manufacturing Company. (Lesure.)

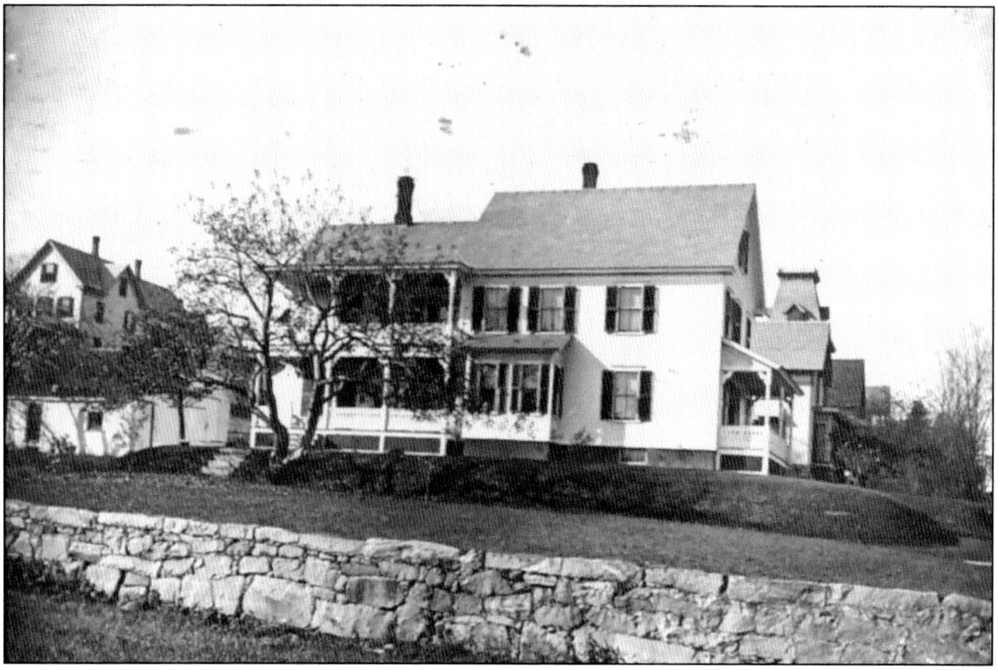

This *c.* 1911 photograph shows the home of Charles B. and Lucie E. Marden. Charles B. Marden was employed at the New Home Sewing Machine Company. The house is located at 41 Putnam Street.

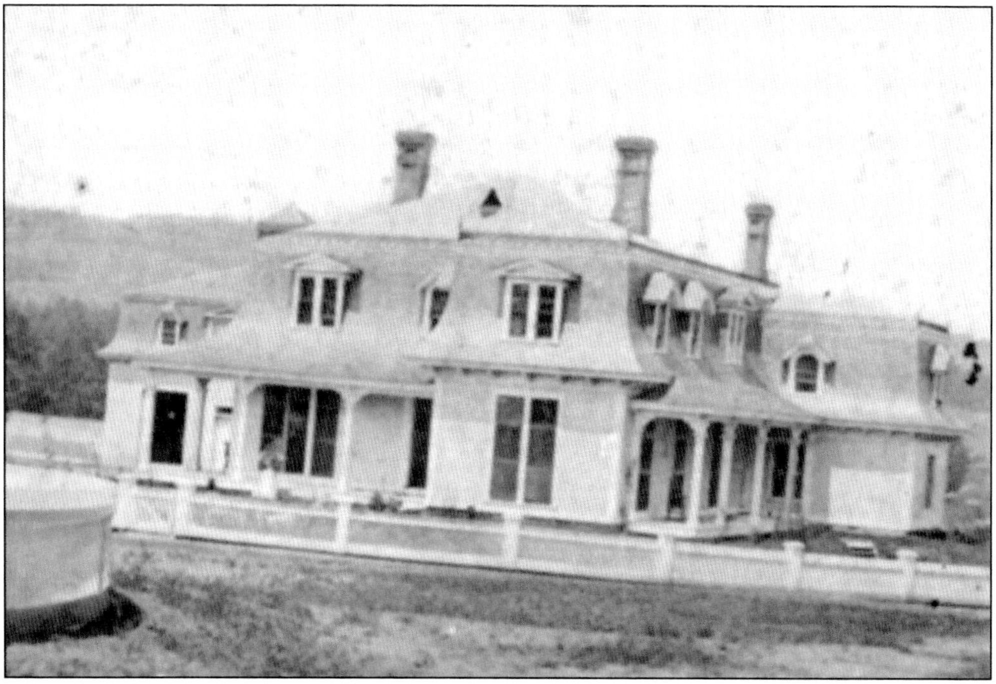

The Cheney Mansion, shown here about 1875, was located on North Main Street, north of Oxbow Road. Nathaniel Cheney, a wealthy industrialist from New York, built the mansion as a summer home around 1872. The mansion burned and the carriage house was remodeled by Charles Lundgren.

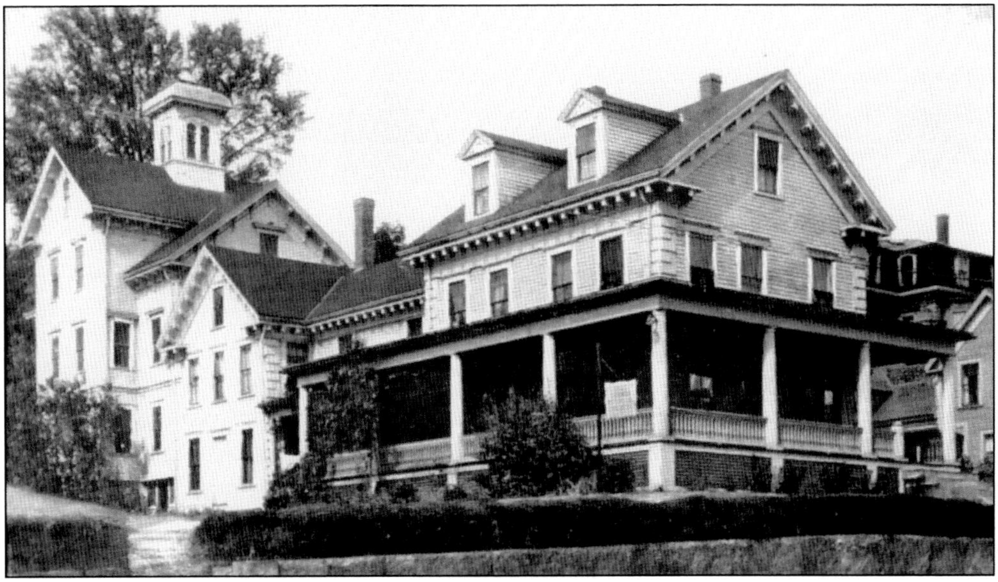

Shown here is the Stephen French home on North Main Street. French was a cofounder of the New Home Sewing Machine Company. It is shown here in the 1950s as the Orange Historical Society, which is currently housed there.

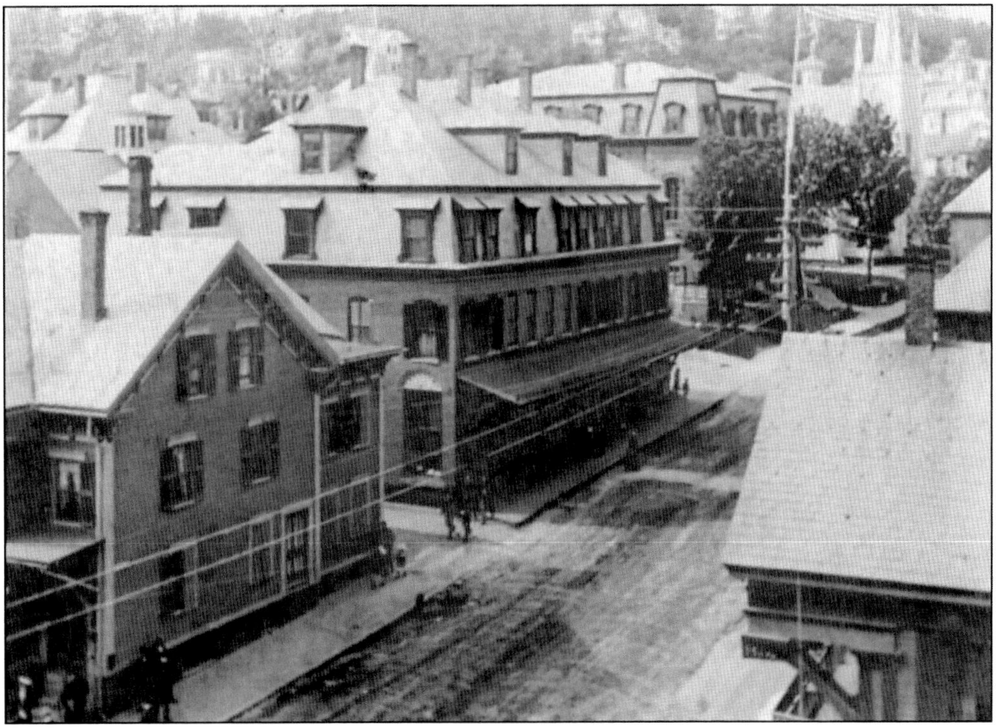

Looking north on North Main Street about 1903, the Whipple Block that faced West Main Street is seen at the left. Abraham's Temple is next with the post office located at the far end. Abraham's Temple was named after Abraham Putnam, who built it. The town hall and the Universalist Church are also visible. The Goddard Block at the corner of North Main and East Main Streets is at the lower right.

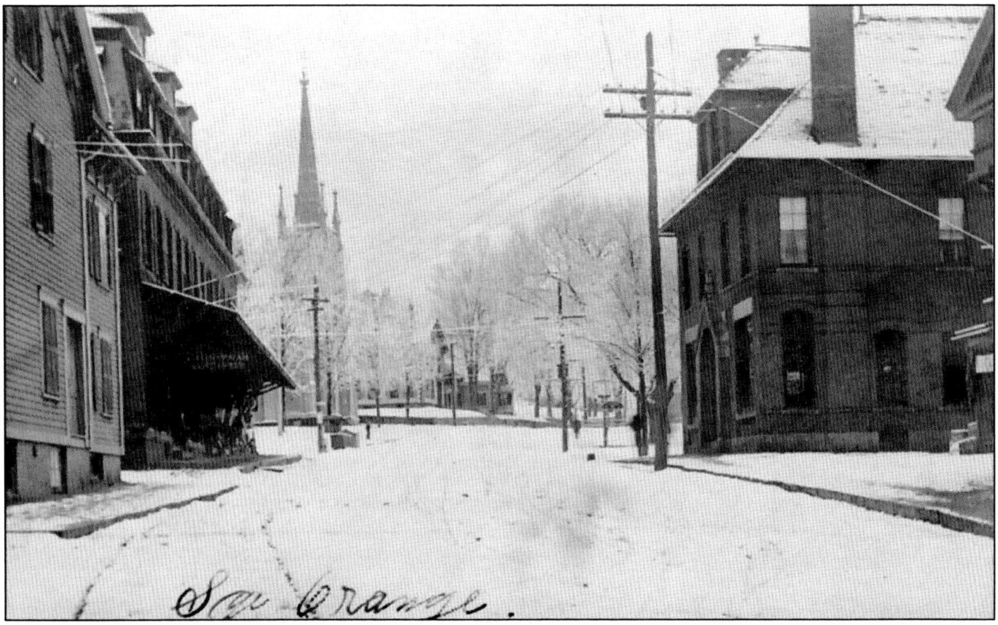

Looking north on North Main Street, the large brick building on the right is the bank building. It housed both the Orange National Bank and the Orange Savings Bank until 1902 when the savings bank moved to its own quarters on West Main Street.

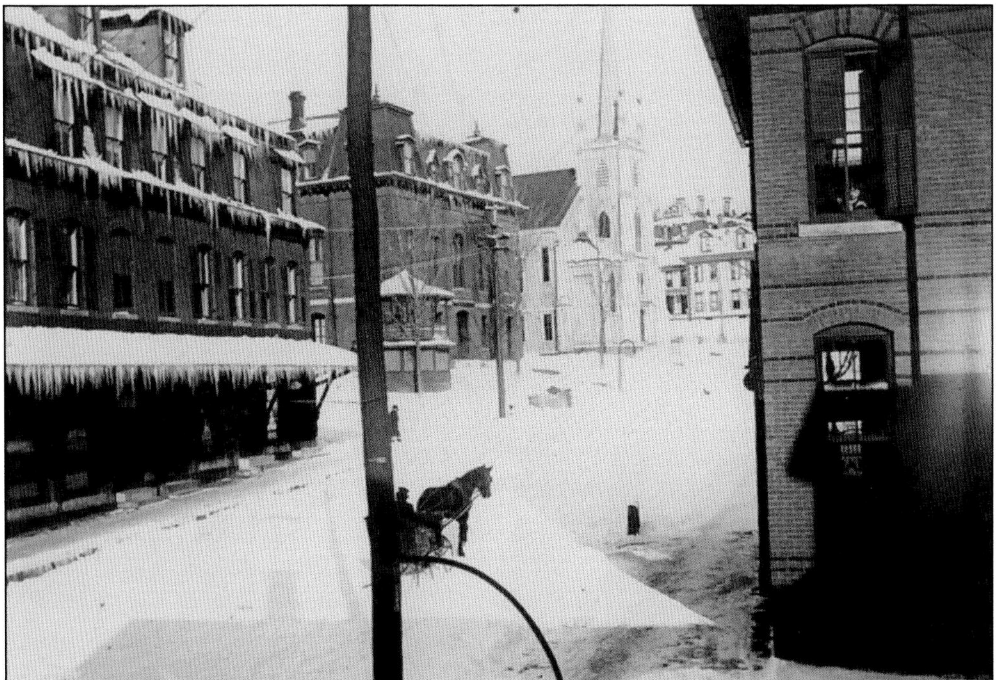

The bandstand next to the town hall is clearly visible in this wonderful mid-winter view looking north on North Main Street. Abraham's Temple, the town hall, the Universalist Church, and the Stephen French house are on the left. Notice the youngster peering out of the upper window of the bank building on the right.

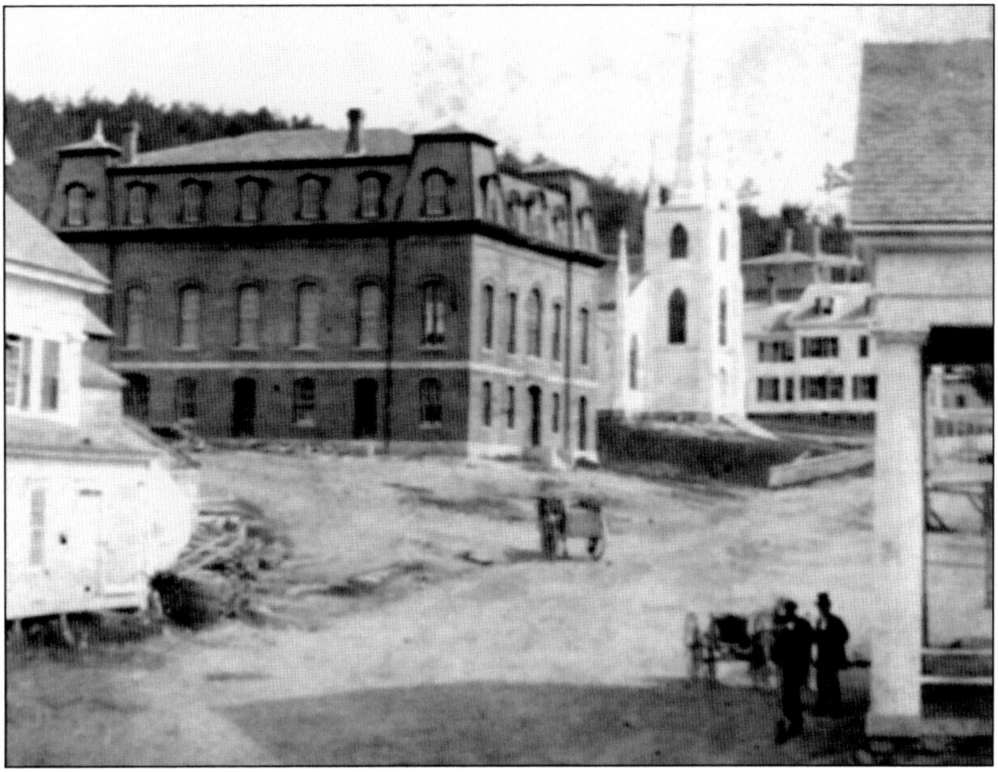

This view from the 1870s of North Main Street looking north shows the town hall, the Universalist Church, and the Stephen French house. At right, with columns, is the old Goddard Block on the corner of North Main and East Main Streets. Prospect Street is to the left beside the town hall. (Lesure.)

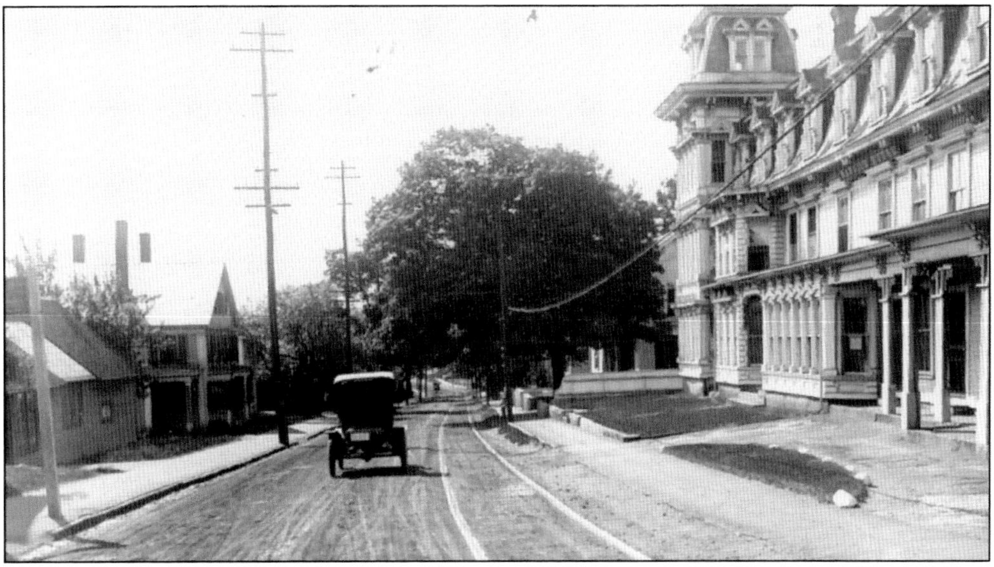

This view from about 1914 of West Main Street is looking west from in front of the Putnam House and shows the Mansion House on the right. Notice the trolley tracks. One could ride the trolley to Athol from 1895 until 1934. (Underwood.)

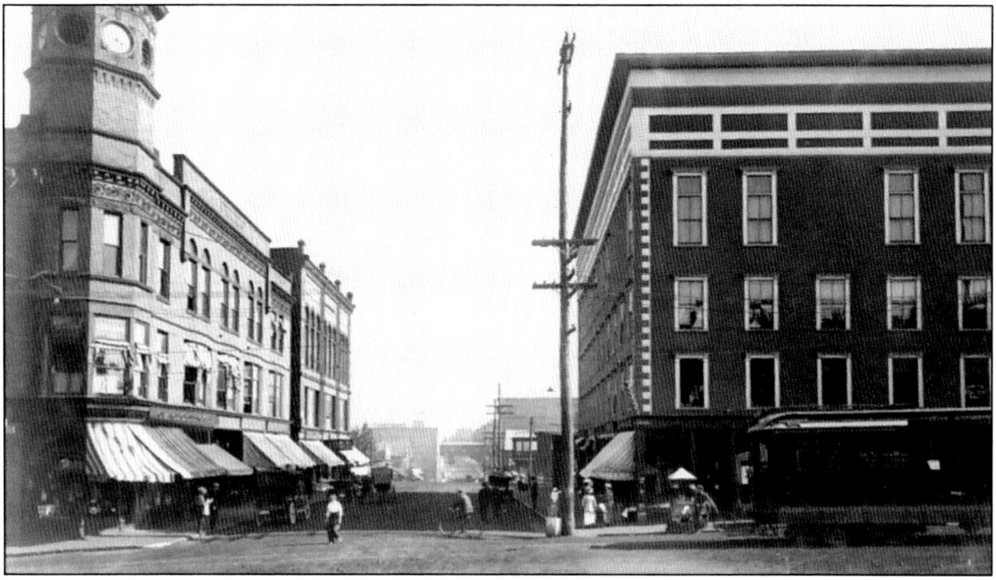

South Main Street as viewed looking south from the square is the subject of this view from about 1914. The Mann Block, with its tall clock tower, appears at the left at the corner of East Main Street. The Mann Block and the Masonic Block, also visible at the left, were built after the fire of 1891. They replaced the Congregational Church and Waite Block. At the right is Lambs Block. (Underwood.)

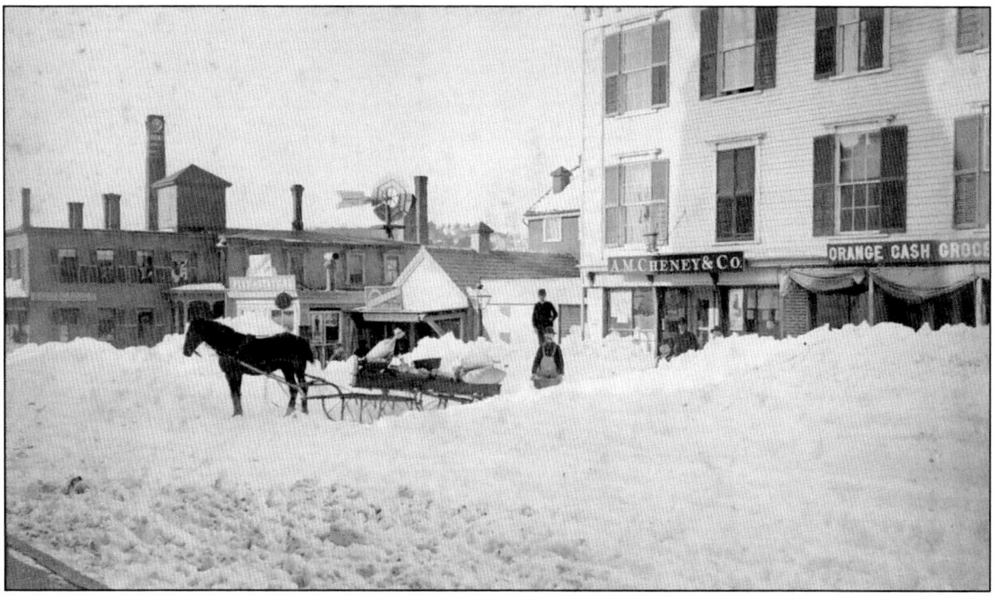

Judging from the amount of snow, this view of South Main Street looking southwest could easily be a photograph of the Blizzard of 1888. Cheney and Company and the Orange Cash Grocery were located in the southern end of Lambs Block. A. M. Cheney was a druggist.

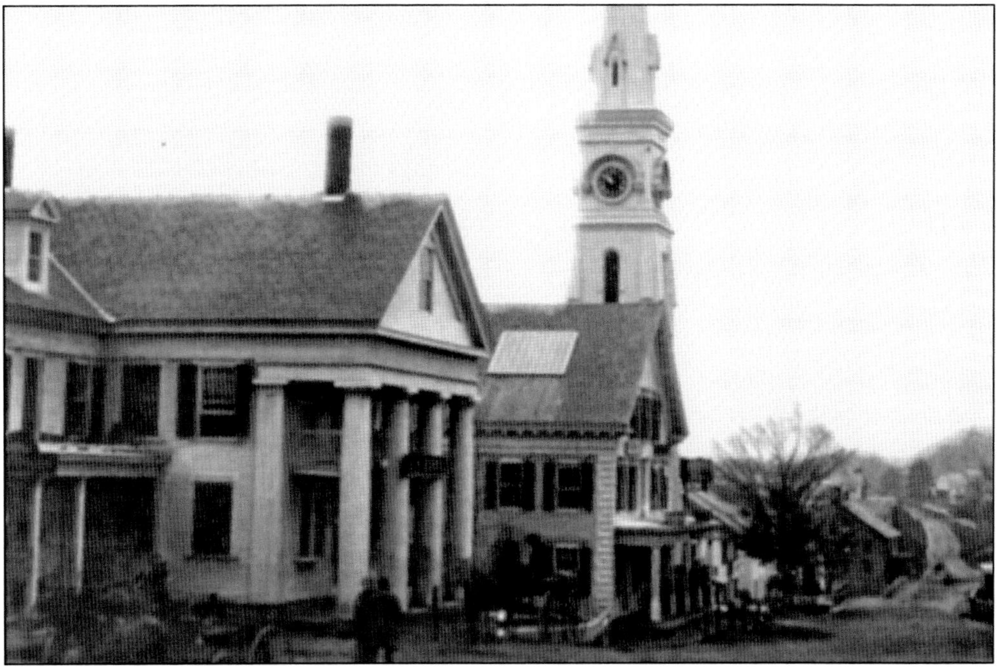

Looking south to South Main Street from North Main Street in the mid-1870s, the old Goddard Block, with columns, appears at the left. Next is the old Bank Block with the steeple of the Congregational Church visible above its roof. East Main Street is between the Goddard and Bank Blocks. (Union.)

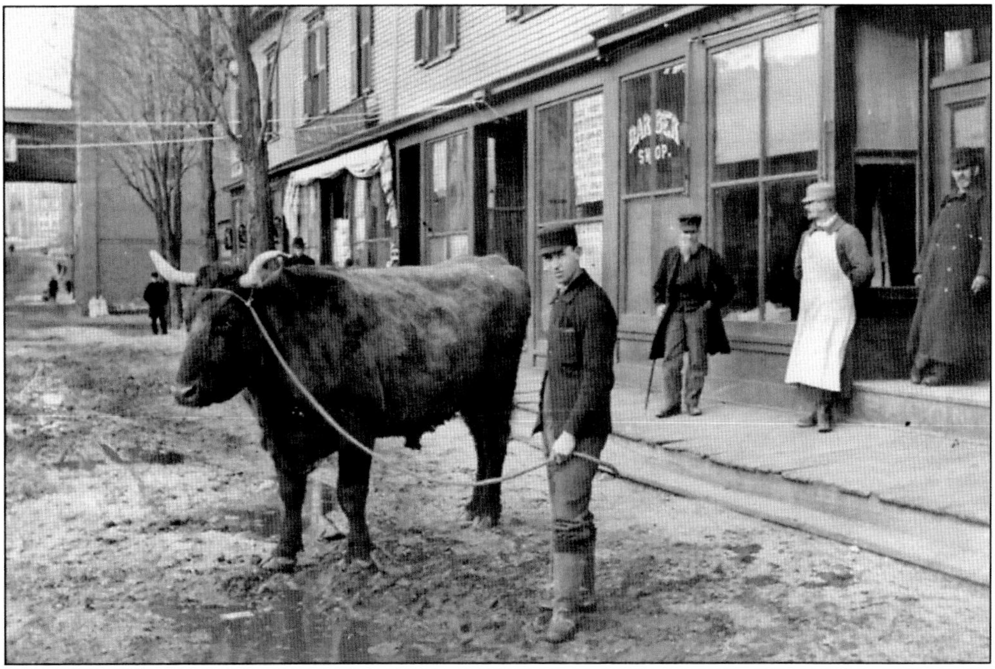

This gentleman is proudly displaying his prized ox in front of the Bingham Block at the corner of South Main and East River Streets. The passageway over South Main Street, visible at the left, connected buildings of the New Home Sewing Machine Company. (Harris and Johnson.)

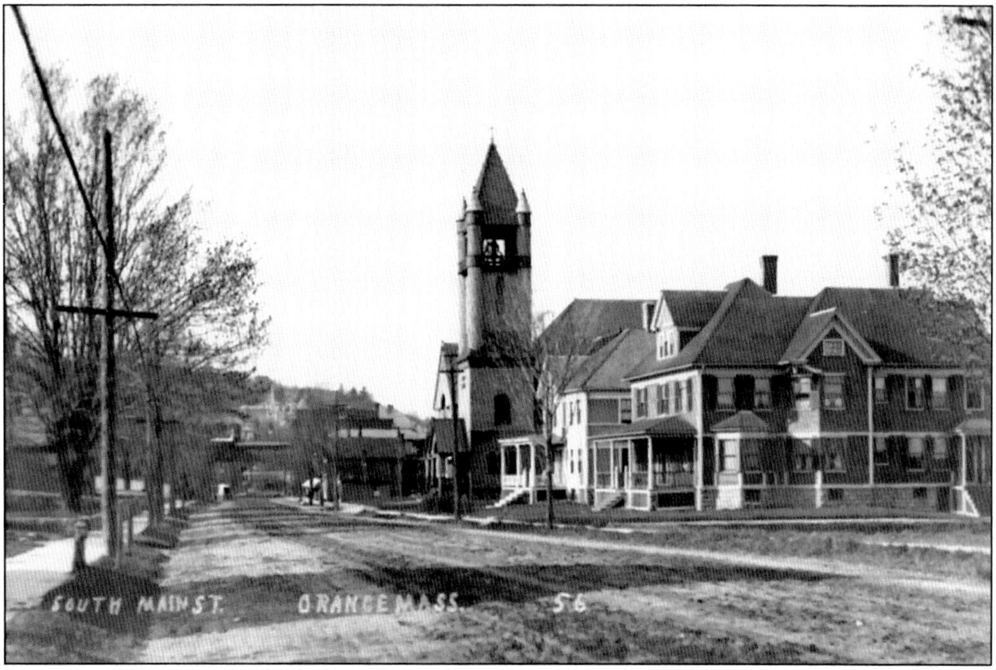

This view is looking north on South Main Street. The Congregational Church, with its large steeple, dominates the scene. The steeple was lost to the hurricane of 1938. The scene is from around 1915. (Eastern Illustrating.)

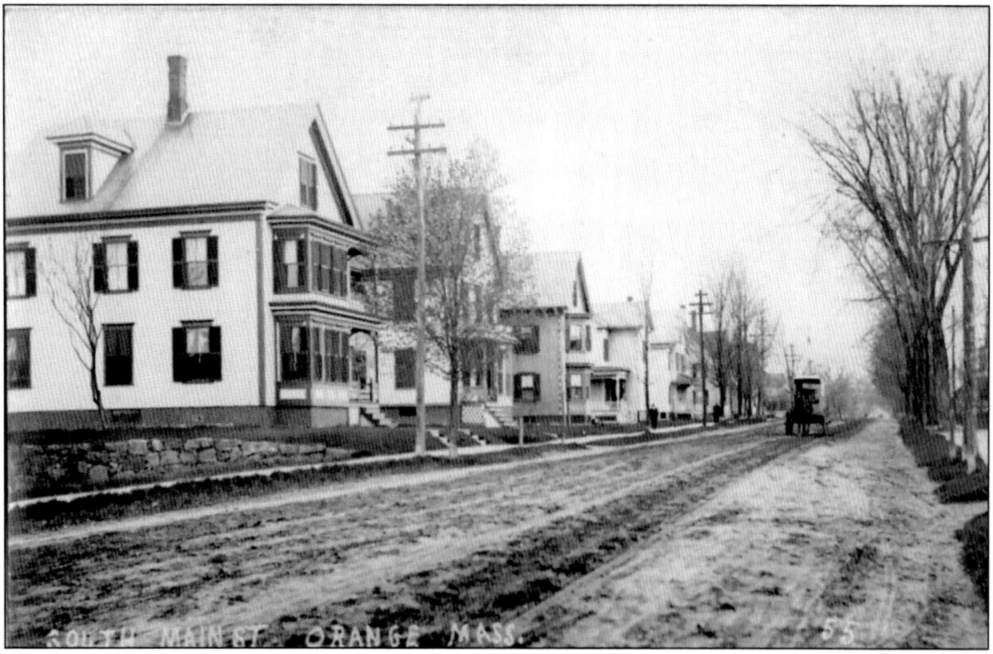

South Main Street looking south is shown about 1910 in this image. The first house is 129 South Main Street.

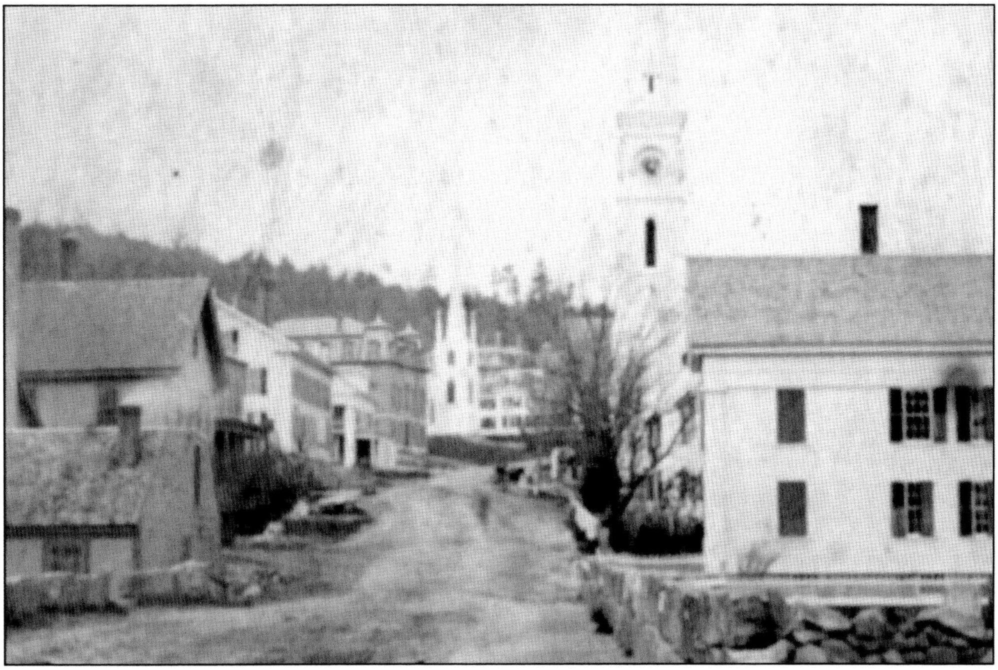

Taken from the old stone arch bridge over the Millers River on South Main Street, this mid-1870s photograph looks north. The old Whipple Block appears on North Main Street with only a white column visible. The town hall and Universalist Church are visible in the distance. The large building on the right is on the corner of Water Street in what is now Memorial Park. (Lesure.)

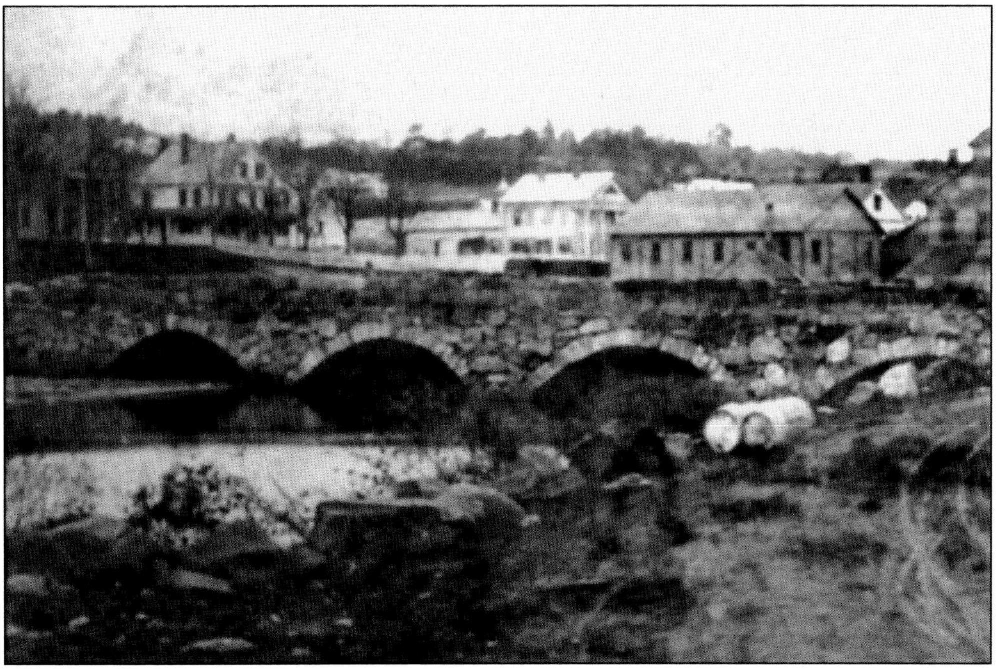

The old stone arch bridge over the Millers River is shown in this mid-1870s view looking southwest from near the present-day fire station. The houses in the background are along West River Street.

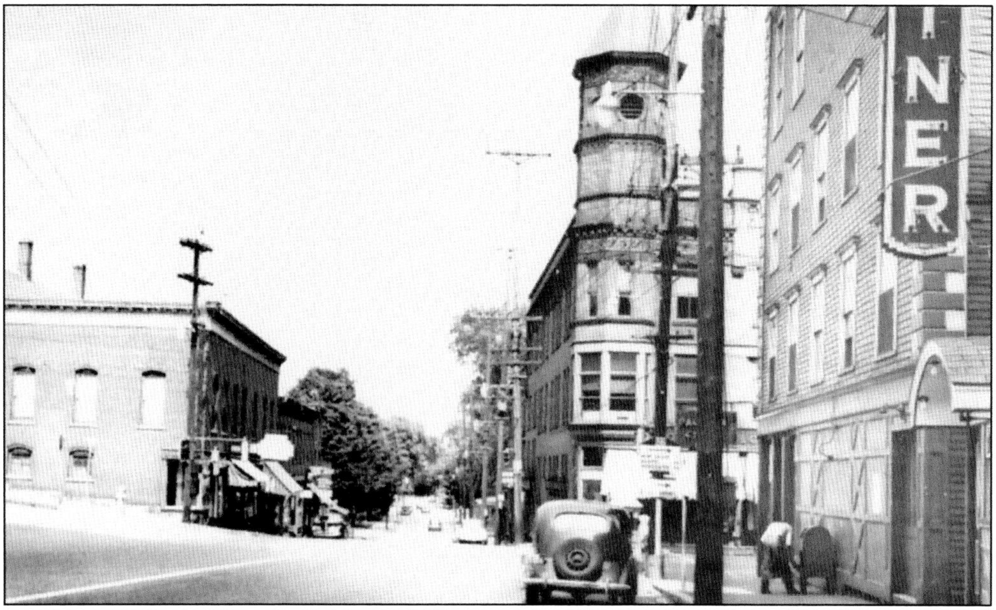

The Mann Block, with its tall clock tower, is clearly visible in this view of East Main Street looking east from the square around 1950. The Mann Block that replaced the Waite Block after it was destroyed by fire in 1891 was, itself, destroyed by fire in 1954. (Fairbanks.)

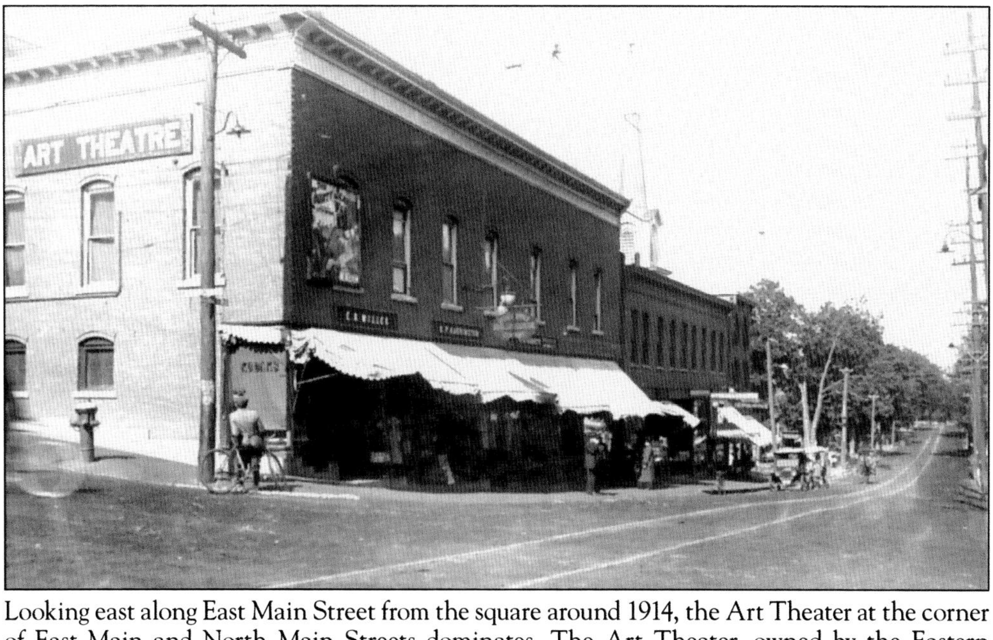

Looking east along East Main Street from the square around 1914, the Art Theater at the corner of East Main and North Main Streets dominates. The Art Theater, owned by the Eastern Theater Company and managed by H. J. Sheerer, showed moving pictures. It fronted on North Main Street that extends to the left where the fire hydrant appears. The steeple of the Baptist Church can be seen rising above the buildings.

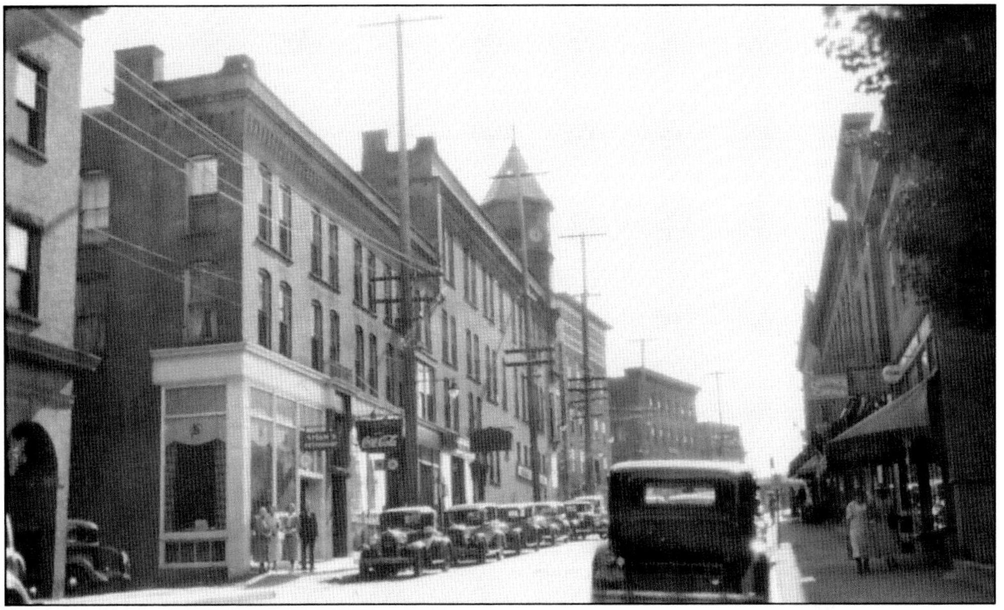

The hustle and bustle along East Main Street is evident in this pre–World War II view looking west toward the square. The Mann Block clock tower, Lambs Block, and the Odd Fellows Block are all visible at the center of the image.

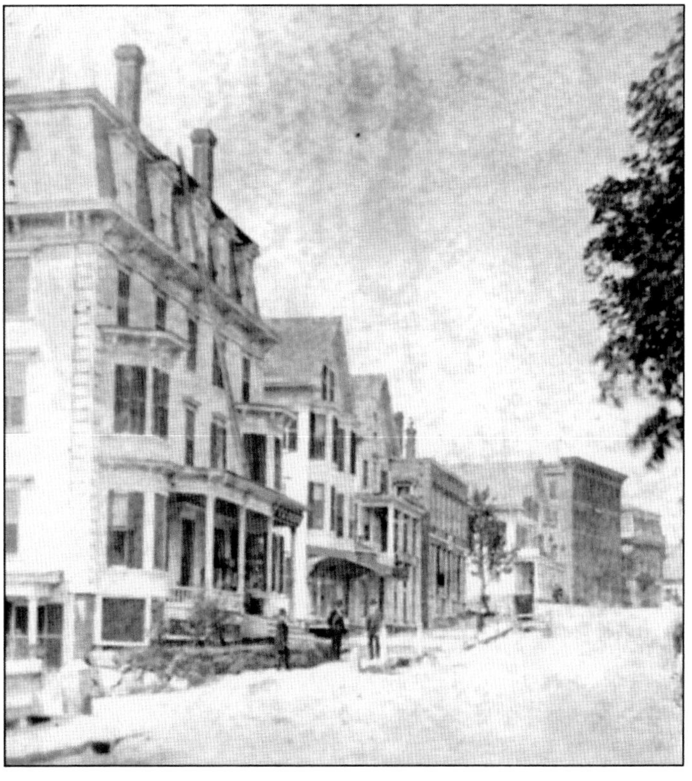

Looking toward the square along East Main Street in this early image, the only recognizable structure is the Putnam Opera House Block, later called the Odd Fellows Block, on West Main Street.

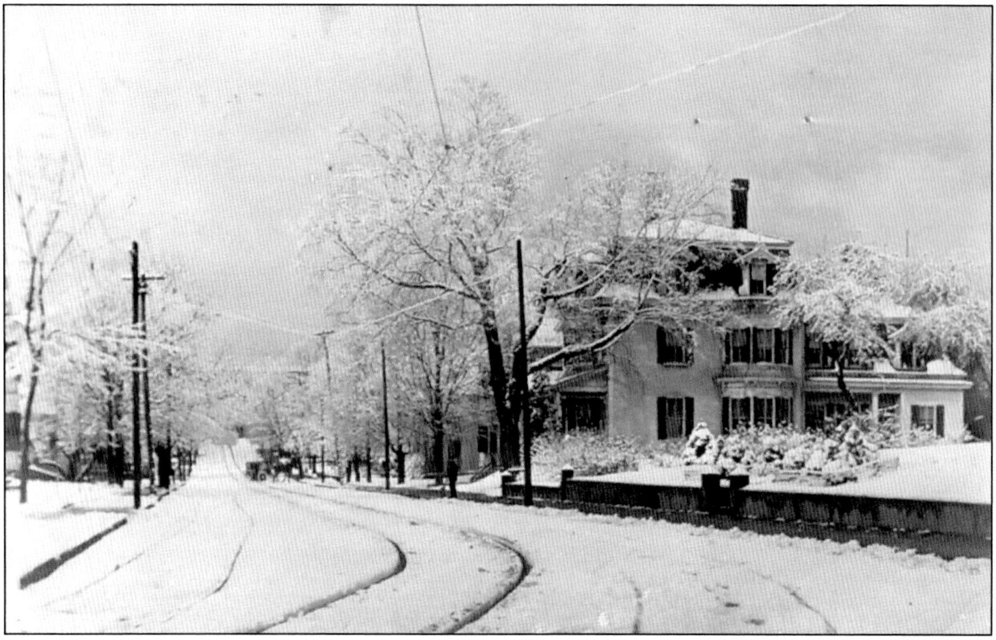

Winter 1908 is shown in this snowy image on East Main Street looking west from in front of the Wheeler Mansion. The house in the foreground is 61 East Main Street. Note both horse and buggy and trolley tracks are visible in the snow.

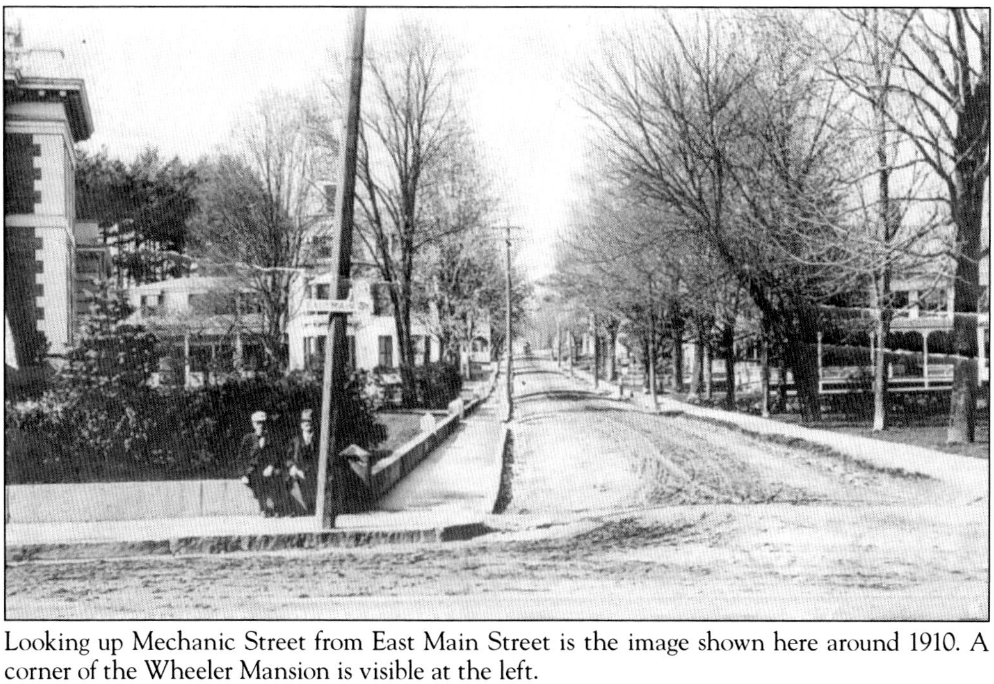

Looking up Mechanic Street from East Main Street is the image shown here around 1910. A corner of the Wheeler Mansion is visible at the left.

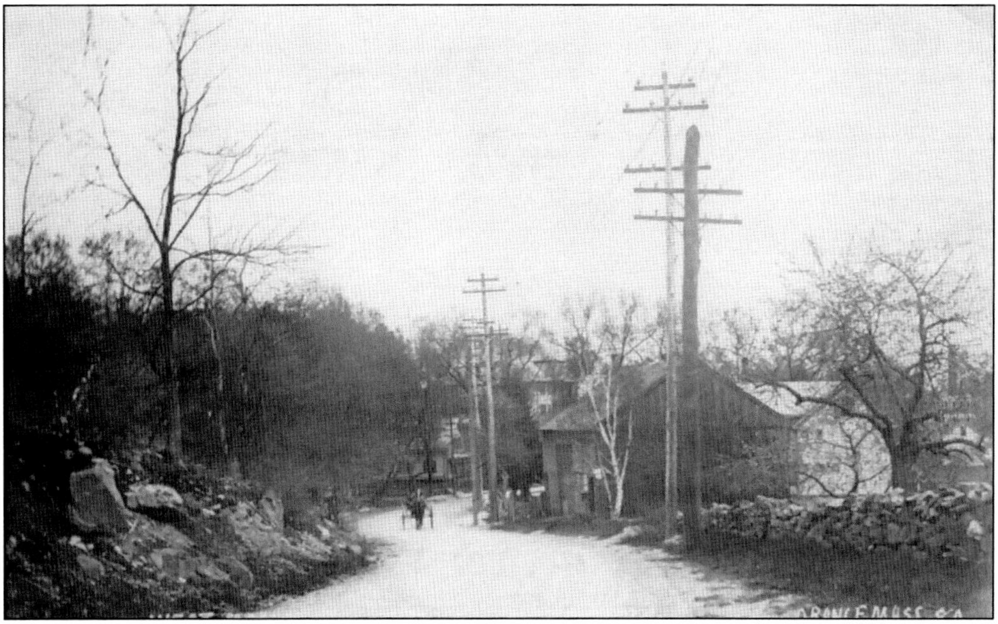

When entering Orange from the west on West Main Street around 1910, a close look through the trees at the far right reveals the windows of the Minute Tapioca Company building in this photograph.

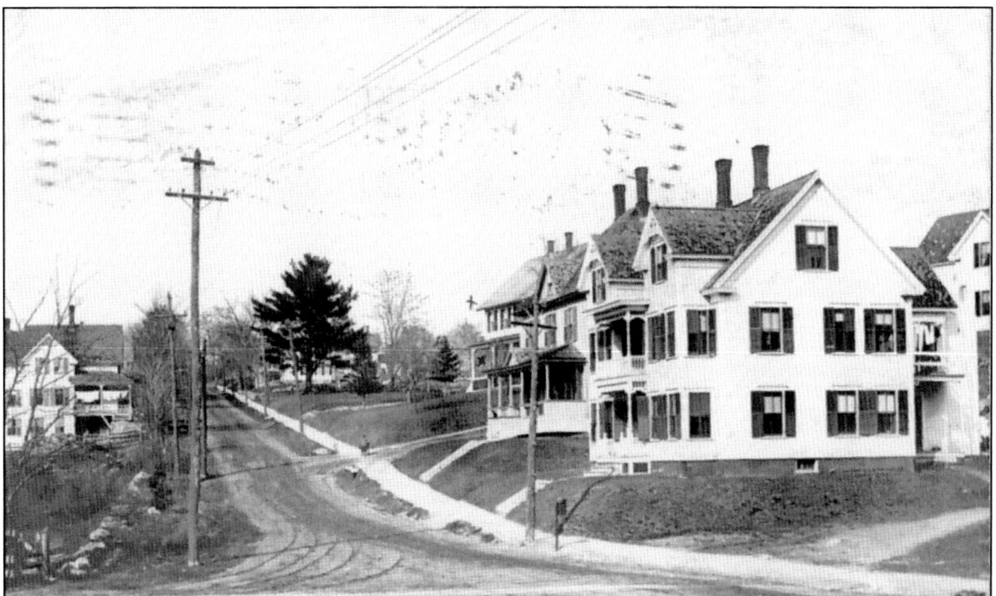

North Main Street looking north at the Dexter Street intersection is seen in this image from about 1910. Dexter Street branches to the left.

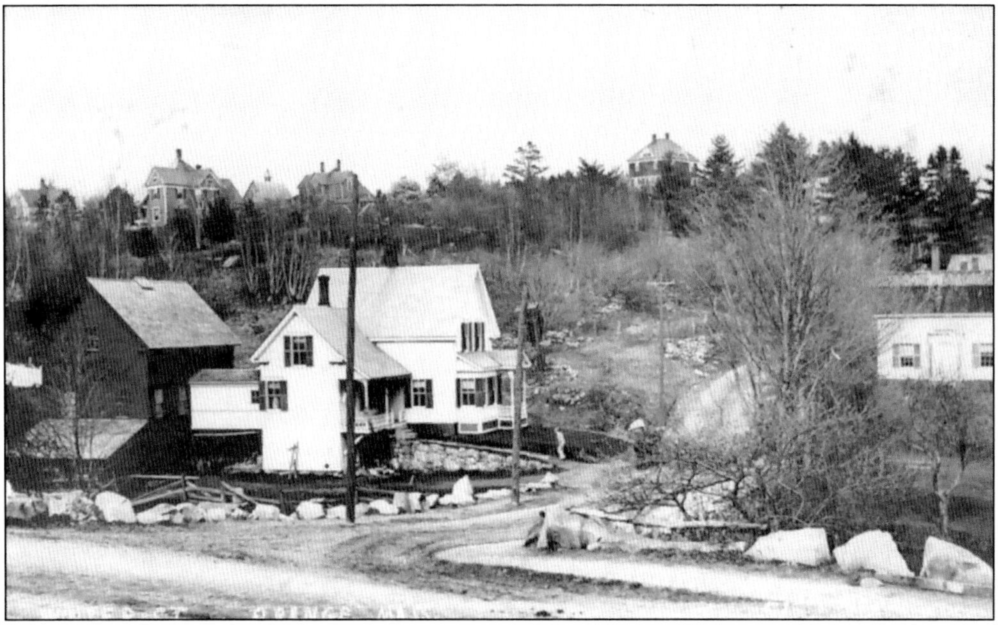

Winter Street is seen here around 1910 from North Main Street.

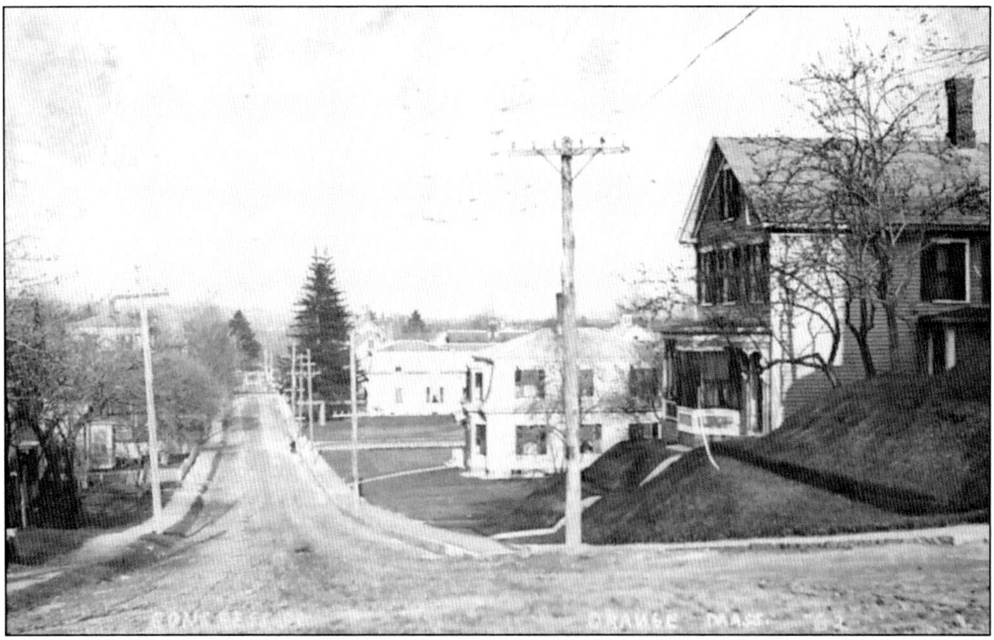

Walter Cole's home at 47 Congress Street, at the right near the intersection with Pleasant Street, is shown in this image from about 1910. Cole was employed at the New Home Sewing Machine Company.

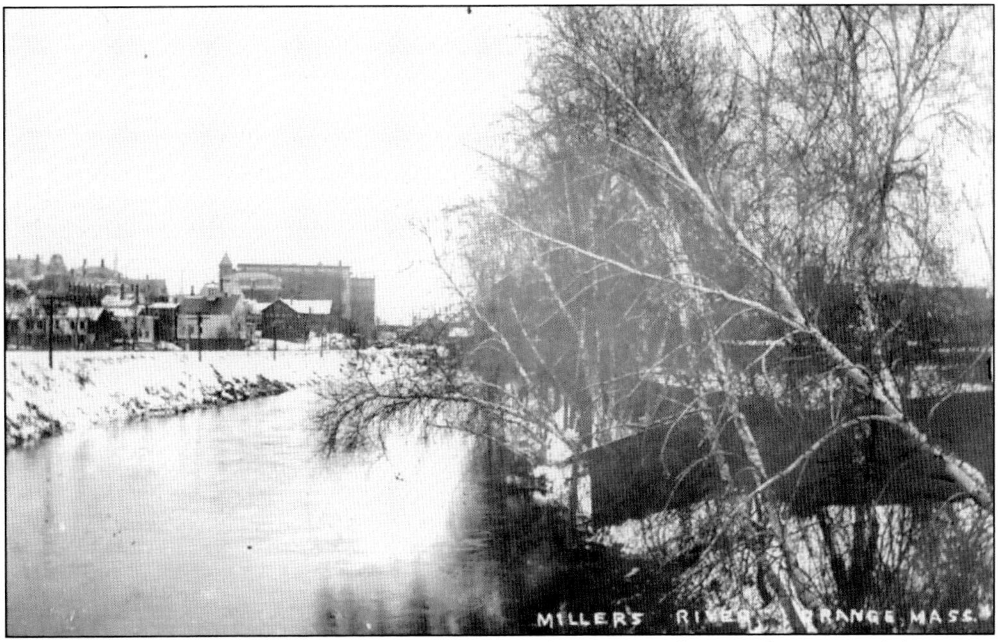

The Millers River flows through Orange and was the source of power for many of the major industries. Tradition has it that the Nipmuck Indians named the river "Baygwage," and that the name Millers River stems from the death of a Mr. Miller who drowned while attempting to cross it on his way to Northfield. This scene is looking east toward the center. Clearly visible is the clock tower of the Mann Block at the corner of East and South Main Streets.

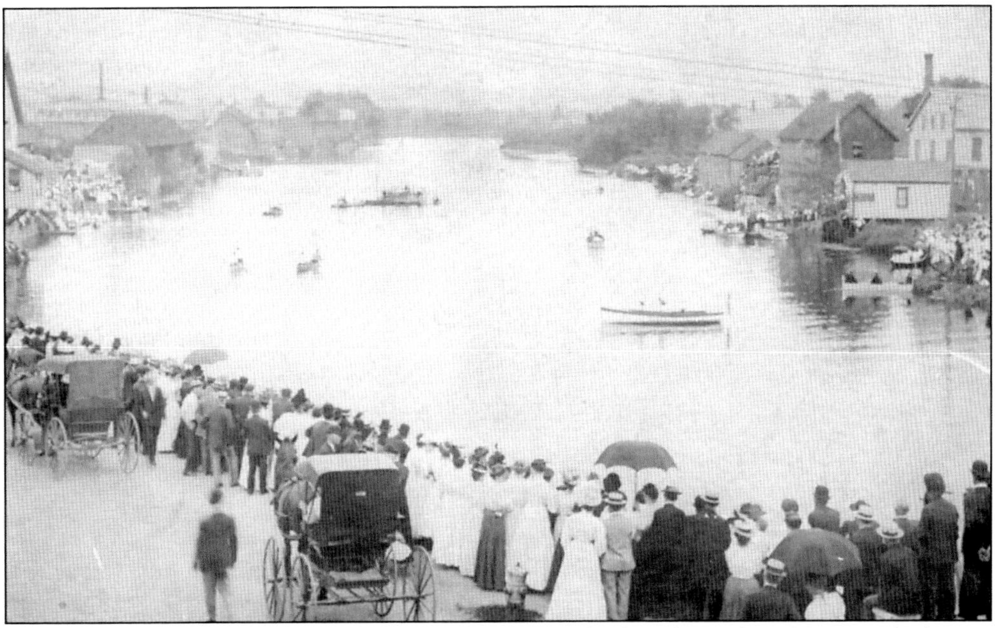

Viewed from the northern end of the South Main Street bridge, this early 1900s image looks east over the Millers River. The present day River Rat canoe race ends here.

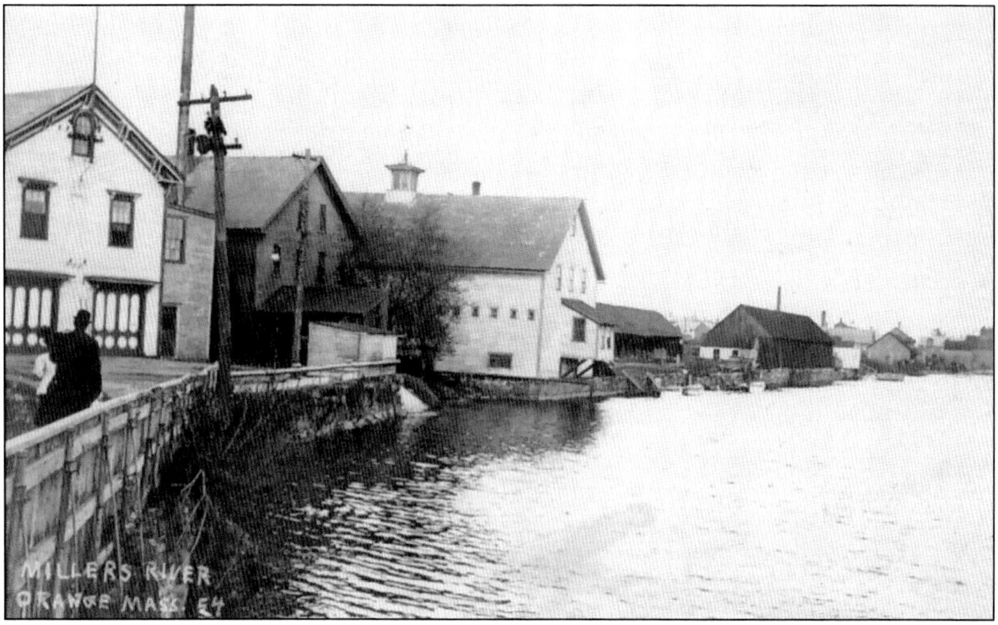

Looking east along the northern bank of the Millers River from the South Main Street bridge shows the fire station on Water Street on the left about 1910.

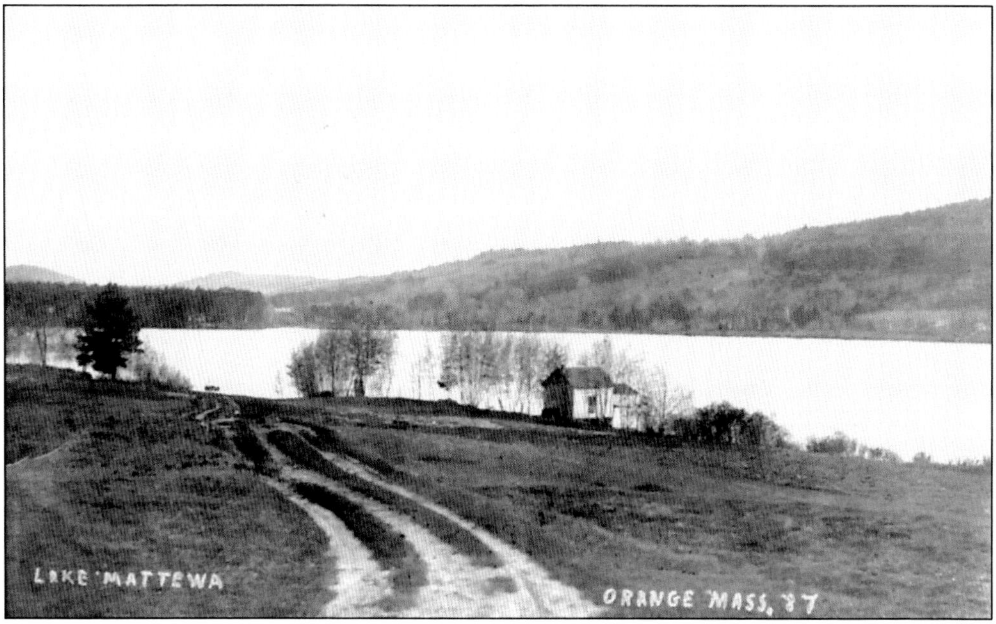

As it does today, Lake Mattawa provided a welcome respite from the work-a-day world in the early part of the 20th century. This view looks east across the lake. Present-day Route 2 runs horizontally along the hills seen across the lake. Early documentation and maps from around 1905 refer to Lake Mattawa as North Pond. (Eastern Illustrating.)

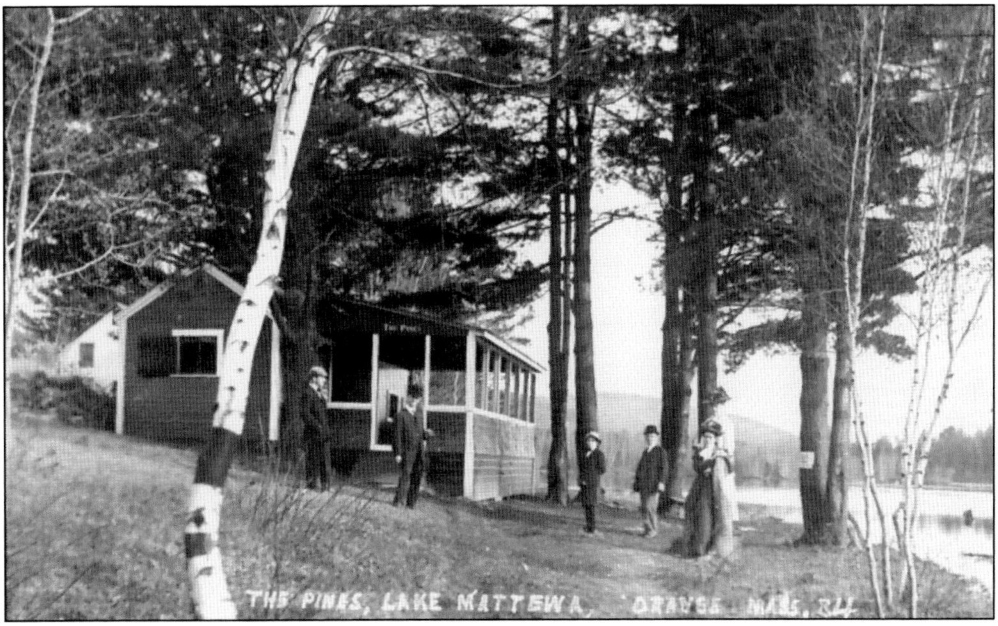

The Pines, seen here on the shore of Lake Mattawa in this image, was typical of the get-away camps surrounding the lake. (Eastern Illustrating.)

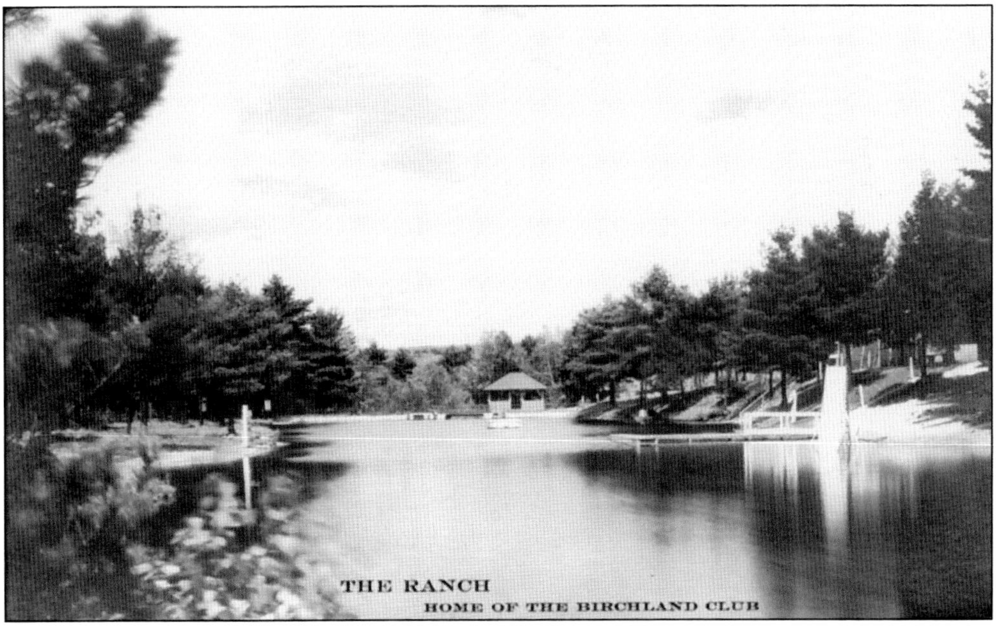

The Ranch, a recreation facility for employees of the Minute Tapioca Company, provided a great venue for relaxation. Complete with pavilions, swimming pool, tennis courts, and ball fields, the facility was very popular. This 1940s view shows the dam that formed the swimming pool. The facility was on East River Street where the present day Leisure Woods Mobile Home park is located.

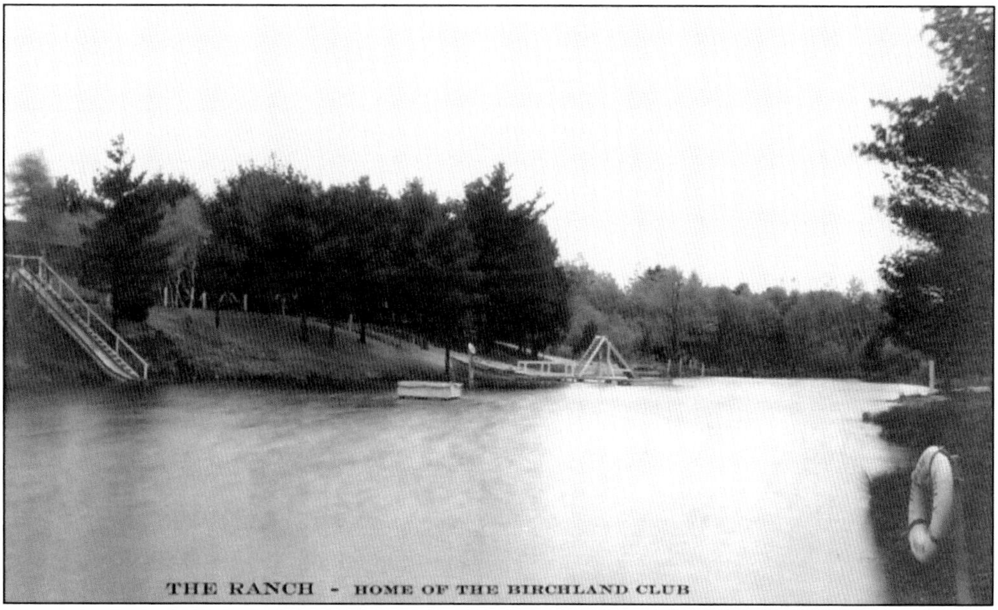

The swimming pool at the Ranch recreational facility is shown complete with waterslide to the left in the above photograph. The very popular young children's pool is shown below.

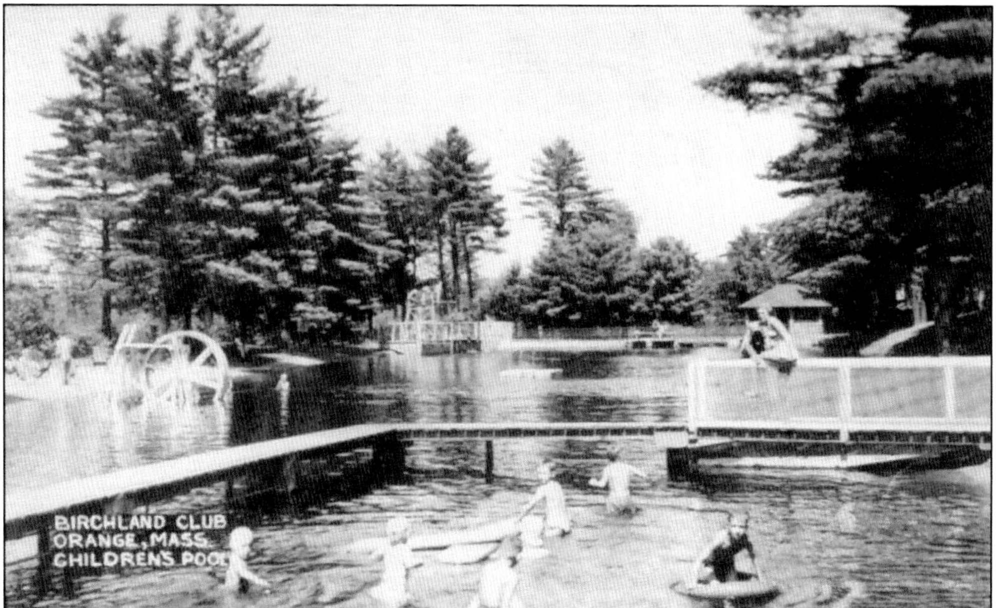

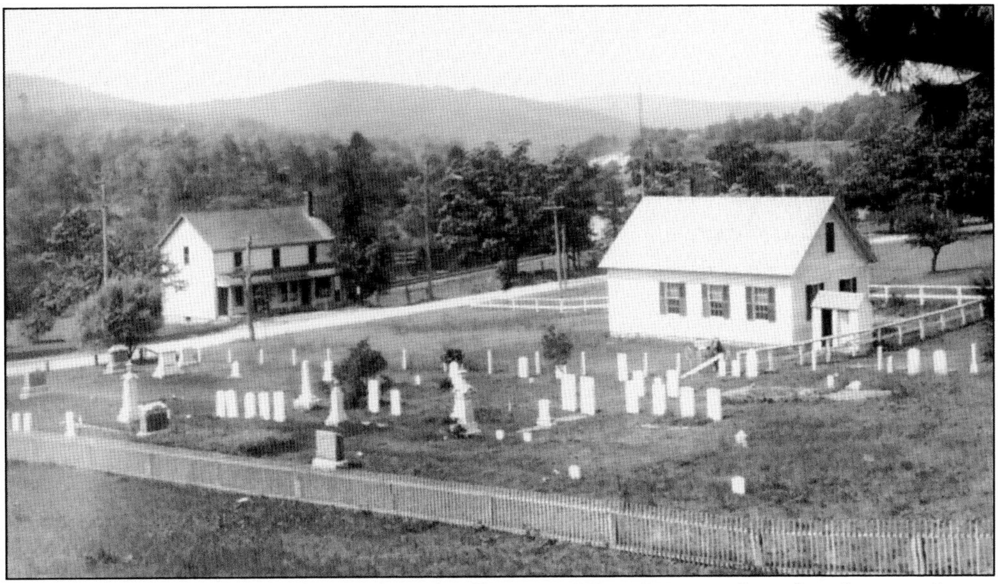

Fanny L. Smith was the teacher at the schoolhouse in West Orange when this photograph was taken, around 1914. Notice the interesting placement of the school adjacent to the cemetery. Across the road, today known as Route 2A, is the Haynes General Store.

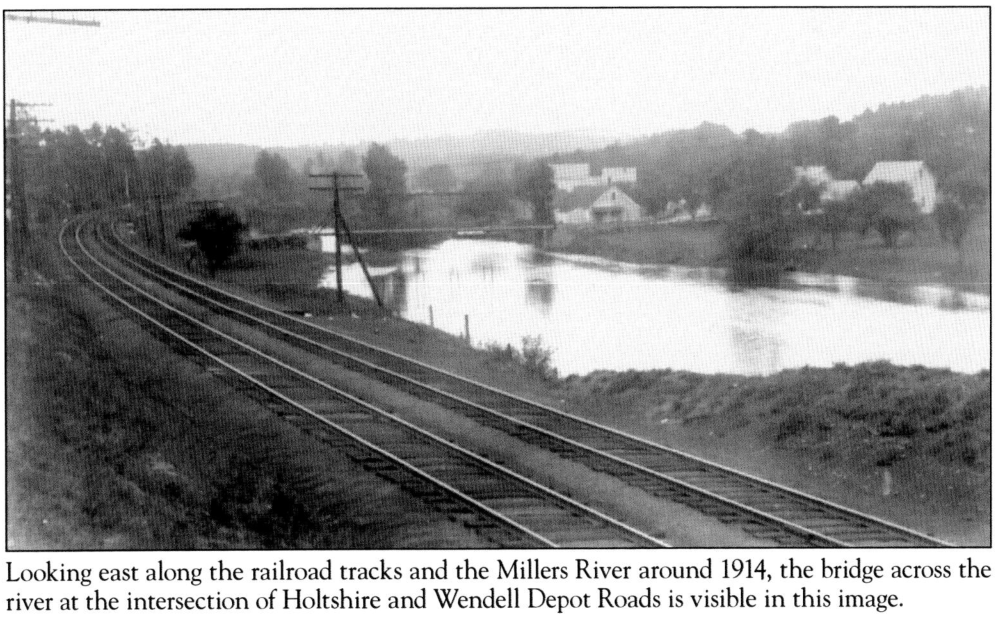

Looking east along the railroad tracks and the Millers River around 1914, the bridge across the river at the intersection of Holtshire and Wendell Depot Roads is visible in this image.

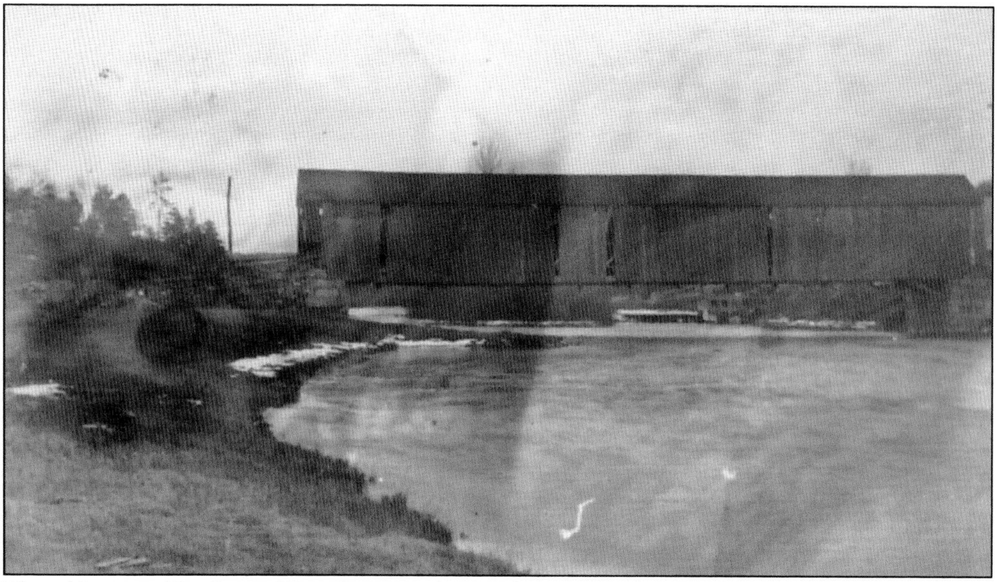

The old covered bridge at West Orange, shown above around 1907, collapsed and was replaced with the steel bridge shown below. The steel bridge is visible in the view looking east on page 69. It has since been replaced with the concrete and steel bridge that is still in place today.

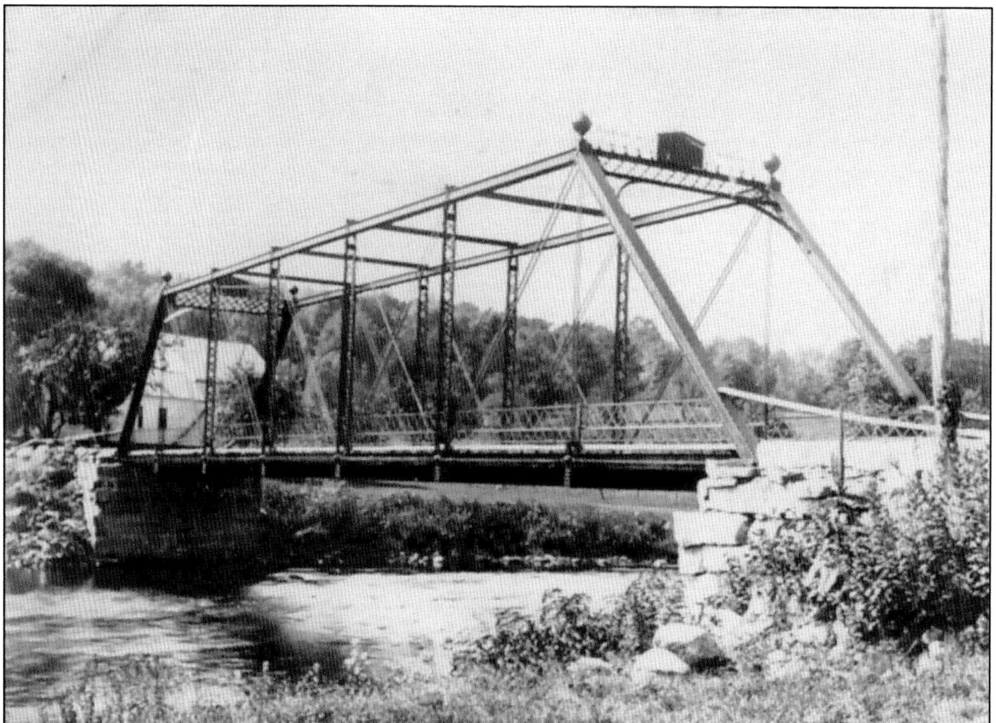

Three

Orange's Centennial Celebration

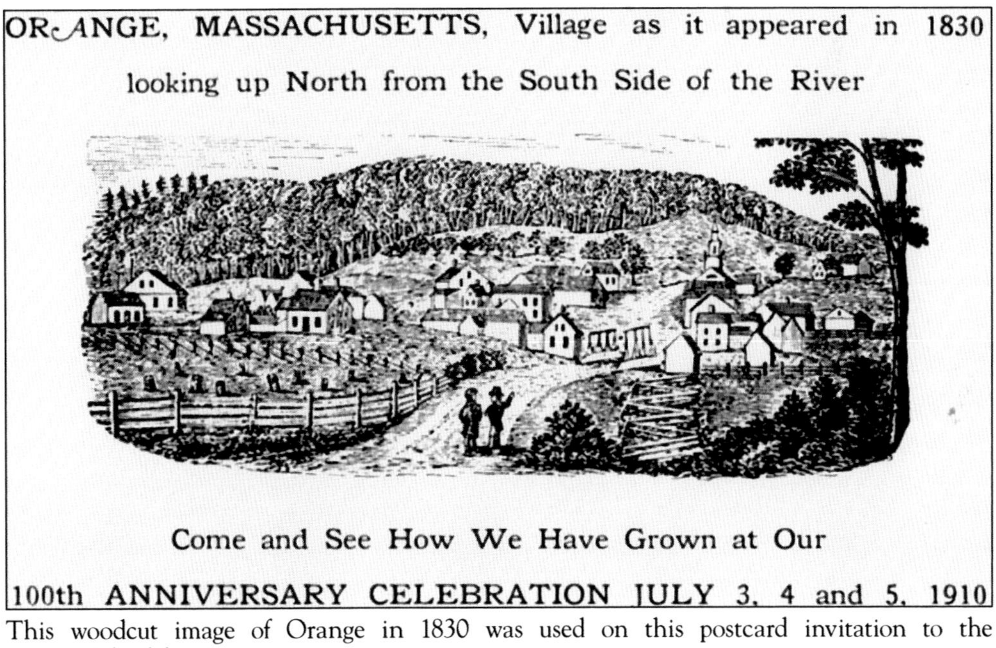

This woodcut image of Orange in 1830 was used on this postcard invitation to the centennial celebration.

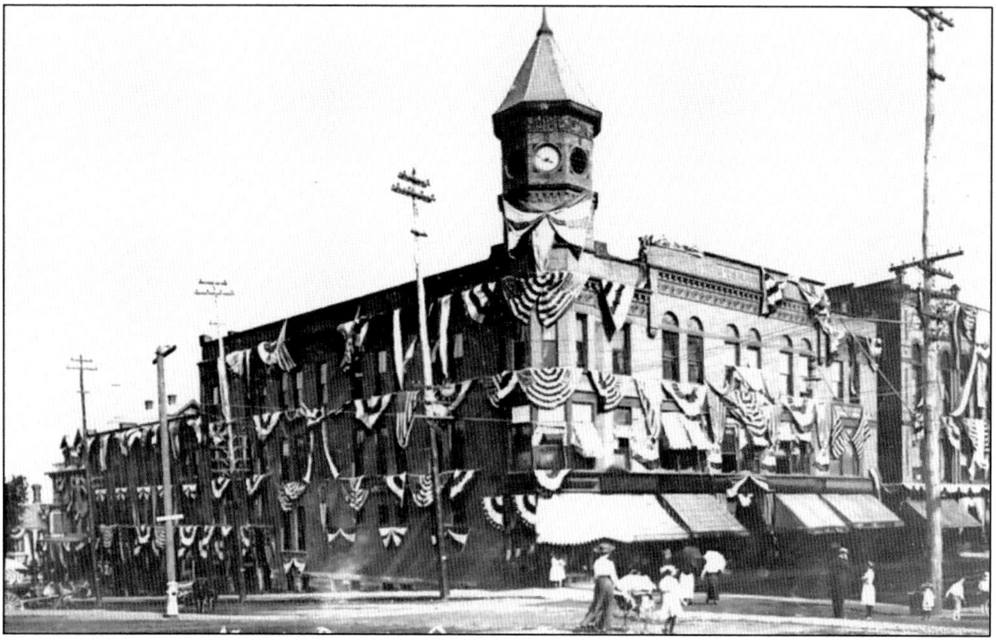

The Mann Block was festively decorated for the centennial celebration. It must have been a daunting task to place the bunting high upon the clock tower. (Underwood.)

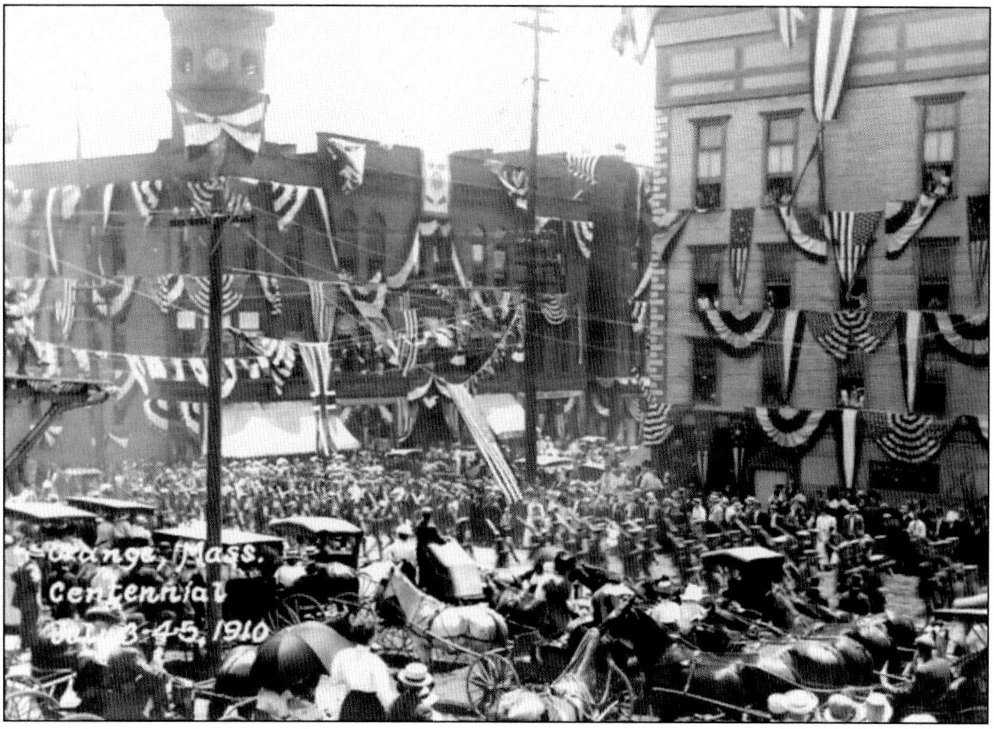

Some of the crowd, estimated to top 20,000 over the three-day celebration, can be seen in the square. Marching units of the Military Dress Parade can be seen making the turn from North Main Street onto West Main Street. This was one of several parades, including an automobile parade, which marked the celebration.

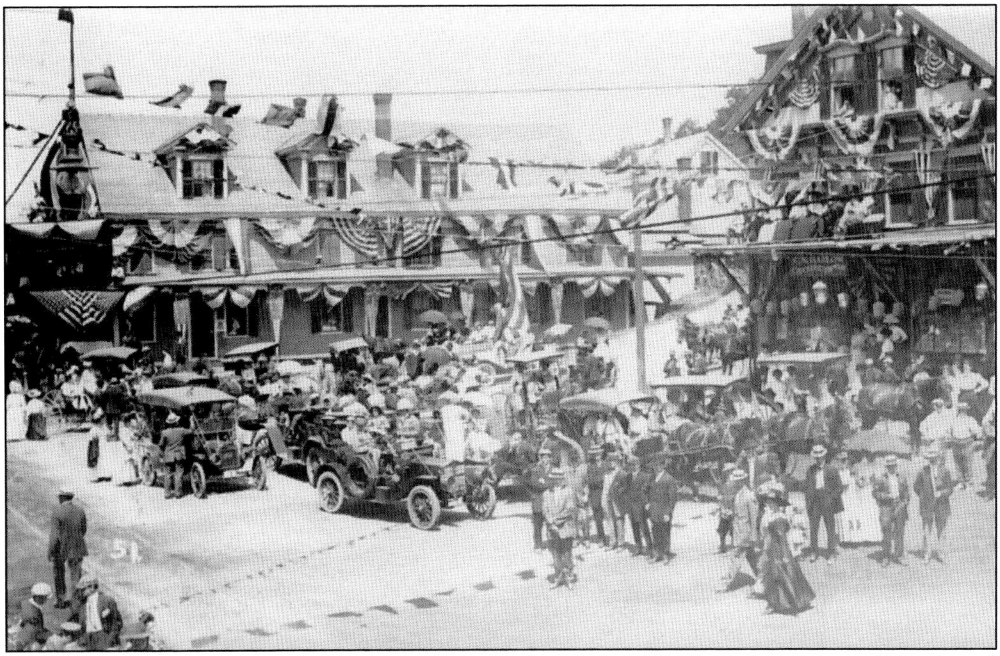

More of the huge crowd can be seen in front of the Harlow Block at the corner of North and West Main Streets. The heavily decorated Putnam House is to the rear. Notice the people sitting on the overhang roof of the Harlow Block. (Eastern Illustrating.)

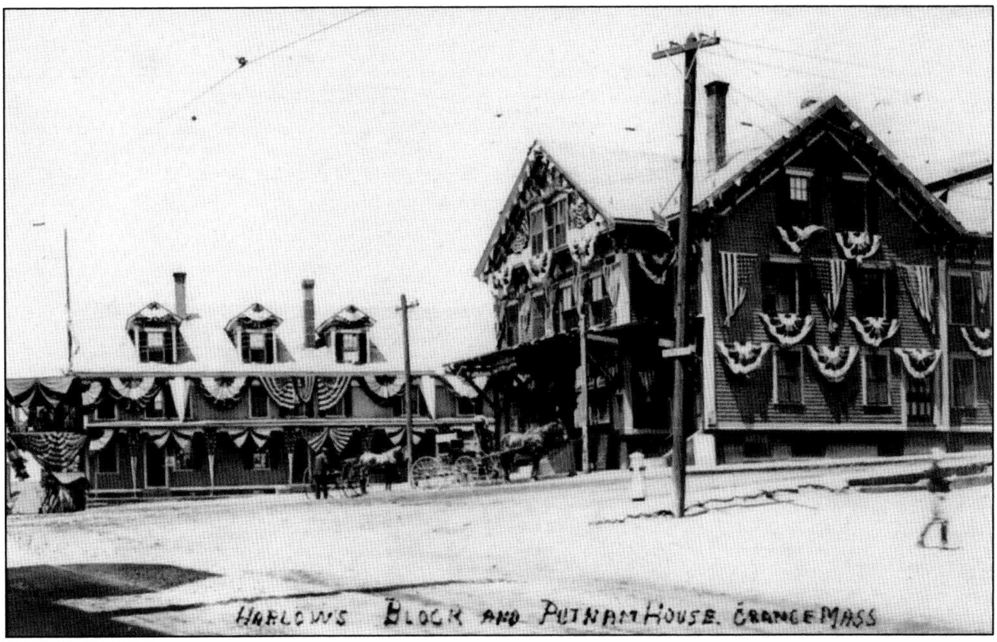

The heavily decorated Harlow and Putnam Blocks are the subject of this centennial celebration image. At the time this photograph was taken, Harlow was the owner of the former Whipple Block. He was a dealer in crockery and tin ware as proclaimed by his sign hanging below the overhang on the front of the building.

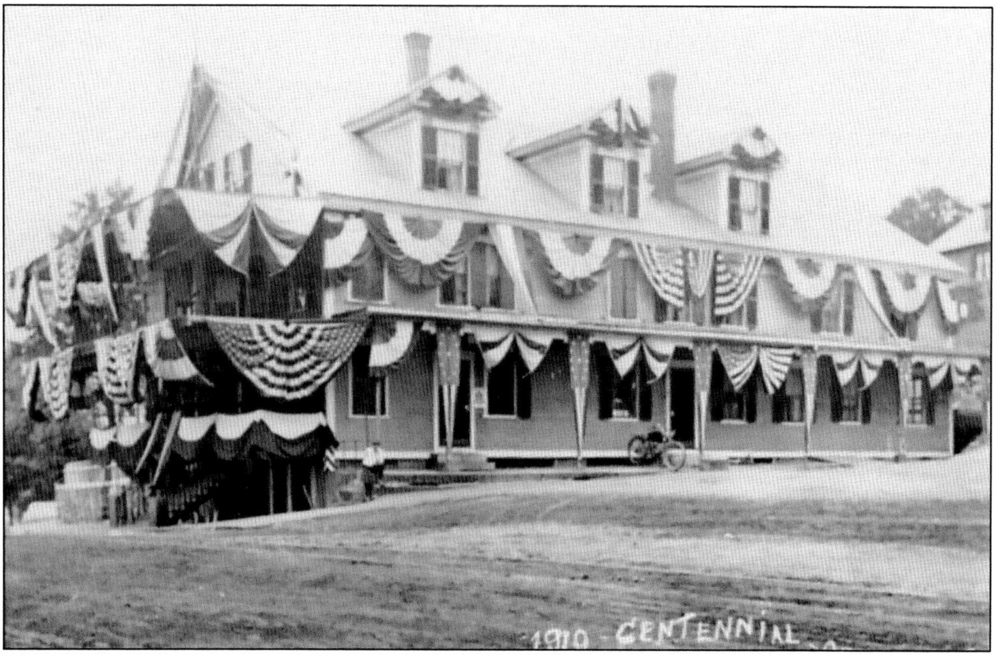

The Putnam House was ready for the centennial celebration. Note the early motorcycle parked along the side of the building.

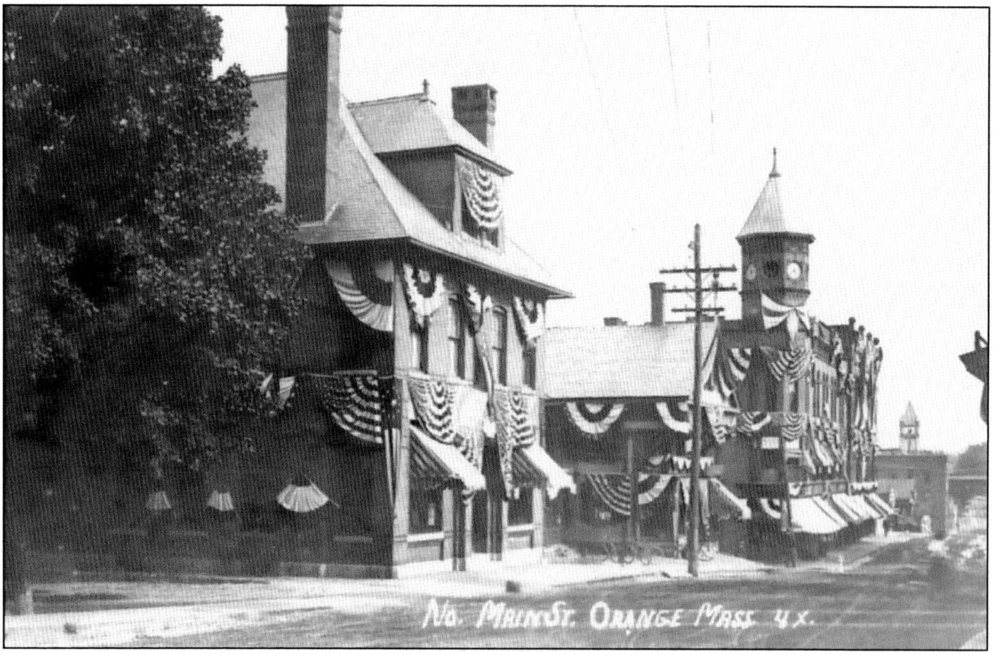

Buildings along North and South Main Streets were adorned with bunting. The Orange National Bank building, Goddard Block, Mann Block, and Masonic Block are shown. The steeple of the Congregational church can be seen in the distance.

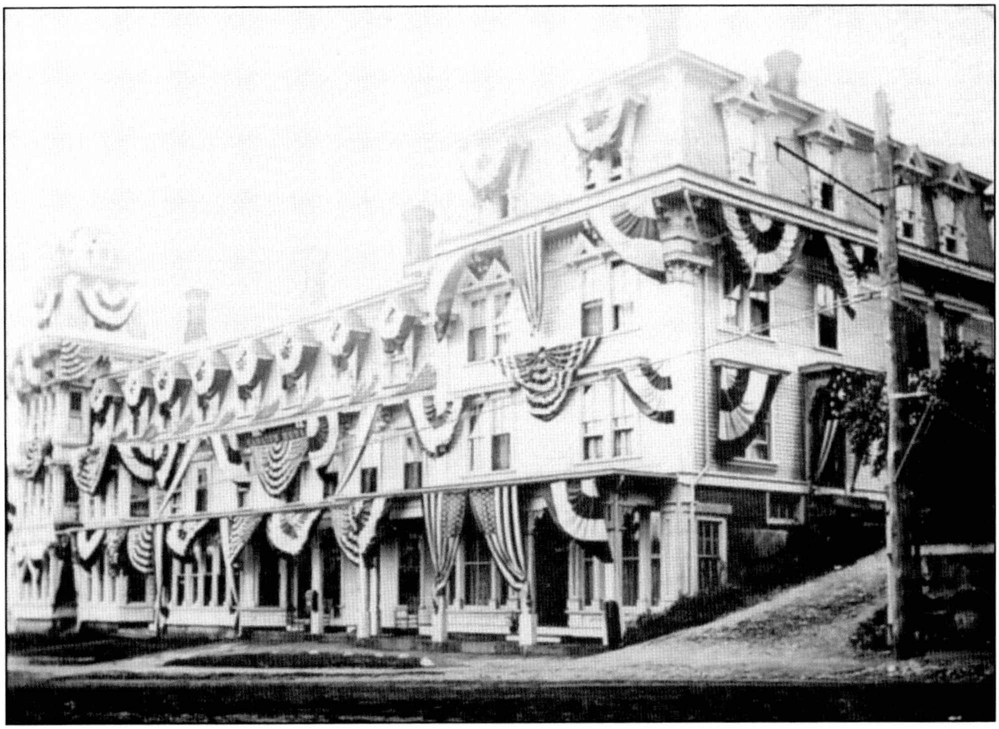

Shown in full celebration dress are the Mansion House on West Main Street (above), and the Central School on North Main Street (below).

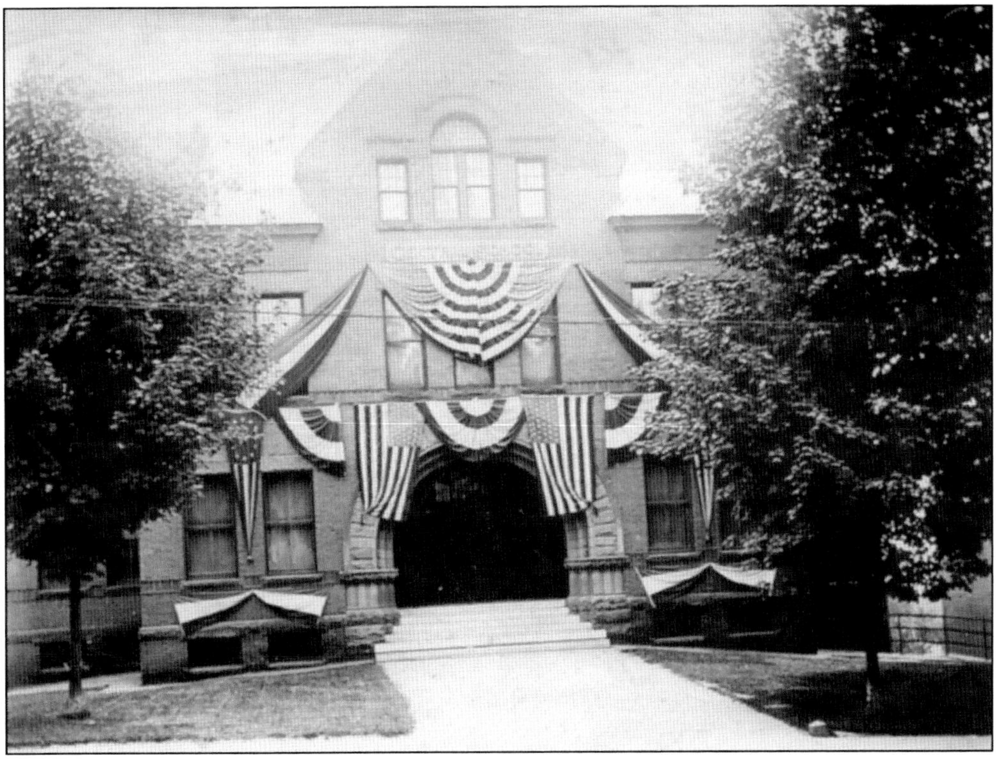

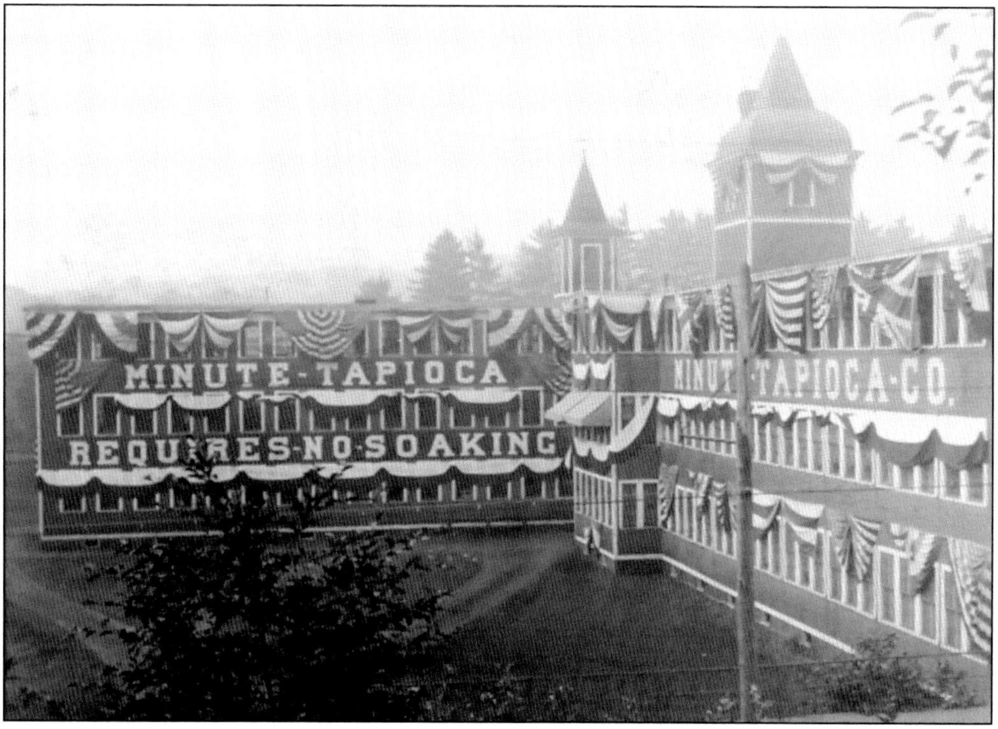

Businesses exhibited their enthusiasm and patriotic spirit for the centennial celebration with prominent displays of bunting and flags. The Minute Tapioca Company on West Main Street is shown above, and the Frederick H. Sprague Company on East Main Street is shown below.

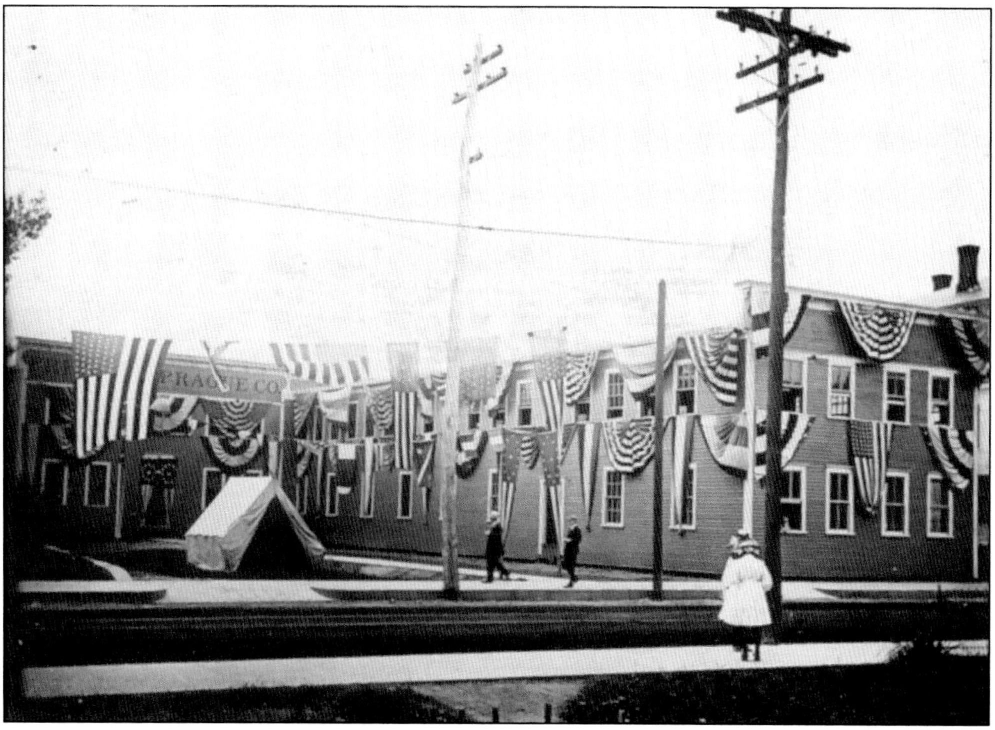

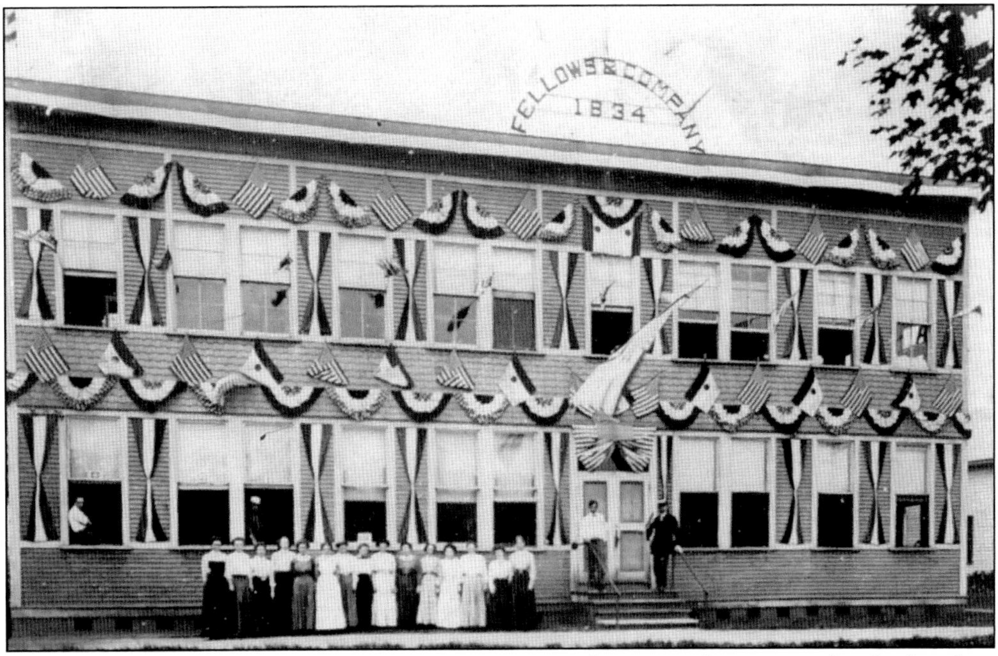

Fellows and Company at 48 West River Street was a shirt manufacturer in this facility. It is shown here, ready for the centennial celebration with employees posed in front.

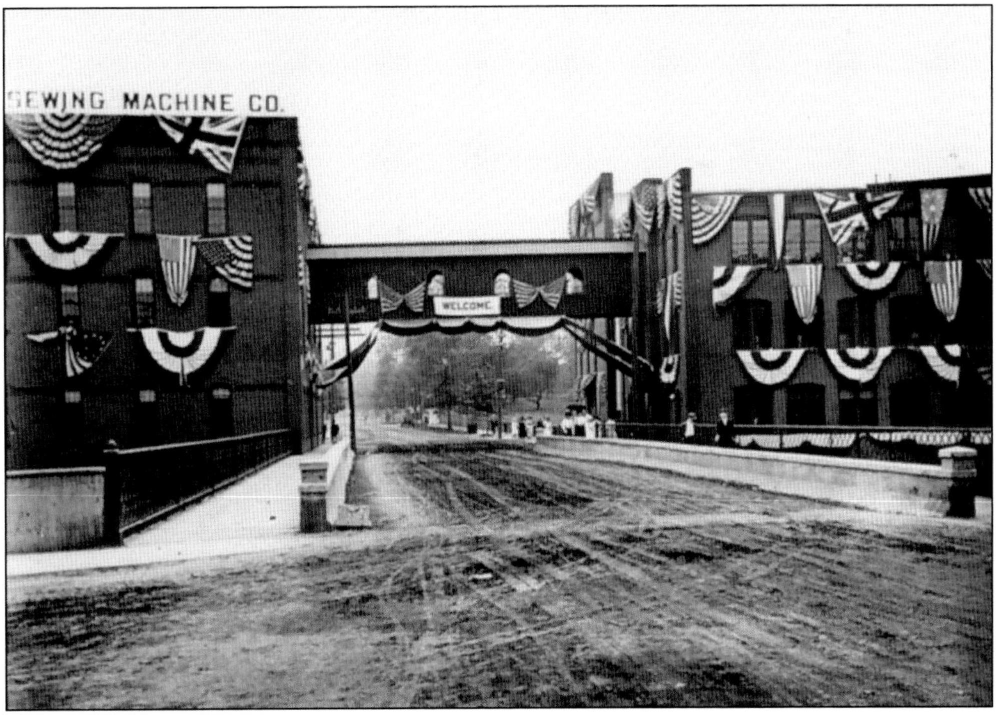

Bunting adorns the New Home Sewing Machine Company's South Main Street passageway along with a banner welcoming visitors. Taken at the corner of Water Street looking south along South Main Street, the South Main Street bridge is in the foreground. The trees in the distance are at the site of the present-day post office.

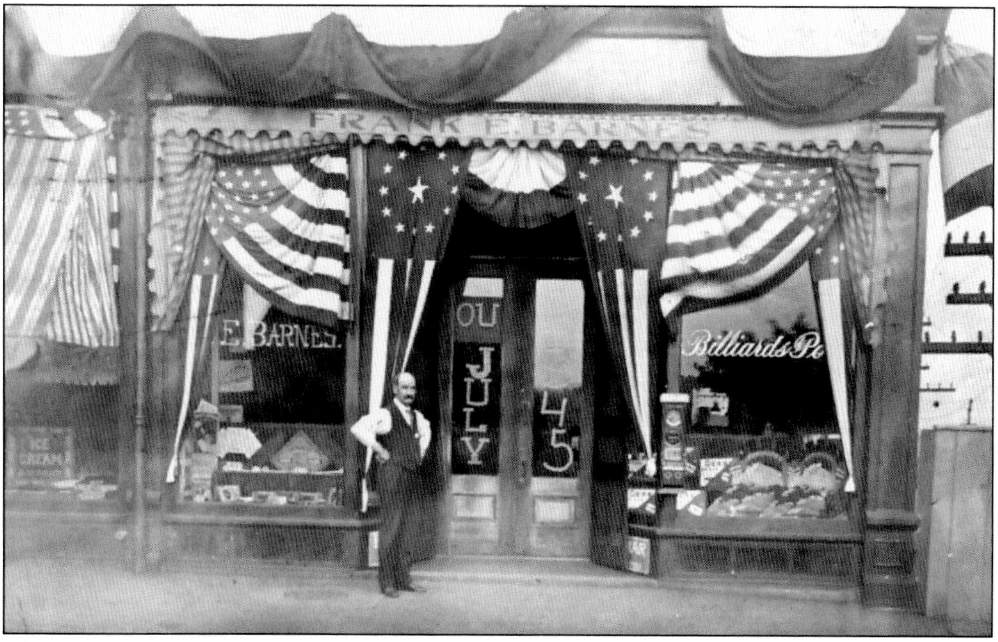

The Frank E. Barnes business at 13 South Main Street was highly decorated for the celebration. This is presently the location of Orange Video.

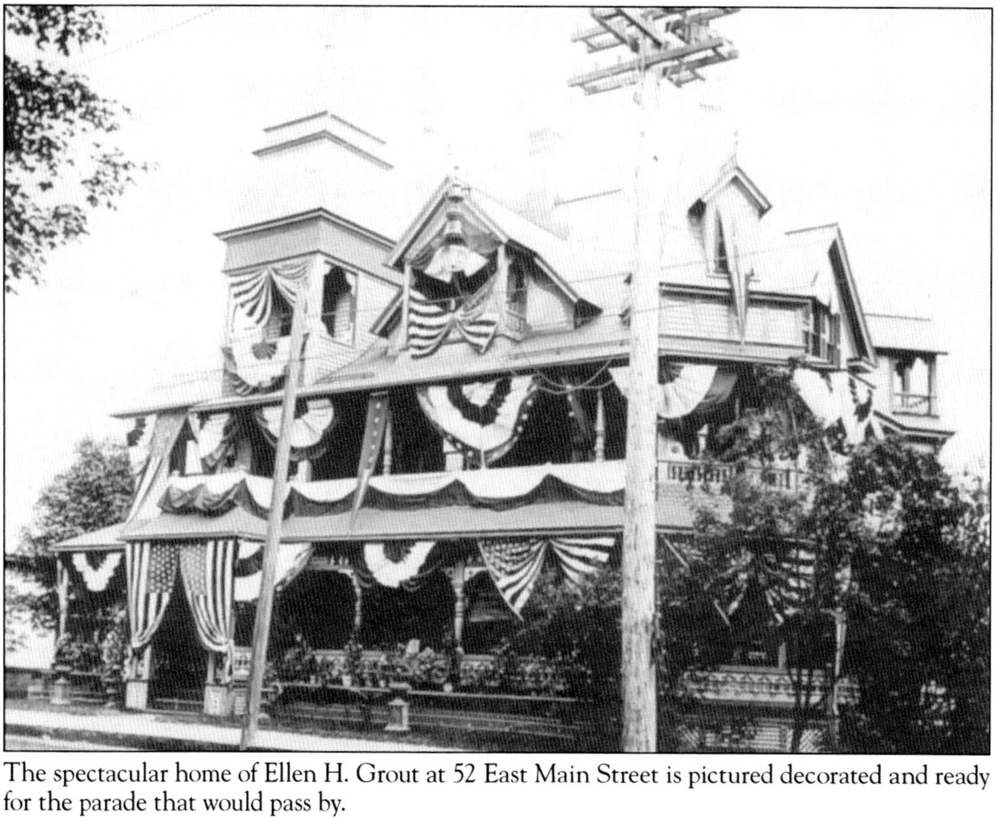

The spectacular home of Ellen H. Grout at 52 East Main Street is pictured decorated and ready for the parade that would pass by.

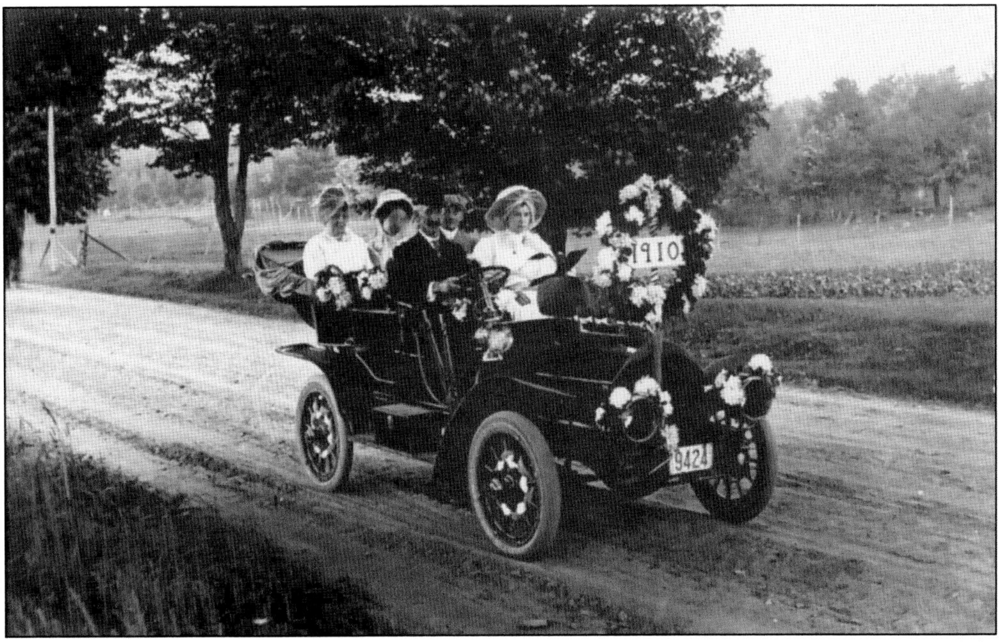

Automobiles were an integral part of the celebration not only for entrants in the automobile parade, but they were also used in advertising. Decorated automobiles toured the surrounding area promoting the upcoming celebration. Flowers, a wreath, and a 1910 sign adorn the automobile pictured above. The automobile below makes the use of oranges as part of its decoration. (Eastern Illustrating.)

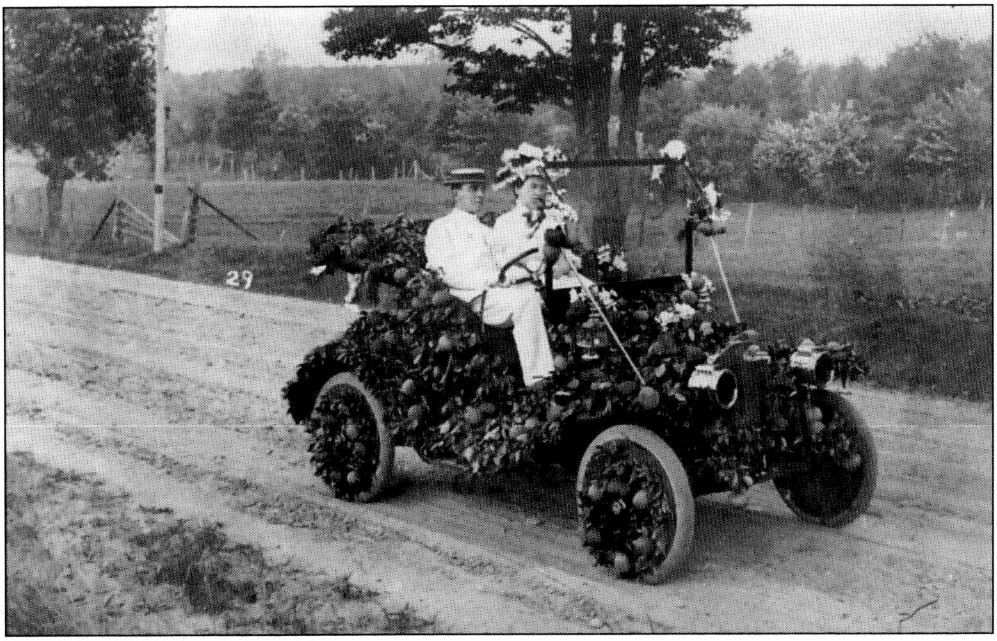

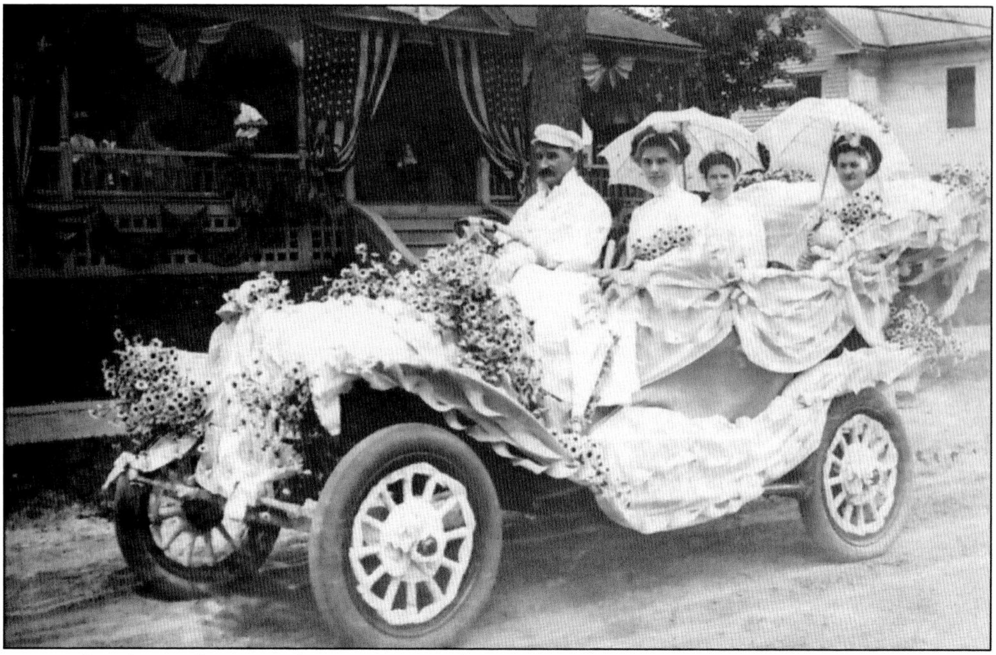

Pictured in front of 142 South Main Street, this proud driver had the pleasure of escorting three lovely ladies in his highly decorated automobile.

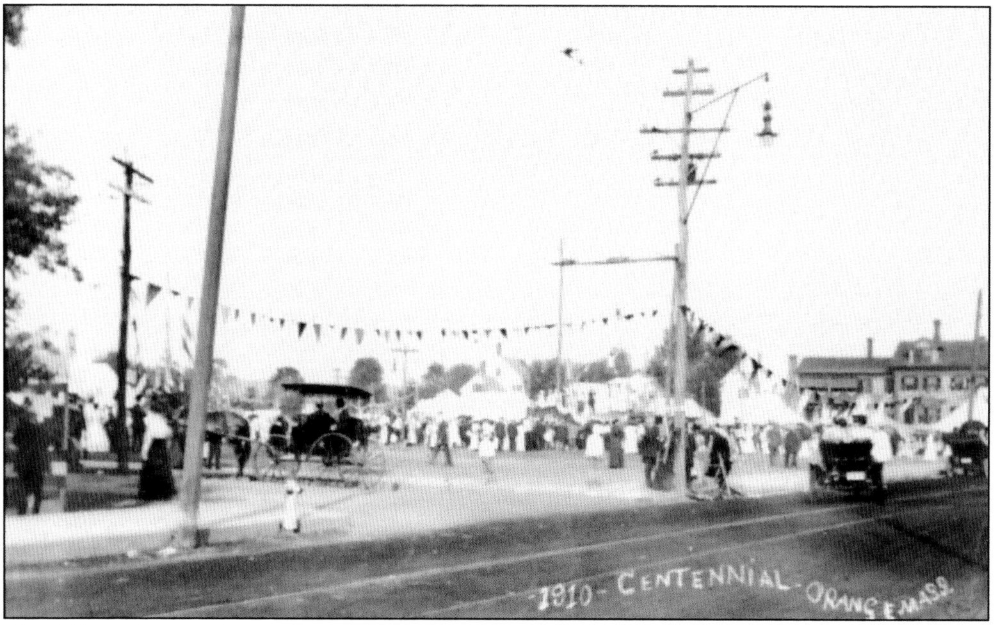

The White City, replete with its white tents, was set up in a vacant lot at the corner of Bacon and East Main Streets, where the armory was later built. The White City provided platforms for speakers, singers, concerts, and vaudeville shows. Also located here were hospitality tents for various government and civic organizations. The horse and wagon appear on Bacon Street with the trolley tracks running along East Main Street.

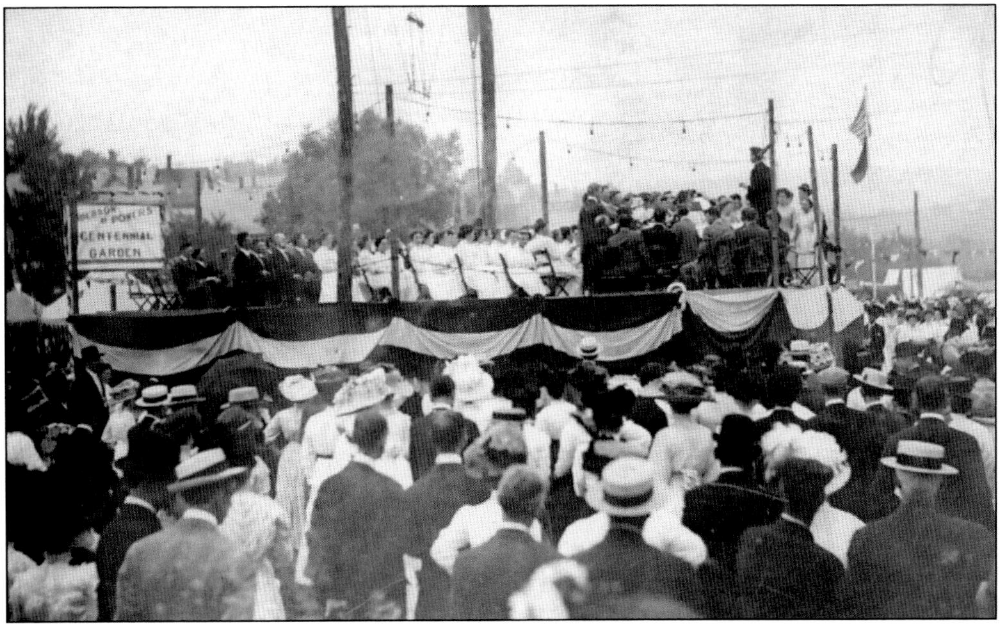

The central speakers and performers platform at the White City is shown in this image.

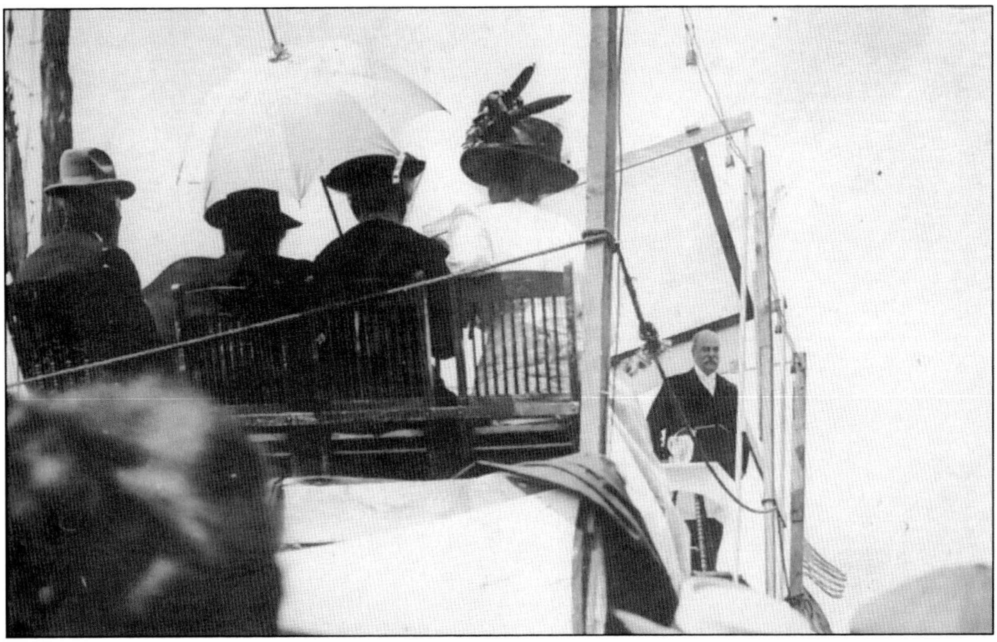

Massachusetts governor Ebenezer Draper addressed the crowd at the White City on Tuesday, July 5, 1910. He is shown here on the central speakers and performers platform. Draper was governor from 1909 to 1911. (Eastern Illustrating.)

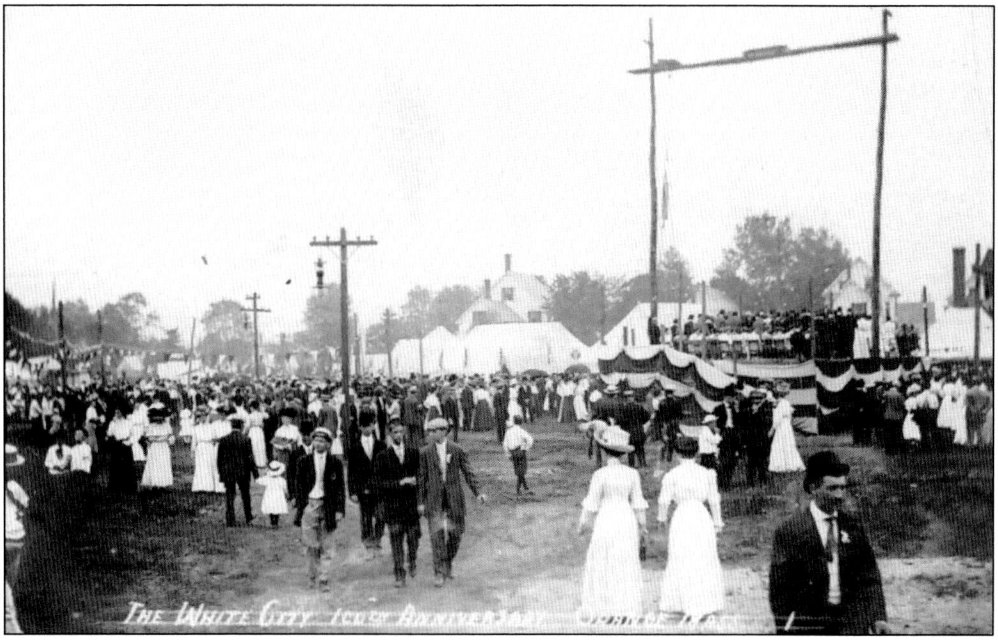

Part of the huge crowd drawn to the White City can be seen in this photograph. The central speakers and performers platform is at the right. Various hospitality tents can be seen in the background.

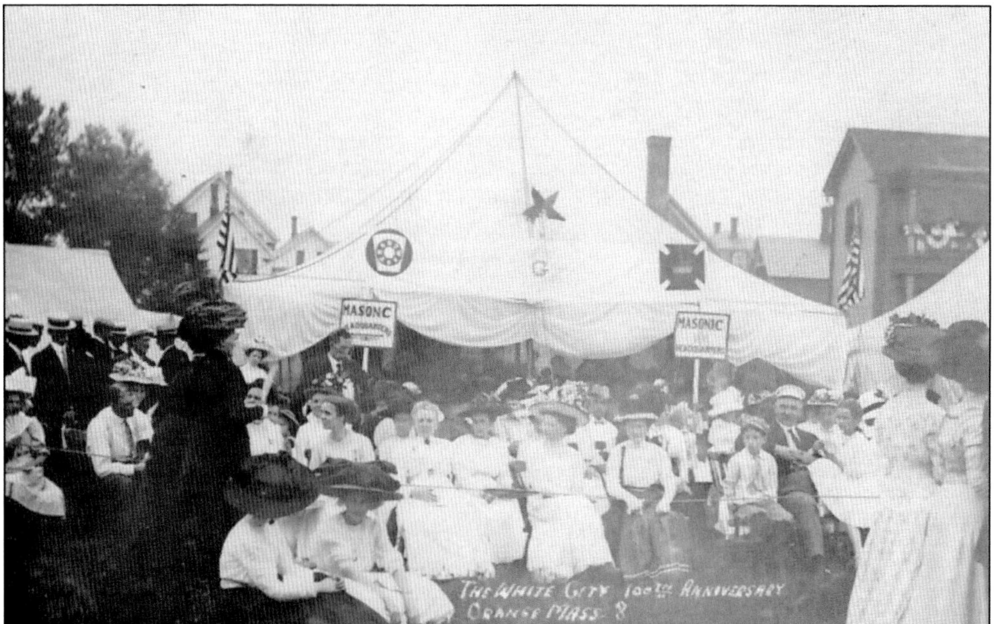

A large crowd has formed in front of the Masonic headquarters at the White City as seen in this photograph.

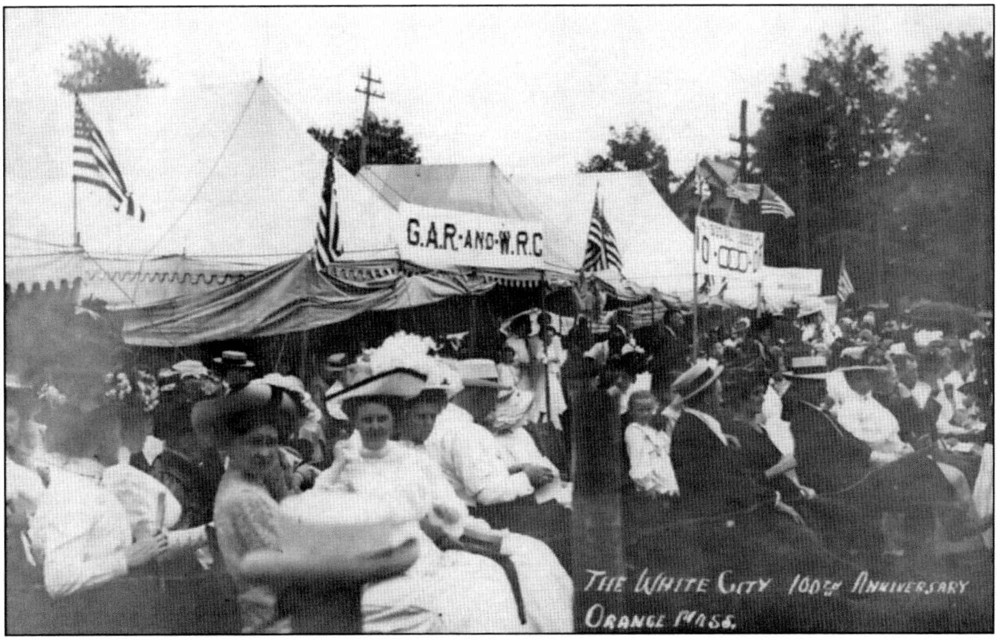

The hospitality tents of the Grand Army of the Republic (GAR) and Woman's Relief Corps (WRC) to the left, and the Social Lodge 182, International Order of Odd Fellows (IOOF) to the right, appear in this photograph. The GAR was a society of men who fought for the north in the Civil War. The WRC began as an auxiliary to the GAR.

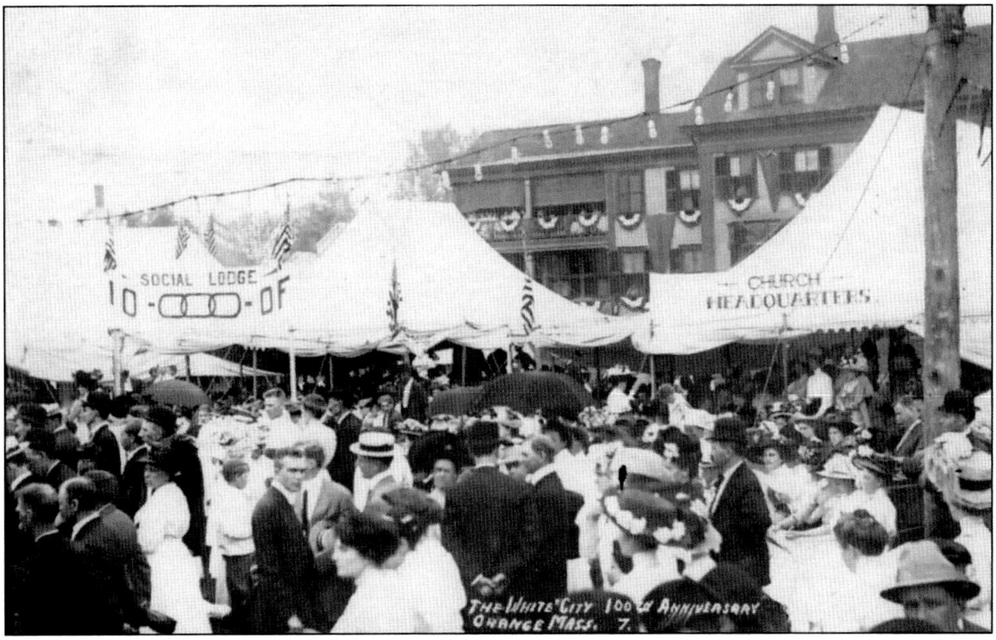

The Social Lodge 182, IOOF, and church headquarters tents are shown with a huge crowd surrounding them. Several churches united to provide a single respite facility for the thirsty and the weary. (Eastern Illustrating.)

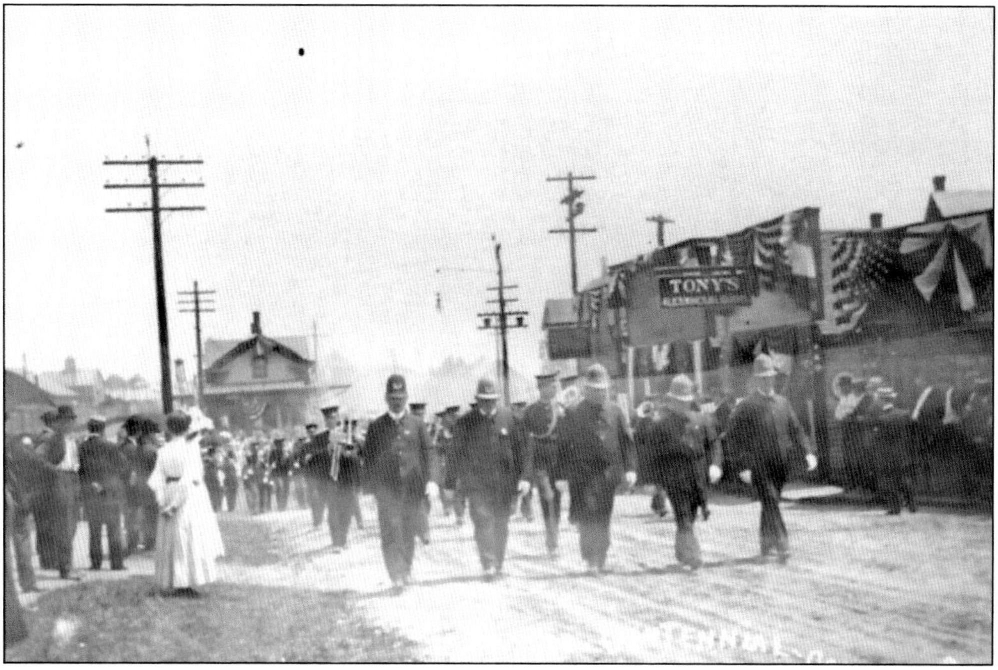

Parades were a central focus of the centennial celebration. Pictured is a marching unit moving along Depot Street (now Railroad Street) toward South Main Street. The railroad station is in the background. The buildings at the right are in what is now Memorial Park.

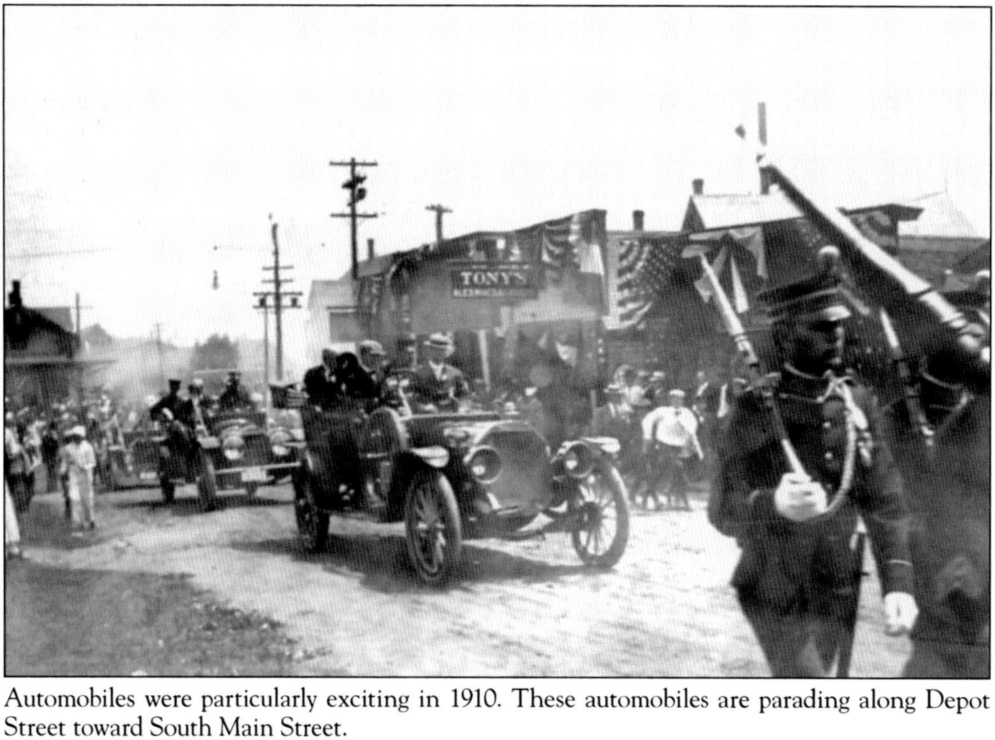

Automobiles were particularly exciting in 1910. These automobiles are parading along Depot Street toward South Main Street.

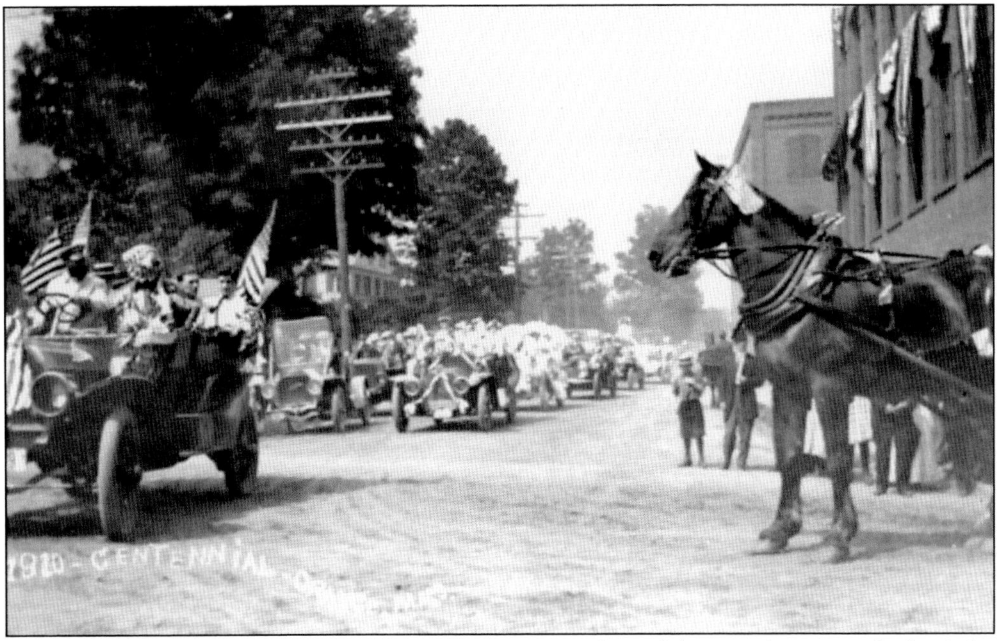

This horse is probably wondering about his part in the celebration because of all of the automobiles. Not to worry though because horses played a very important role in the parade, drawing numerous floats. This scene is on West River Street approaching South Main Street.

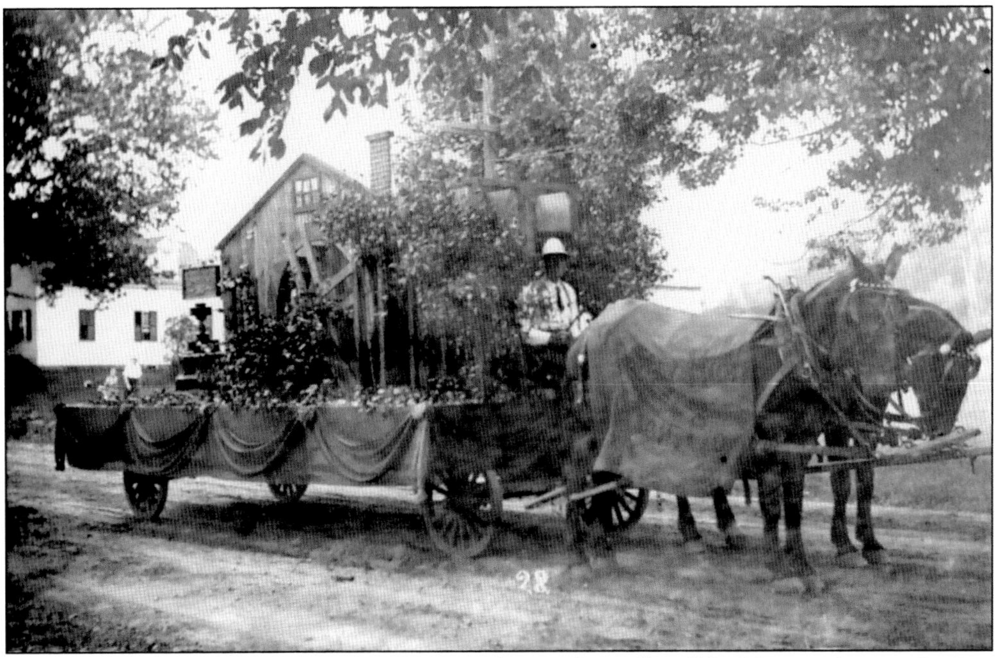

The float of the Rodney Hunt Company, complete with small mill building and waterwheel, is shown in this picture.

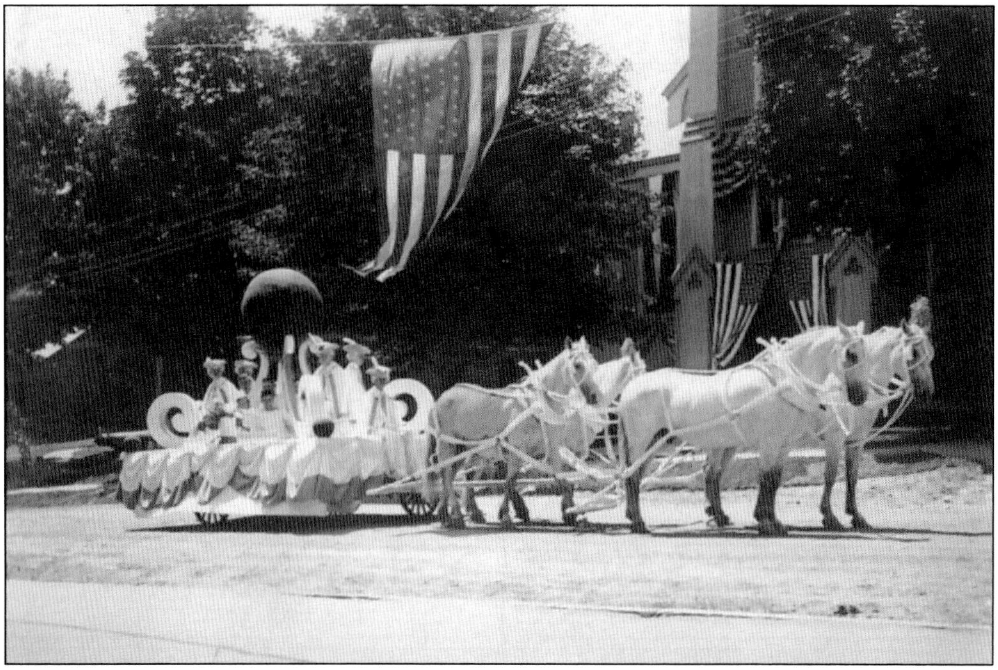

Four magnificent horses drew the float of the Orange Clothing Company. It is pictured in front of the Universalist Church on North Main Street.

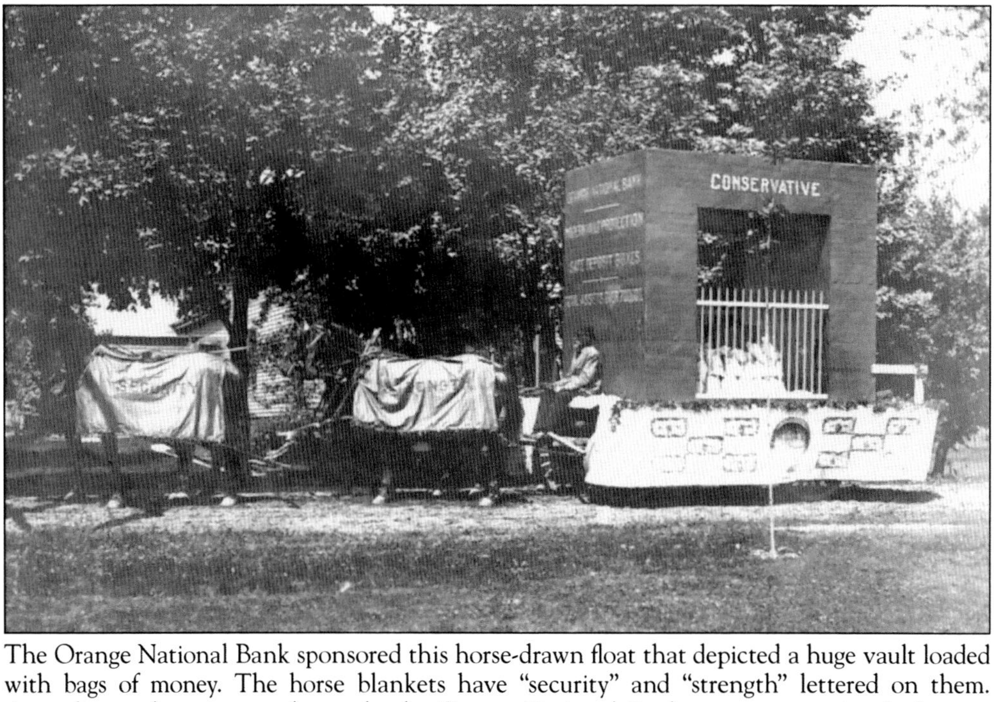

The Orange National Bank sponsored this horse-drawn float that depicted a huge vault loaded with bags of money. The horse blankets have "security" and "strength" lettered on them. According to lettering on the vault, the Orange National Bank was conservative, had assets over $700,000, and offered safe deposit boxes and modern vault protection.

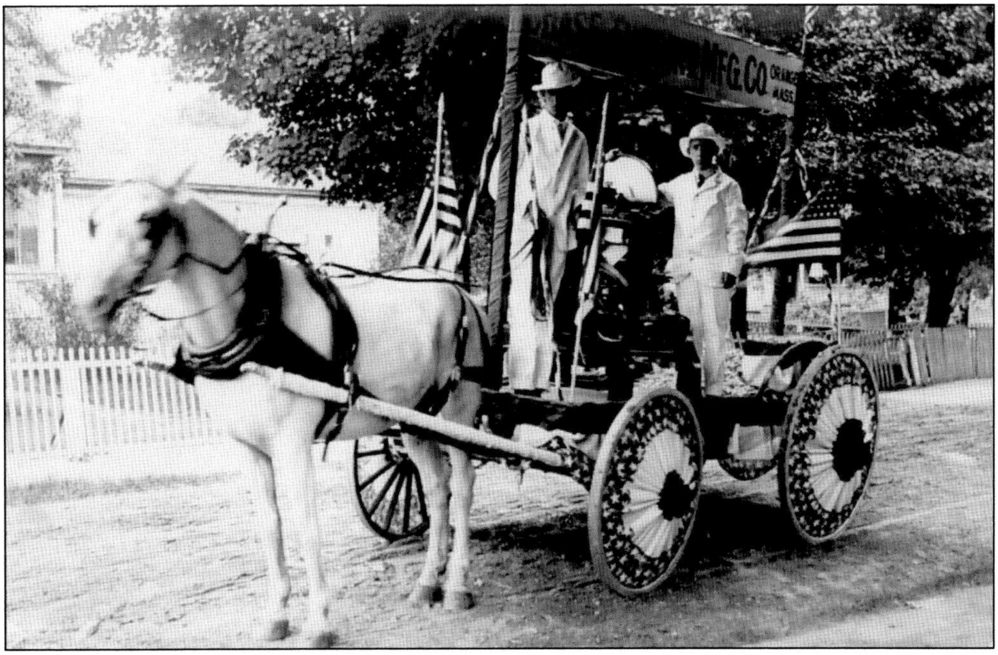

The Chase Turbine Manufacturing Company float carried two gentlemen displaying machinery built by the company.

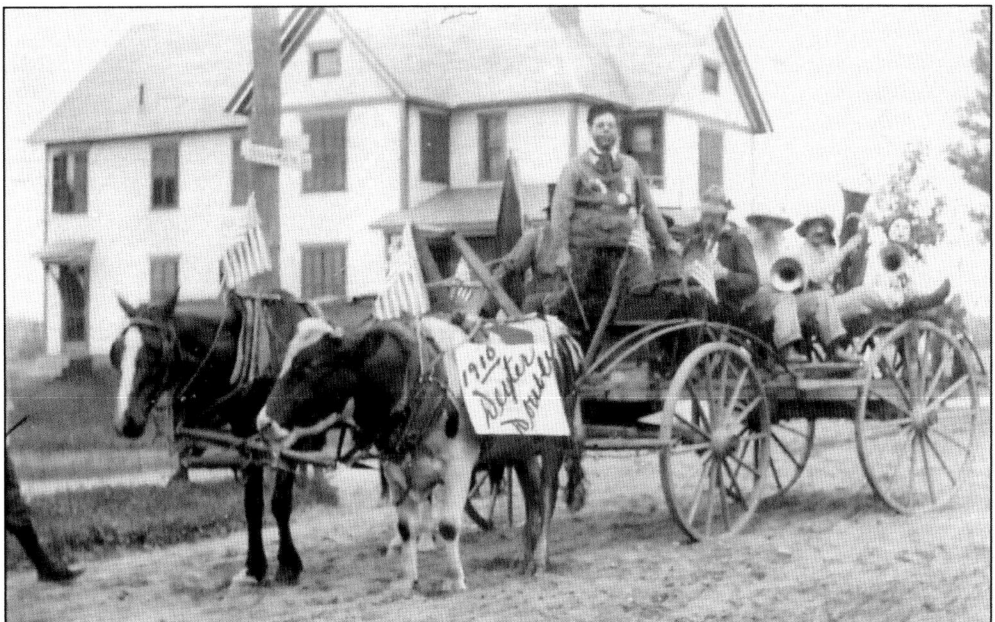

Undoubtedly, the unique horse and ox team owned by Hervey Dexter of Dexter's Stock Farm must have been a crowd pleaser. Dexter Farm was on the east road to North Orange (now North Main Street).

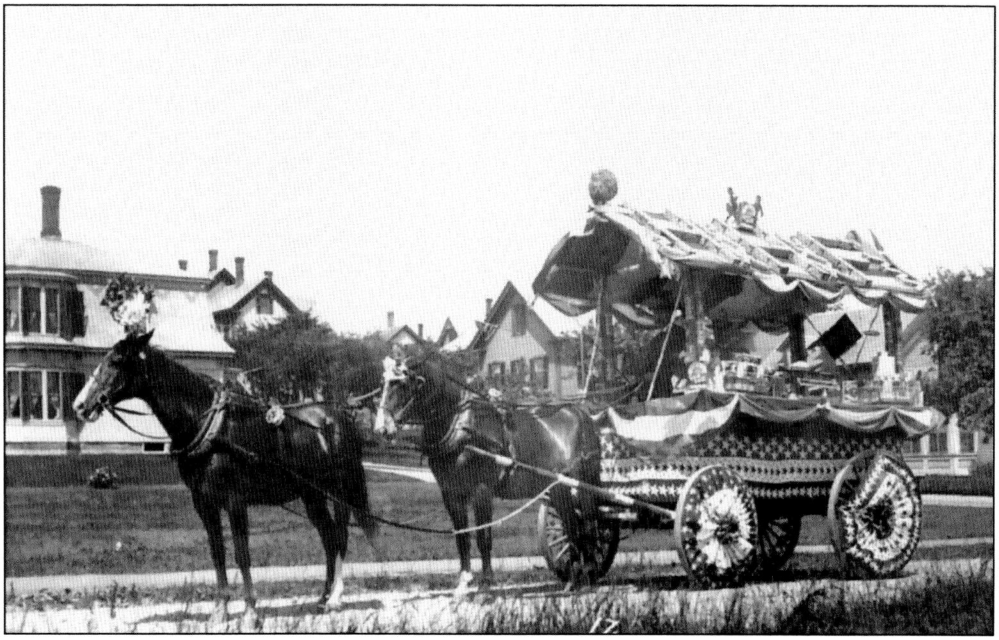

This horse-drawn float with the huge letters HHF on its top, created with boxes of graham crackers, was entered into the parade by Herbert H. Foskett. Foskett was a grocer on East Main Street. (Eastern Illustrating.)

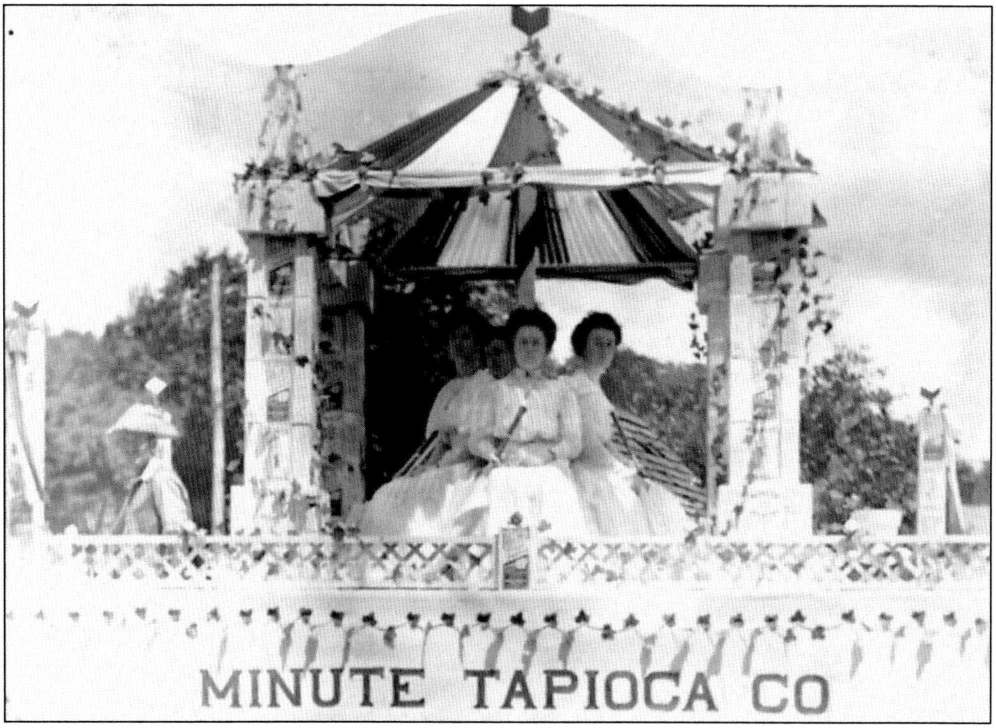

The Minute Tapioca Company float carried four gaily dressed ladies beneath a striped canopy. The canopy was supported by four columns composed of boxes of the company's products. Atop the columns stood a minuteman statue.

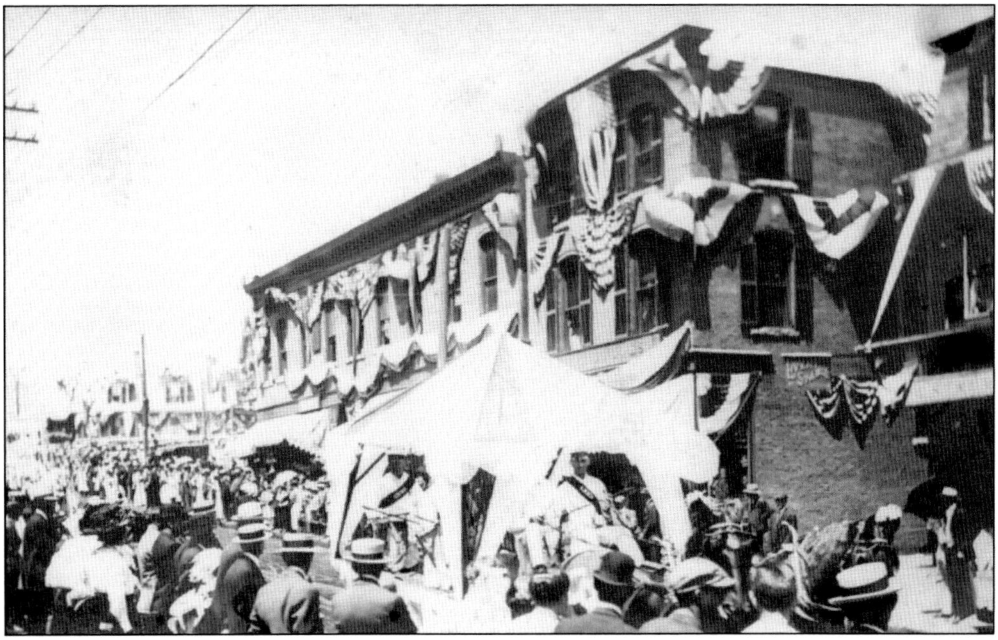

The horse-drawn float of the International Order of Odd Fellows is shown making its way along East Main Street. The Putnam House is in the left background

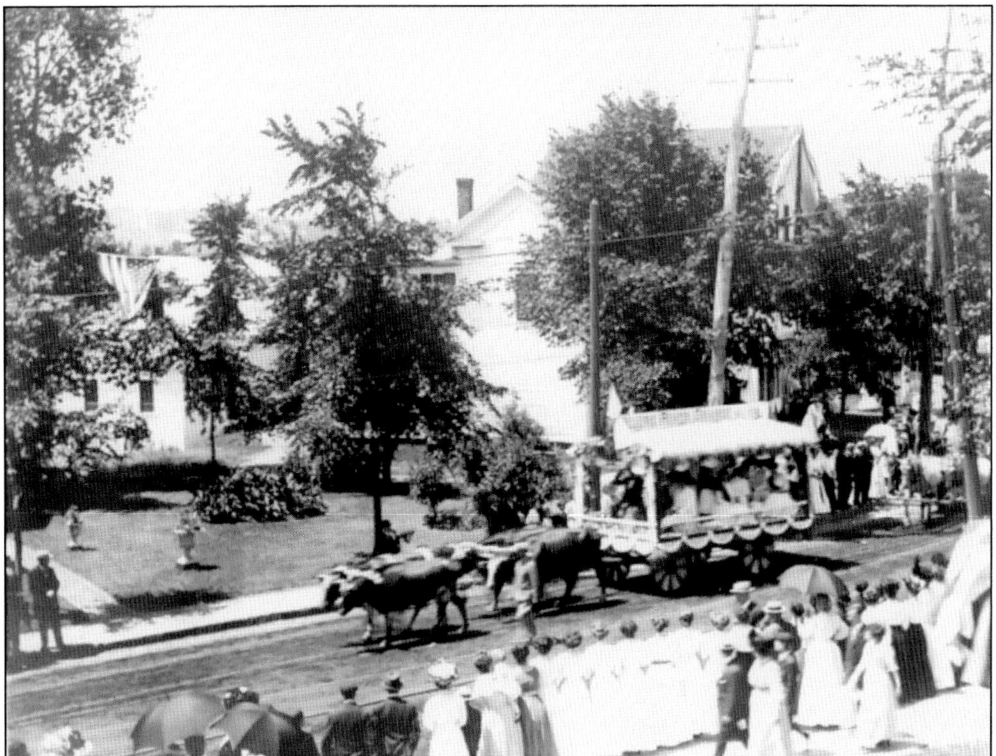

A team of four oxen are shown drawing the Millers River Grange float along East Main Street in this photograph.

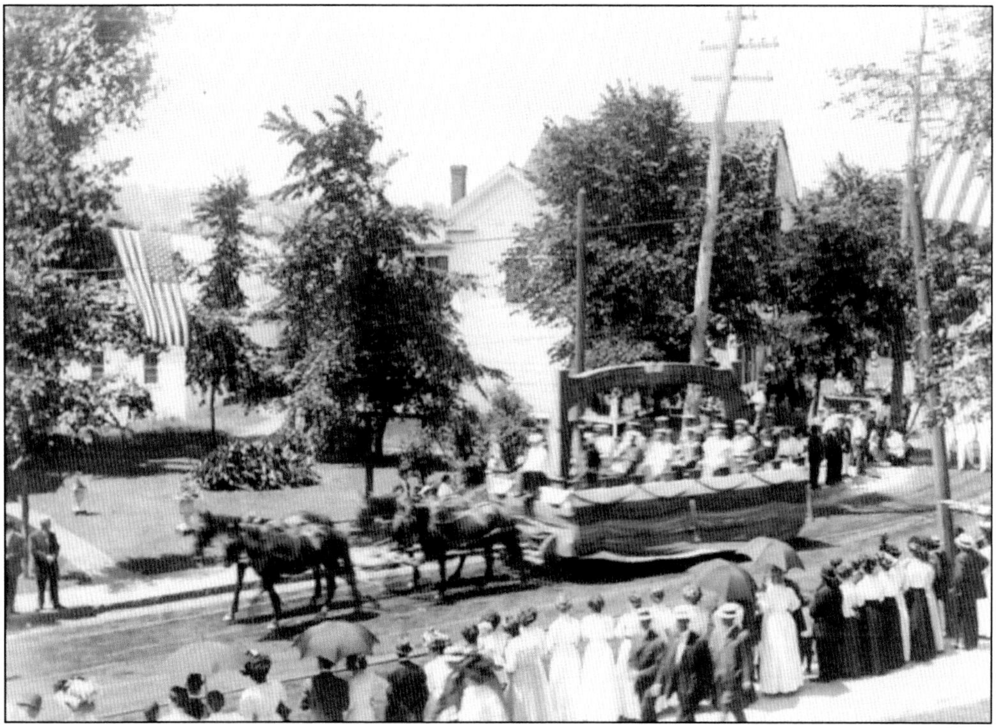

A four-horse team was used to draw the float of the Knights of Pythias. It is shown proceeding along East Main Street.

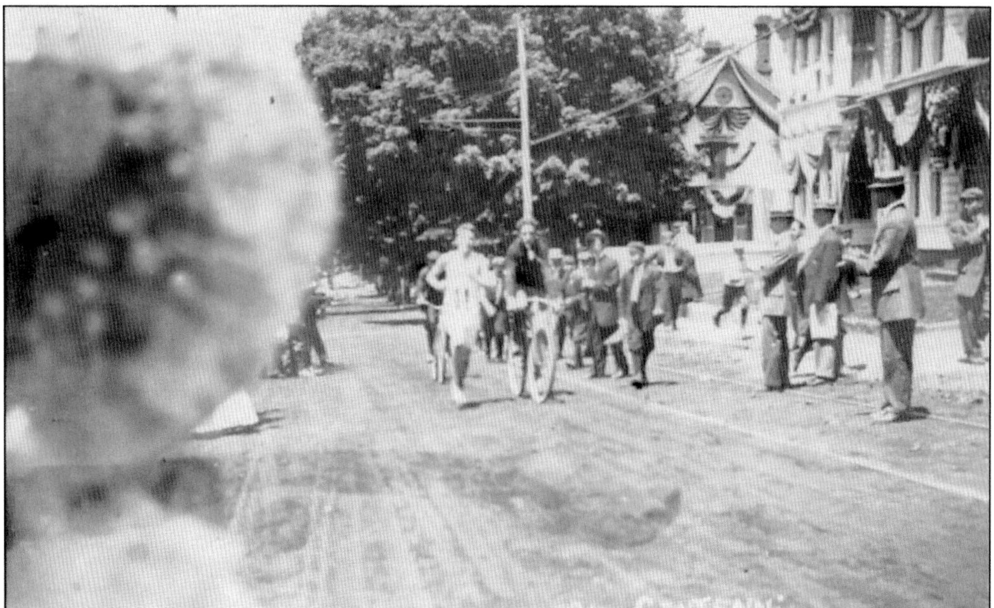

Road races were among the featured events of the centennial celebration. This runner, accompanied by two bicyclists, is shown passing in front of the Mansion House on West Main Street heading for the square.

Four

DISASTER

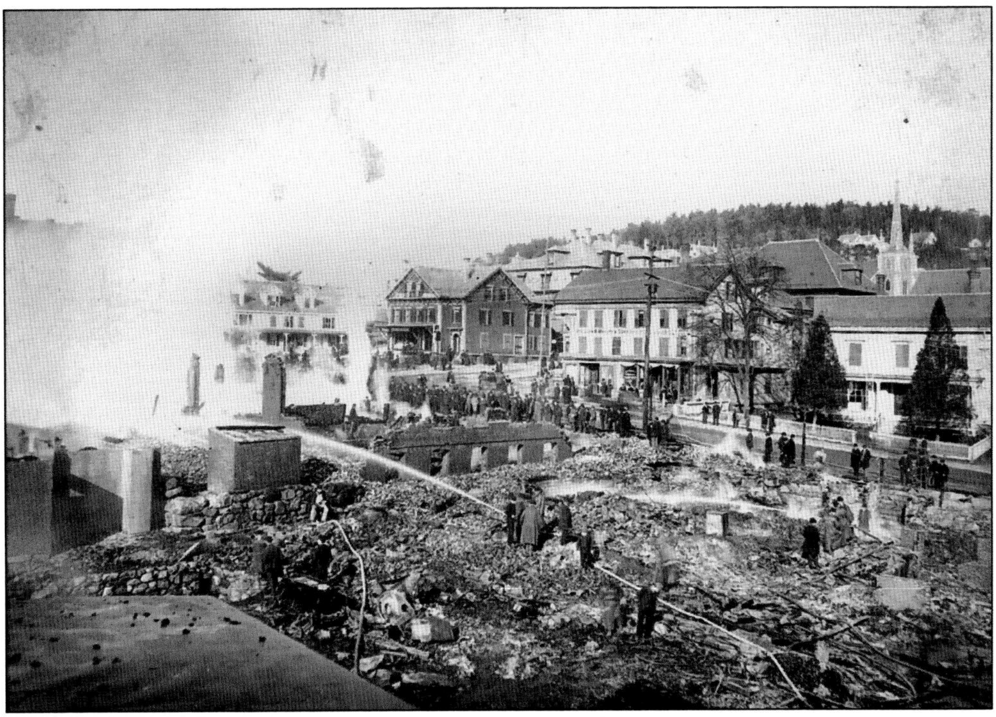

Orange has endured its share of disasters, including fire, flood, and wind. One of the worst was the fire of November 7, 1891. Looking northwest from the American House that stood on the site of the present day Orange District Court parking lot, it can be seen that the Bingham Block at the corner of East and South Main Streets was reduced to ash. The Congregational Church to its left was also completely destroyed. These two structures stretched from East Main Street to the railroad. The Whipple Block at the corner of North and West Main Streets appears at the center of the photograph. (Dunklee.)

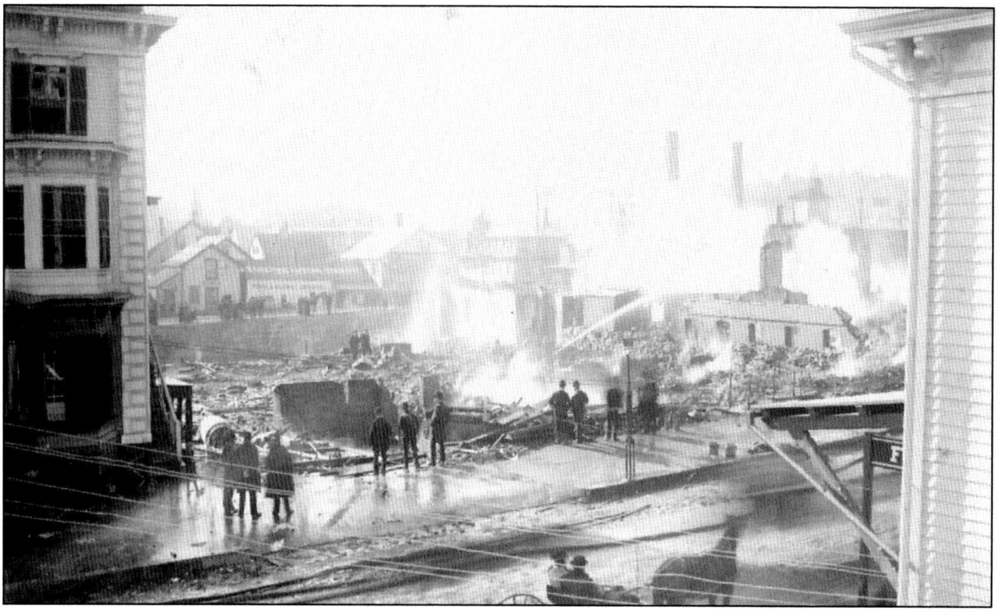

Looking from the Baptist Church southwesterly toward the South Main Street railroad overpass shows that the entire area between East Main Street and the railroad tracks was completely destroyed in the fire of November 7, 1891. The buildings to the left in the distance are in what is now Memorial Park. (Dunklee.)

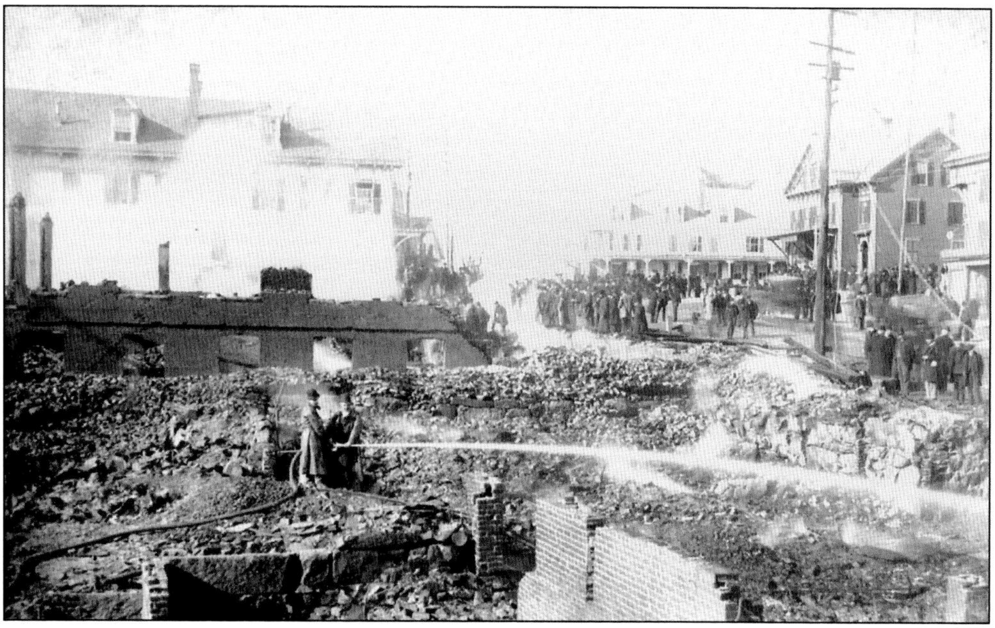

Smoldering ruins of the Bingham Block are being soaked down after the fire of 1891 in this close-up view. Lambs Block at the corner of South and West Main Streets is at the left with the Putnam House and Whipple Block to the right. (Dunklee.)

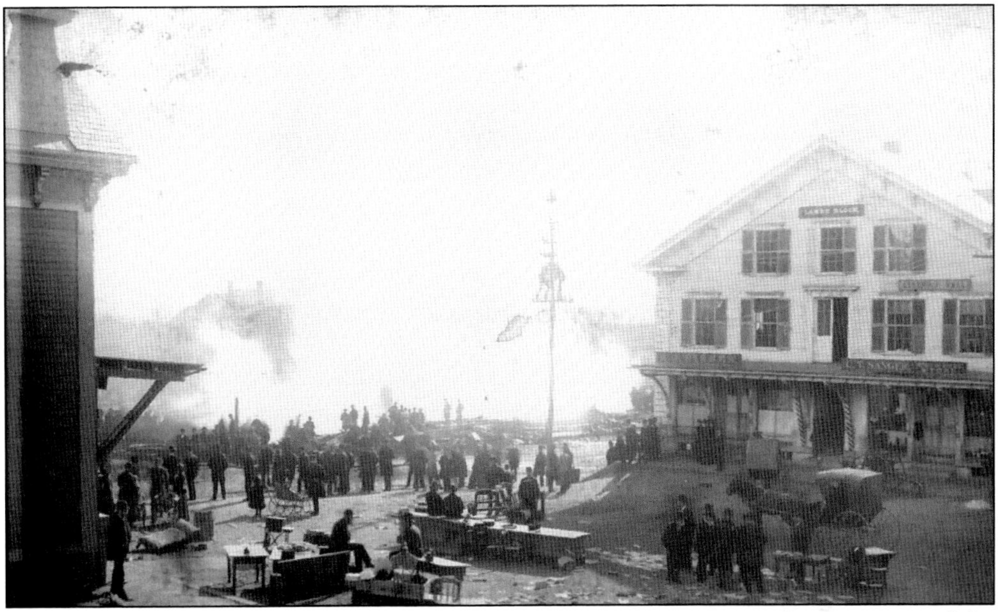

This view of the fire of 1891 is looking from near the Putnam House across the square toward the American House that is hidden by the smoke in the center. Lambs Block is at the right. Notice the furniture and other items that must have been saved from the burning buildings and are now strewn about the square. (Dunklee.)

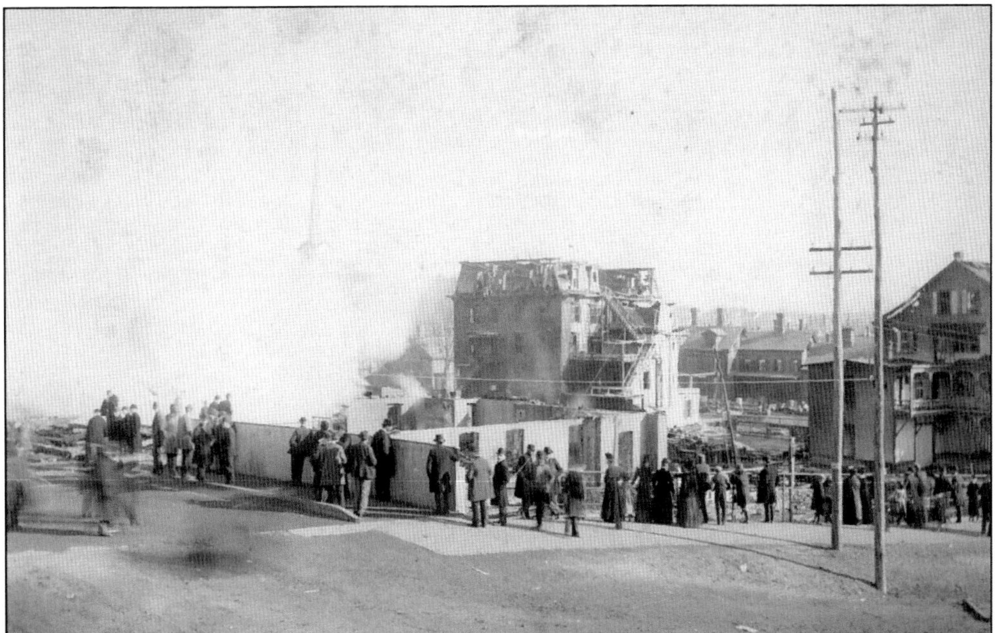

This group of onlookers is peering at the ruins of the Congregational Church from the South Main Street railroad overpass and along Railroad Street. At the center is the Washburn Block at the corner of East Main and Water Streets. It, along with the American House at the right was damaged in the fire. Notice the steeple of the Baptist Church that is visible through the smoke to the left of the Washburn Block. (Dunklee.)

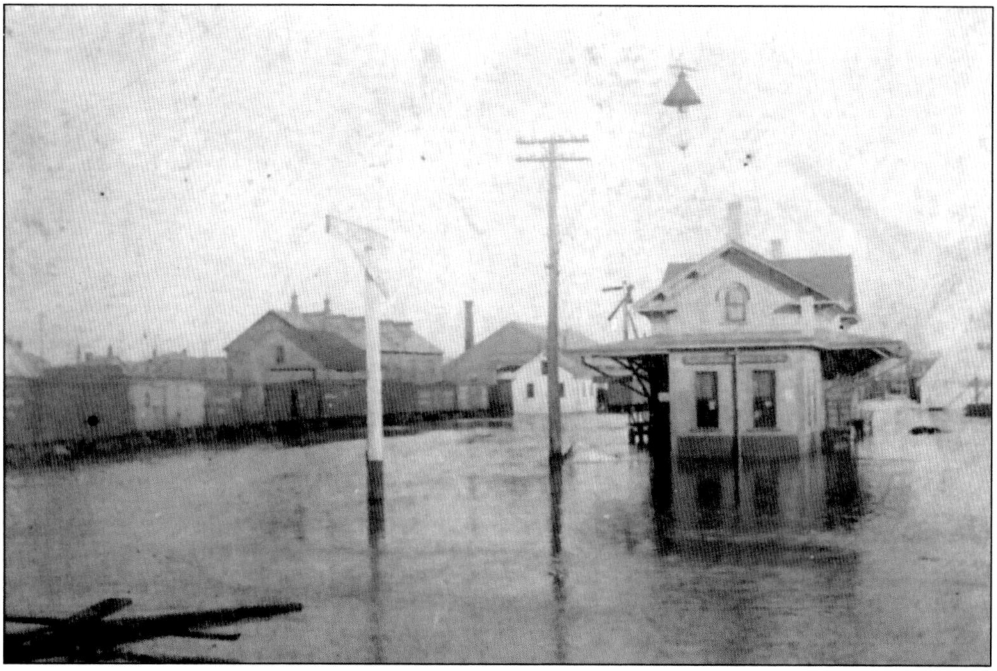

Flood was the enemy February 13–14, 1900. At least two feet of water surrounded the area around the railroad station shown here, looking east from the corner of what is now Memorial Park.

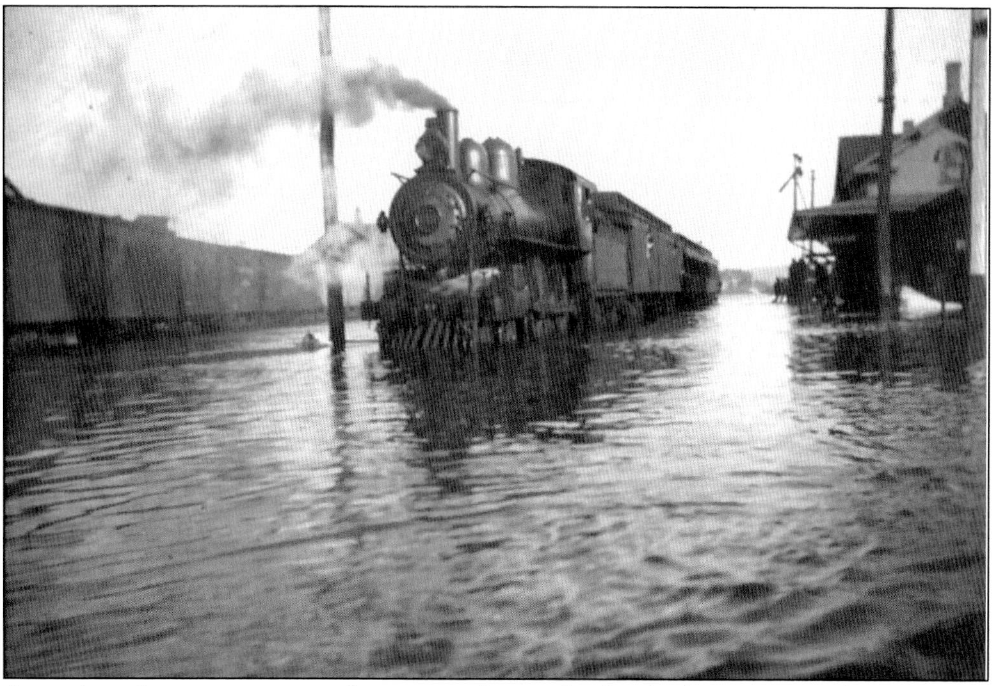

A westbound train eases into the station during the flood of 1900. Note the passengers waiting for the train trying to keep their feet dry by standing on the platform next to the station. (Whitcomb.)

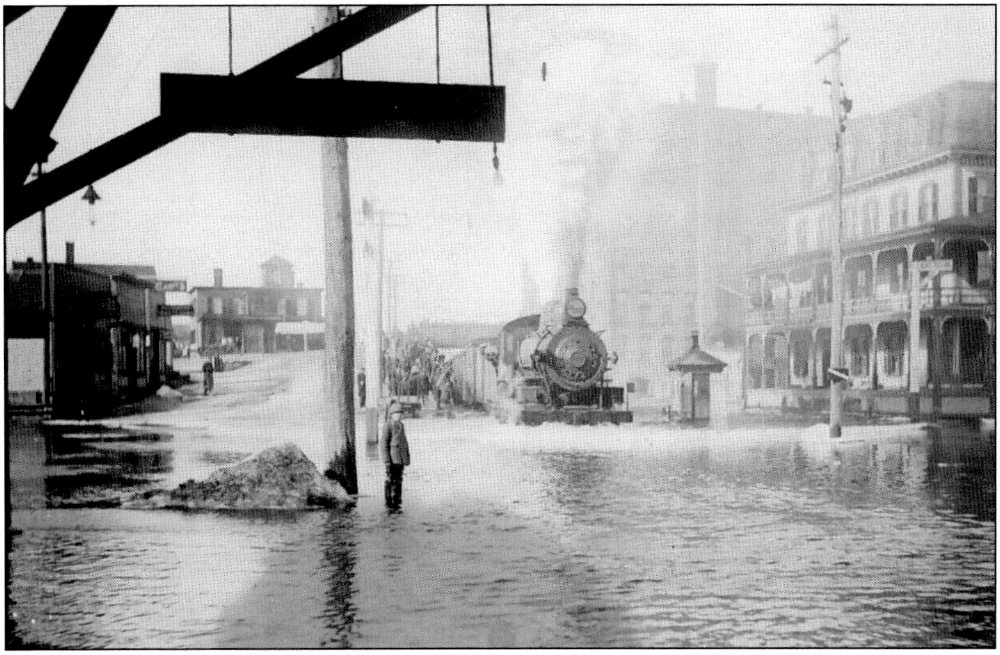

In this view, an eastbound train approaches the station pushing a considerable wave of water ahead of it. The South Main Street railroad overpass can be seen above the train. Note the crowd of onlookers standing along Railroad Street to the left of the train. The American House is at the right.

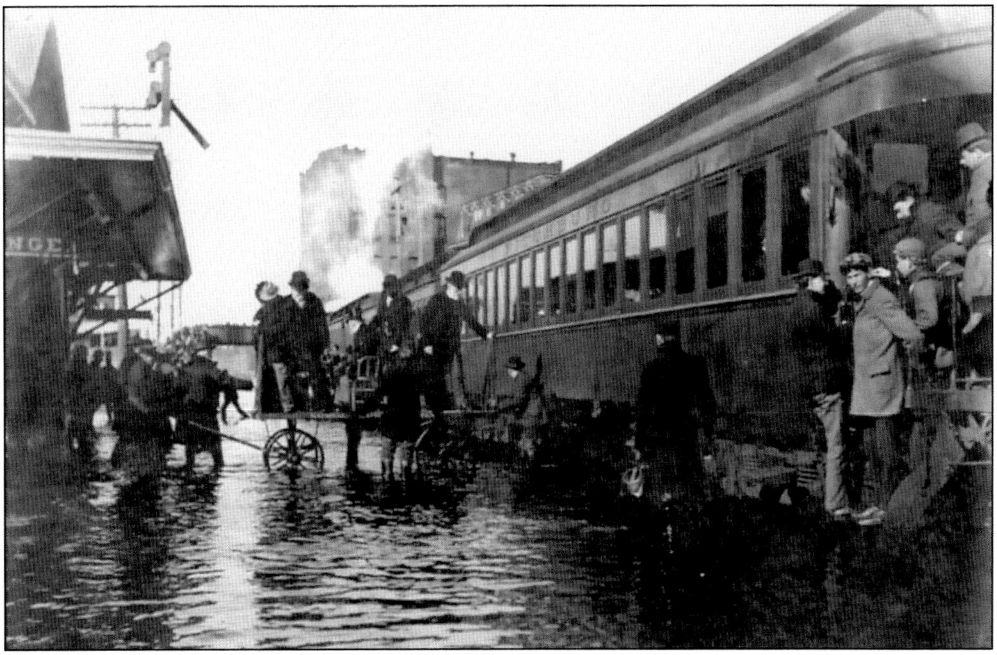

During the flood of 1900, passengers were "ferried" between this westbound Fitchburg Railroad train and the station using a baggage cart. The Masonic Block, where the Orange District Court is now located, can be seen above the train.

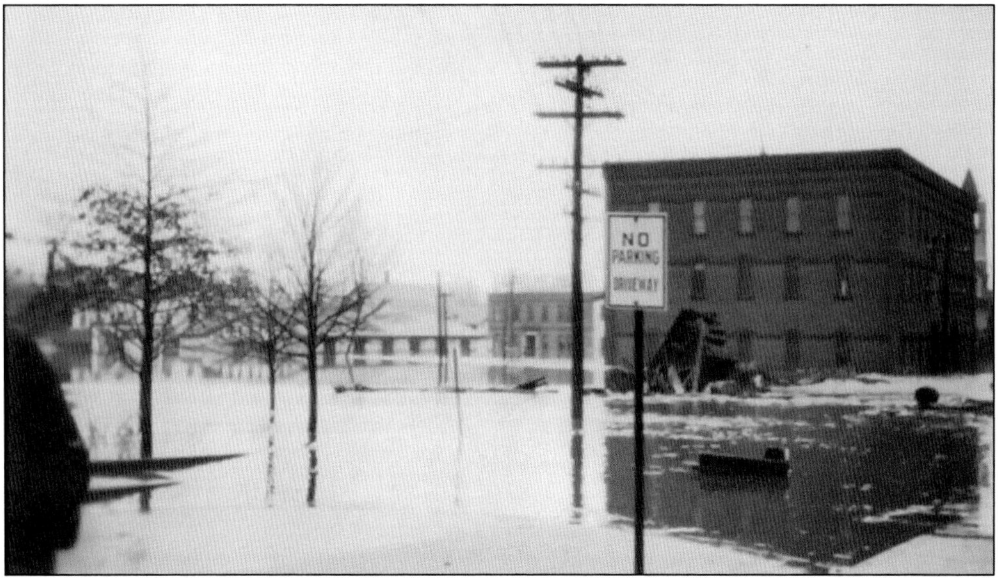

Flood again ravaged Orange in March 1936. Unseasonably warm weather, heavy rainfall, and the ensuing rapid ice melt caused the Millers River to overflow its banks. In this photograph, rubble can be seen piled against the South Main Street bridge. A New Home Sewing Machine Company building, now the Orange Trading Post, lies just across the bridge. The Leavitt Machine Company on East River Street is visible in the background as is the Congregational Church steeple at the extreme right.

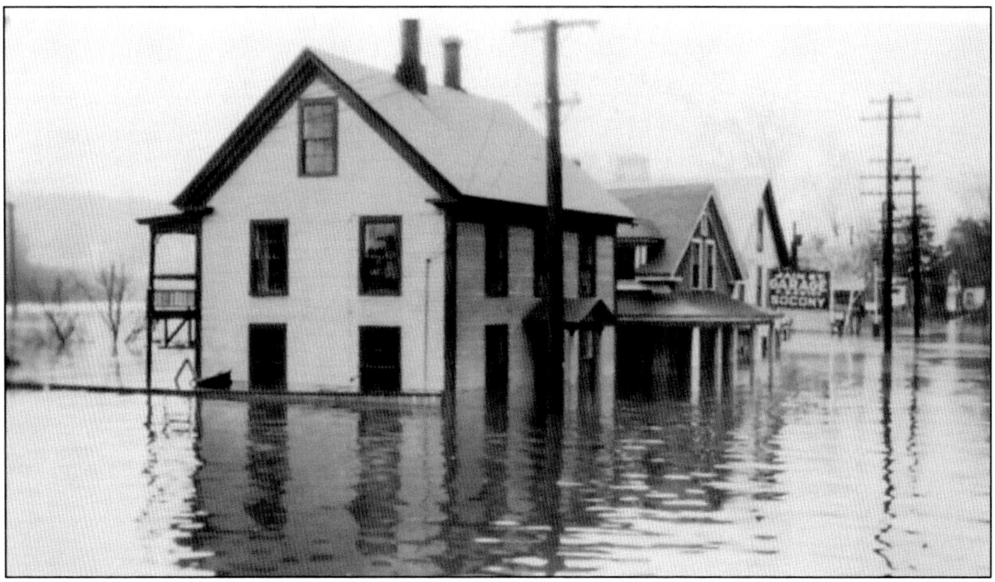

One can get a perception of the depth of the flood waters in 1936 in this view along West Main Street. The Main Street Garage of F. S. Estey at 77 West Main Street is visible beyond the two buildings in the foreground.

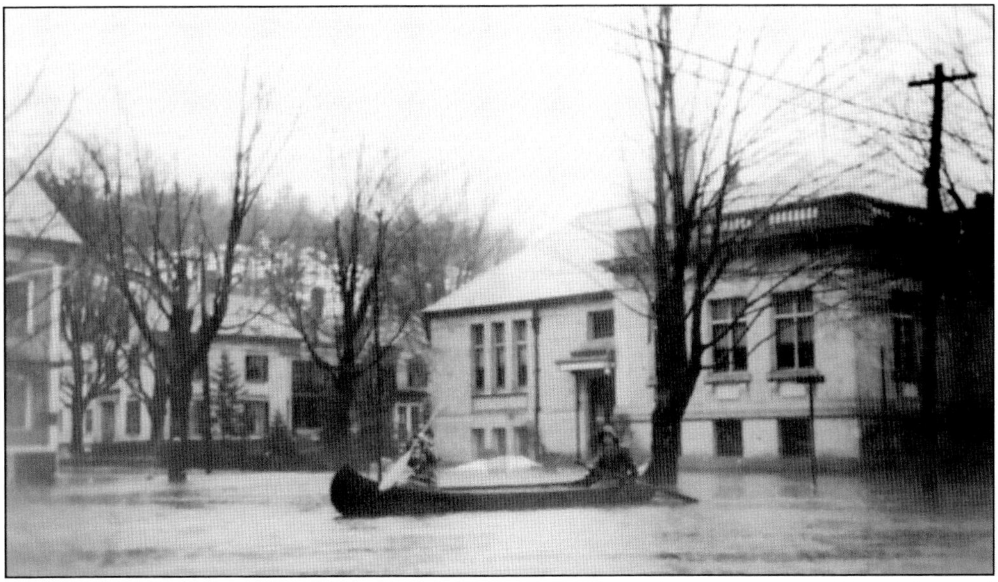

In this scene, a canoe is seen plying the flood waters of 1936 at the intersection of East Main and Grove Streets. The Wheeler Memorial Library, fronting on East Main Street, is at the right.

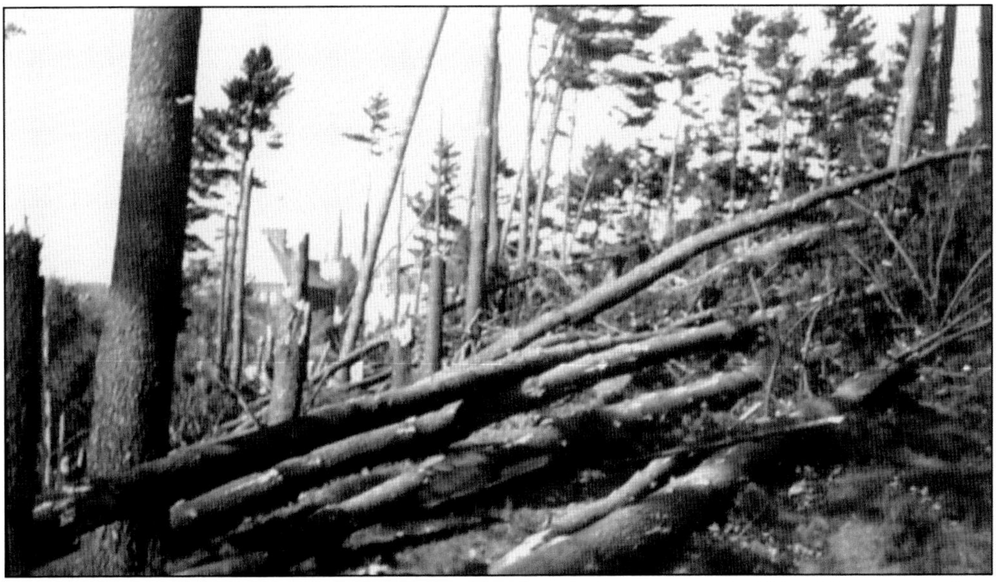

Hurricane winds and flooding devastated Orange on September 21, 1938. The tremendous power of the wind can be seen in this photograph of downed trees in Central Cemetery on Grove Street. Through the downed and broken trees at the left, Central School and the steeple of the Baptist Church on North Main Street may be seen.

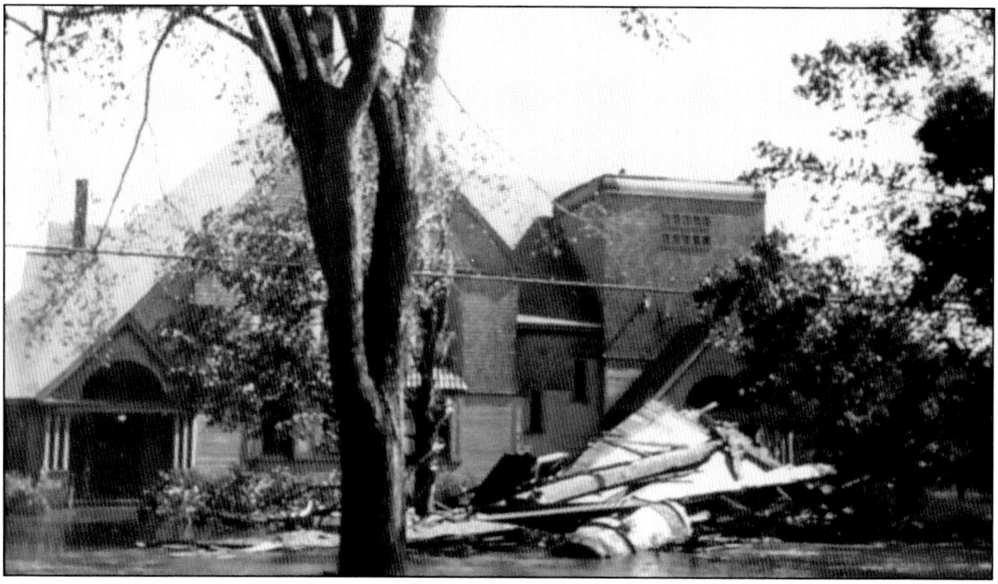

The powerful winds of the hurricane of 1938 toppled the steeple of the Congregational Church as shown in this image.

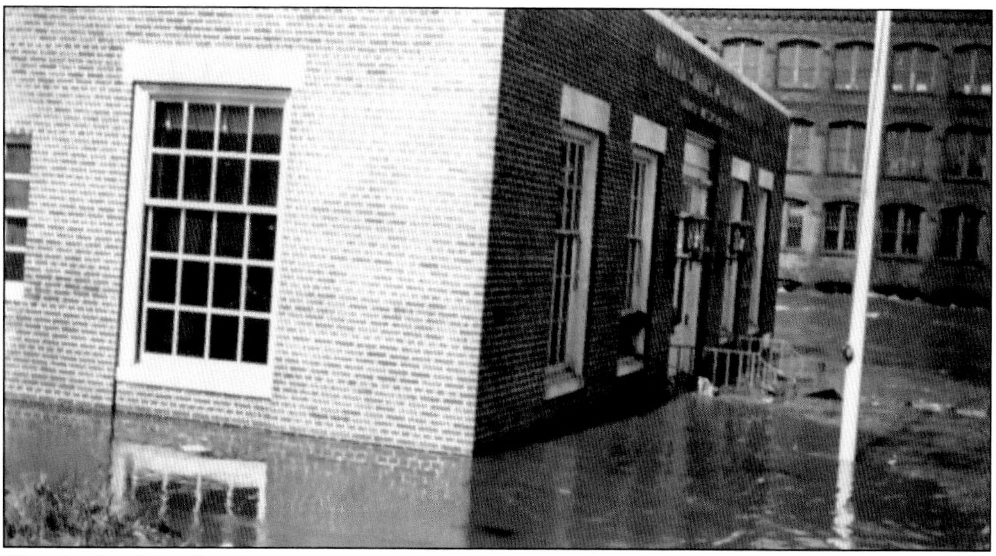

The depth of the flood accompanying the 1938 hurricane is evident in this photograph of the then-new post office at the corner of South Main and West River Streets. Notice the person in the window beside the front door who appears to be attempting to retrieve something from the water with a long pole.

Five

North Orange and Tully

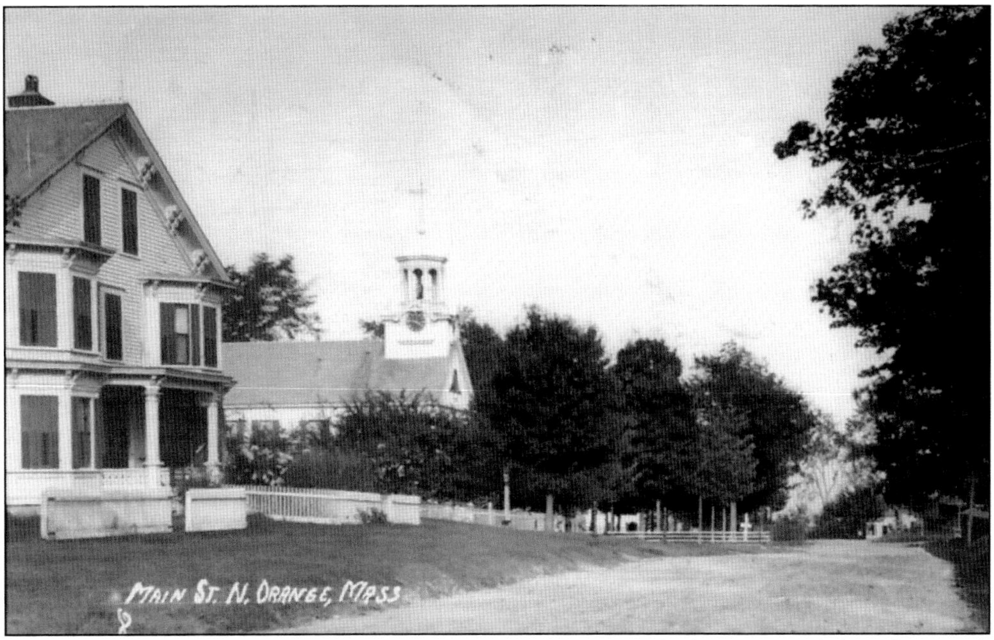

This view of Main Street in North Orange from about 1910 looks east. At left is the North Orange Universalist Church. In the distance to the left of Main Street surrounded by a rail fence is Goddard Park.

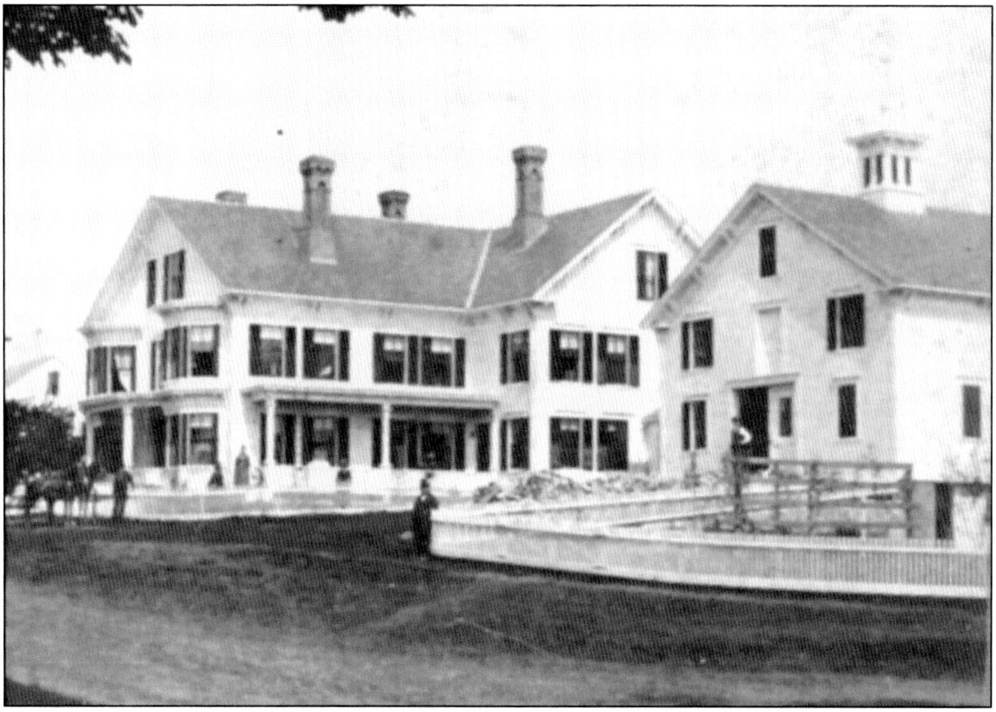

This photograph is of the F. E. Goddard house on Main Street in North Orange around 1880. Located beside the Universalist Church, the house was destroyed by fire around 1967. (Wells.)

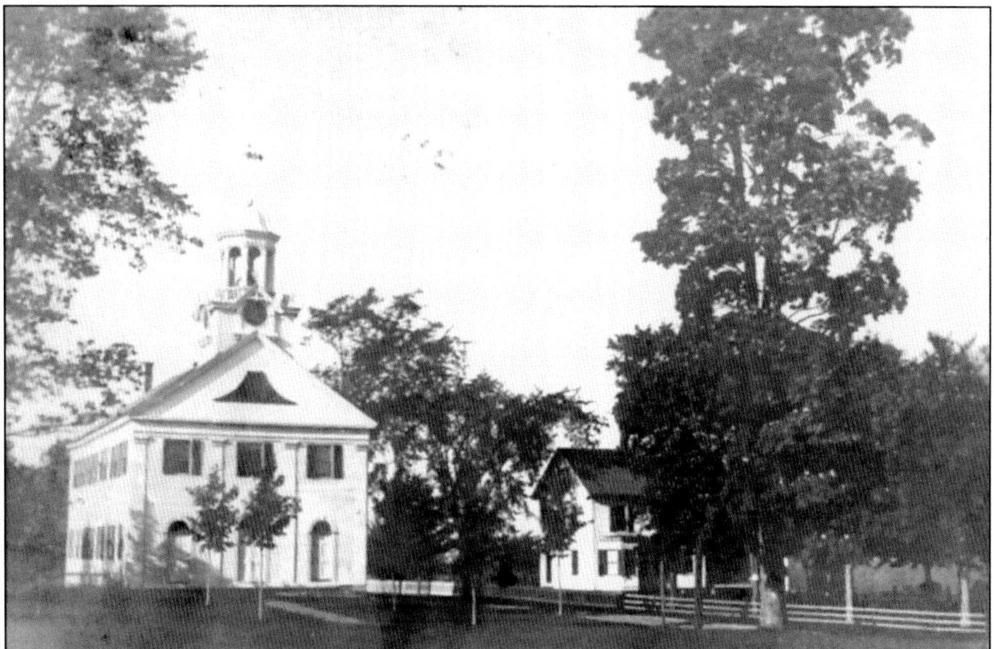

The North Orange Universalist Church, shown here around 1905, still stands regally on Main Street. It was built in 1871. Originally facing east-west, the church was turned 90 degrees in 1832 to its present north-south orientation.

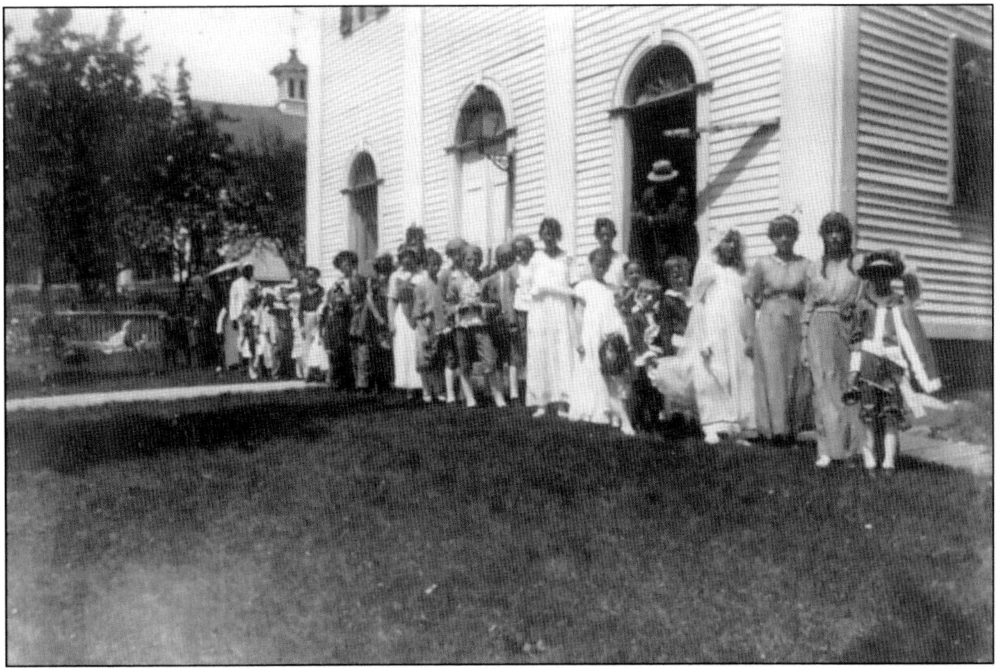

Information on the reverse of this postcard photograph in front of the North Orange Universalist Church indicates that the image is of the children's parade held at the 1915 North Orange reunion.

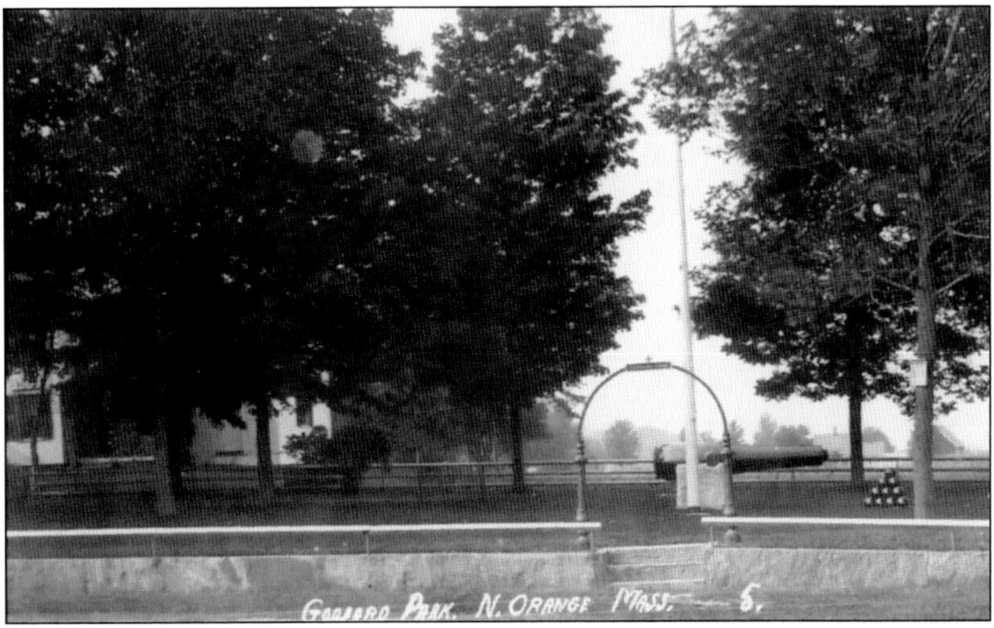

Goddard Park on Main Street in North Orange is the oldest park in the town of Orange. Reunions have taken place here since 1900.

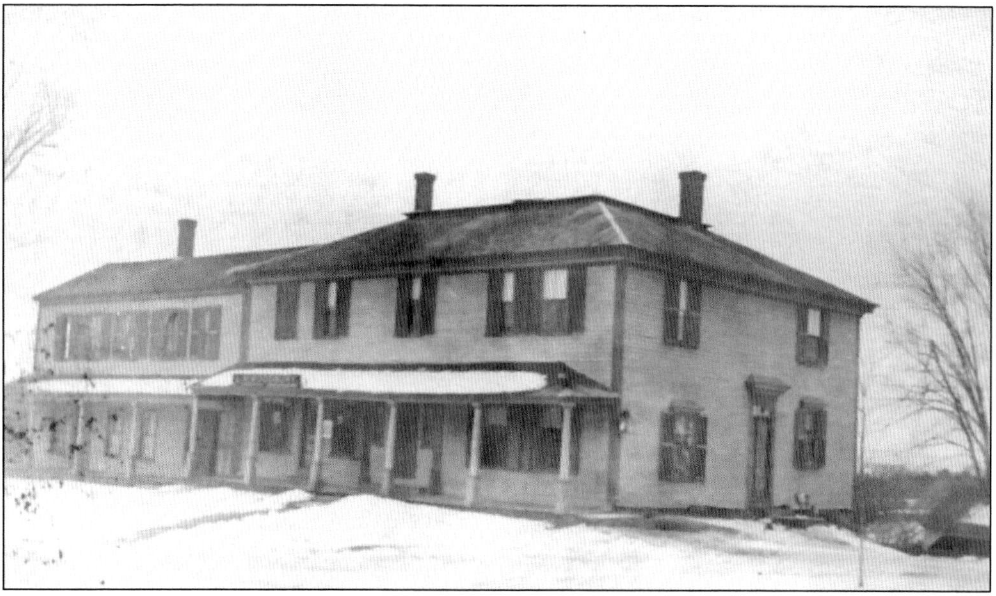

This building was situated across Main Street from Goddard Park. The date of construction is unknown but is generally accepted to be prior to 1800. The facility served North Orange as a tavern, general store, hotel, rooming house, and post office. It was a popular stopover point for stagecoaches when the main thoroughfare between Boston and Brattleboro, Vermont, passed its doors. Known over the years as the Green House because of its color, it was also known as the Green Tavern, the Green House Tavern, and the Central House.

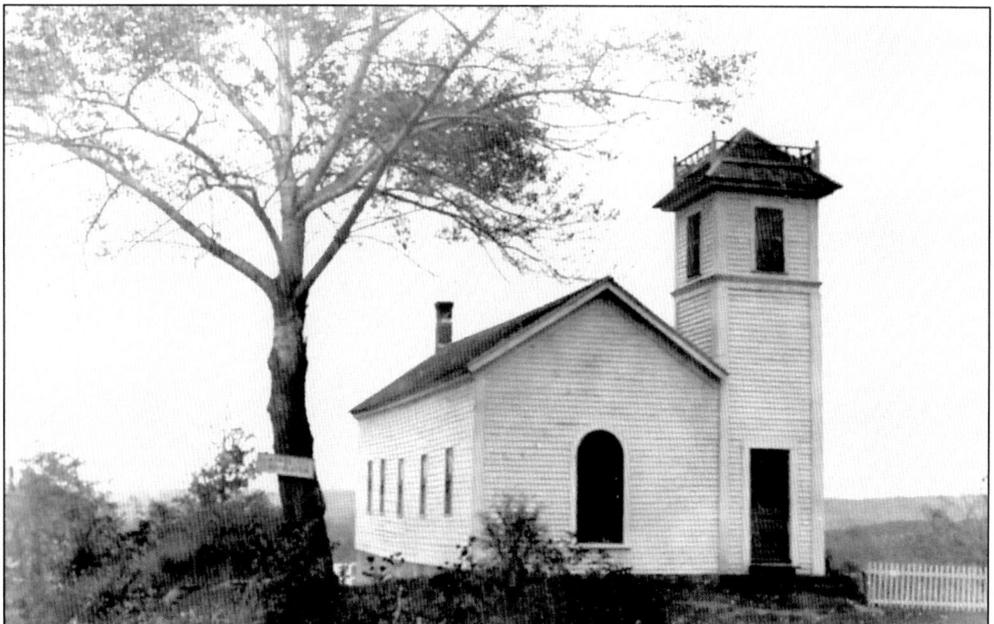

The "Congo" Chapel, as it was known, was the meetinghouse of the Third Congregational Society of Orange, founded in 1843. Originally a home, the chapel was moved at least once before arriving at the intersection of Main Street, Athol Road, and Royalston Road, where this photograph was taken around 1907. The Moore-Leland Library is now located on the site.

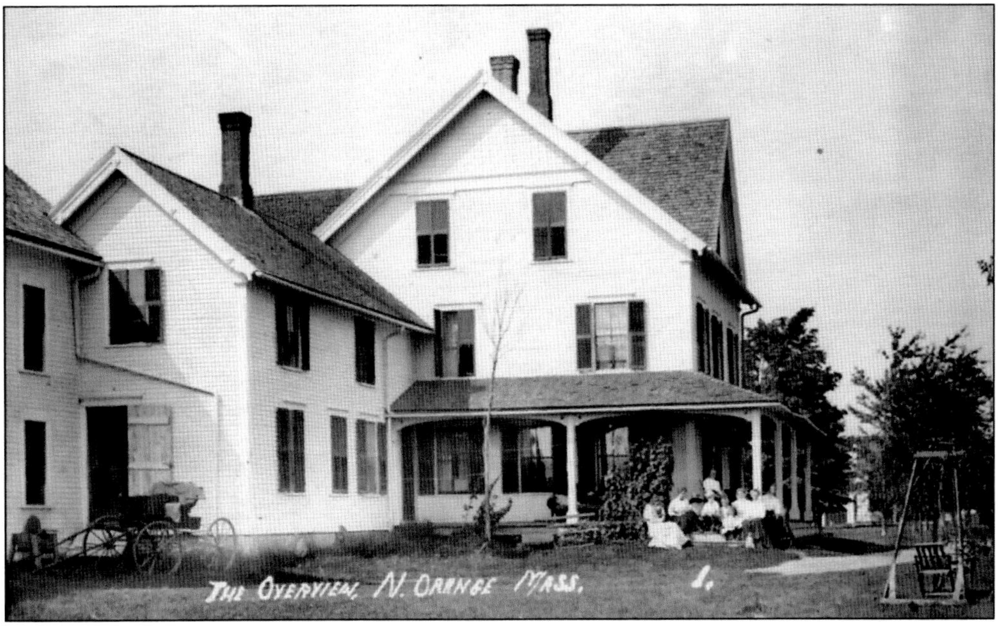

After the closing of the Green Tavern as a public house, the Overview was built by Mrs. F. E. Goddard in 1888. It was first known as the North Orange Hotel and opened in 1895 under the name Overview. It was sold to the Estabrooks family in 1917 as a private residence where, as late as 1950, the family operated a store and post office in part of the house. It is pictured here around 1913.

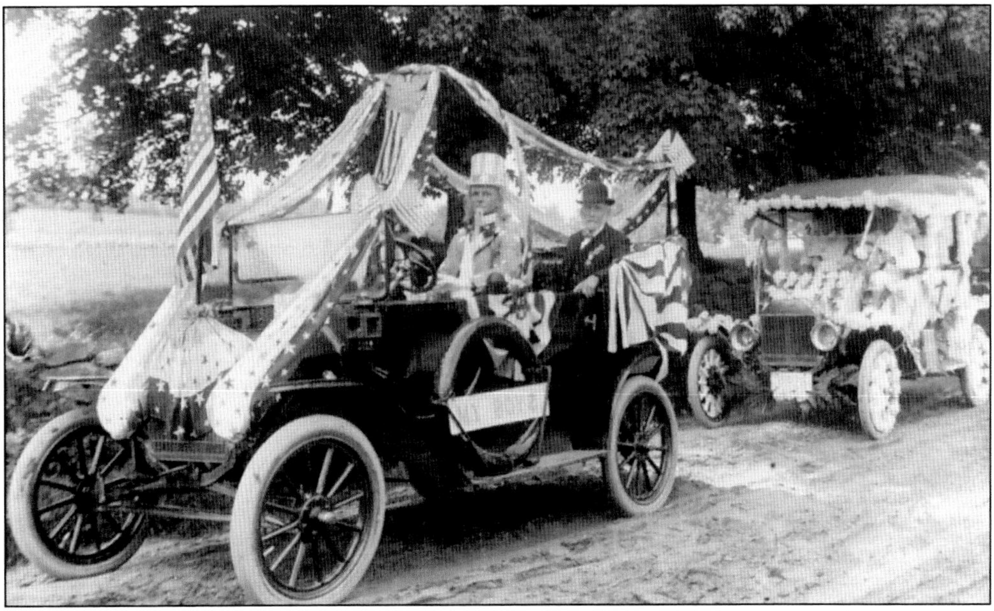

The North Orange Reunion Association has a proud tradition of holding annual reunions that extend back to 1900. The Old Home Day of 1914 was remarkable with its highly successful parade. Among the participants in the parade was Rollin White, driving his automobile dressed as Uncle Sam. (Clapp and Ingalls.)

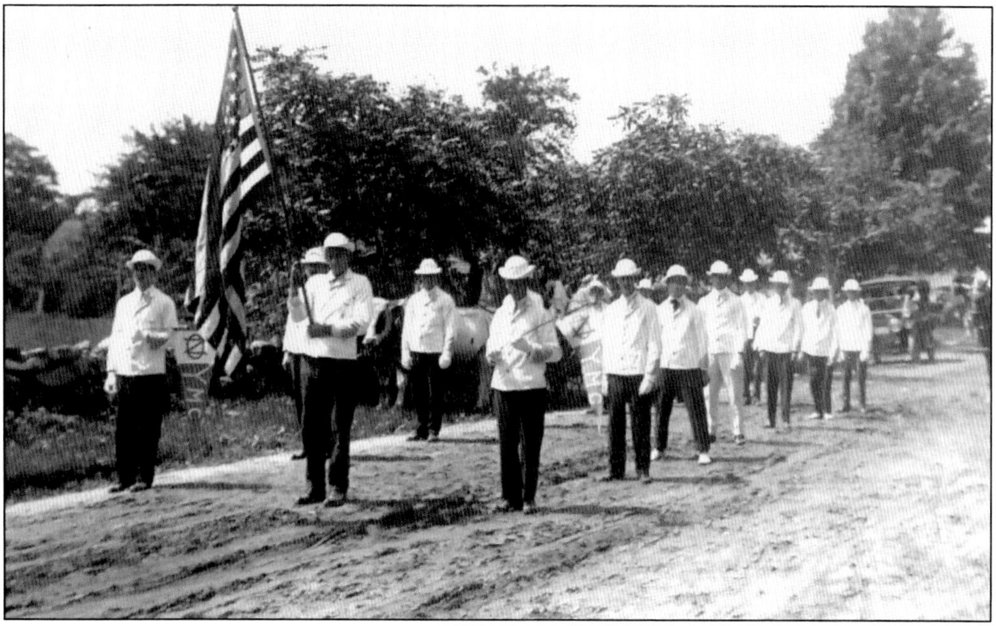

Dressed in white tunics and hats and proudly displaying their banners and flag of the United States, the North Orange Young Men's Club members marched in the 1914 Old Home Day parade. (Clapp and Ingalls.)

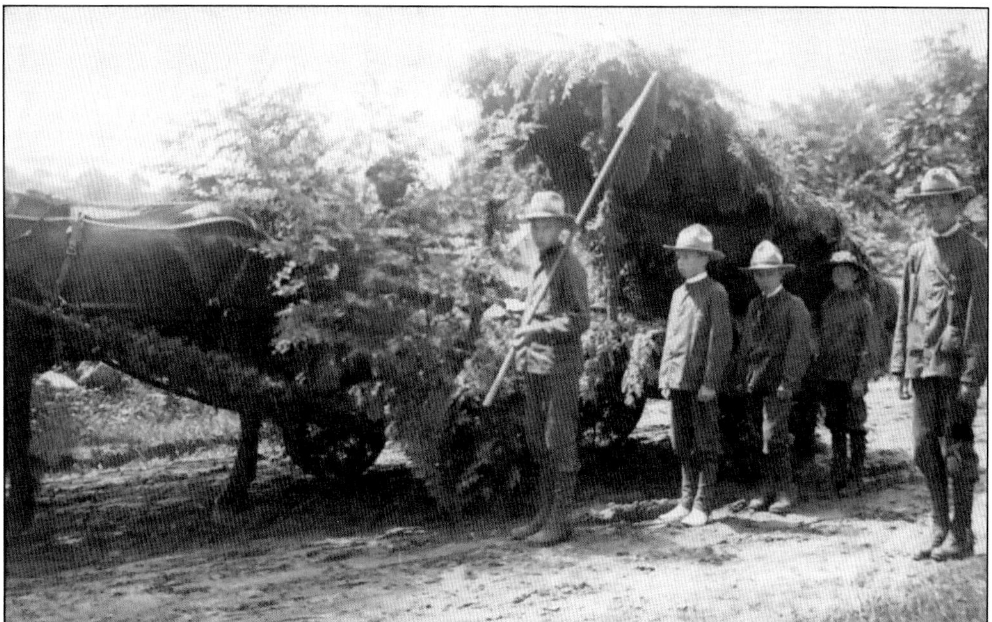

The Boy Scouts were represented in the 1914 Old Home Day parade. The scoutmaster at the time was Rev. Paul Weller. (Clapp and Ingalls.)

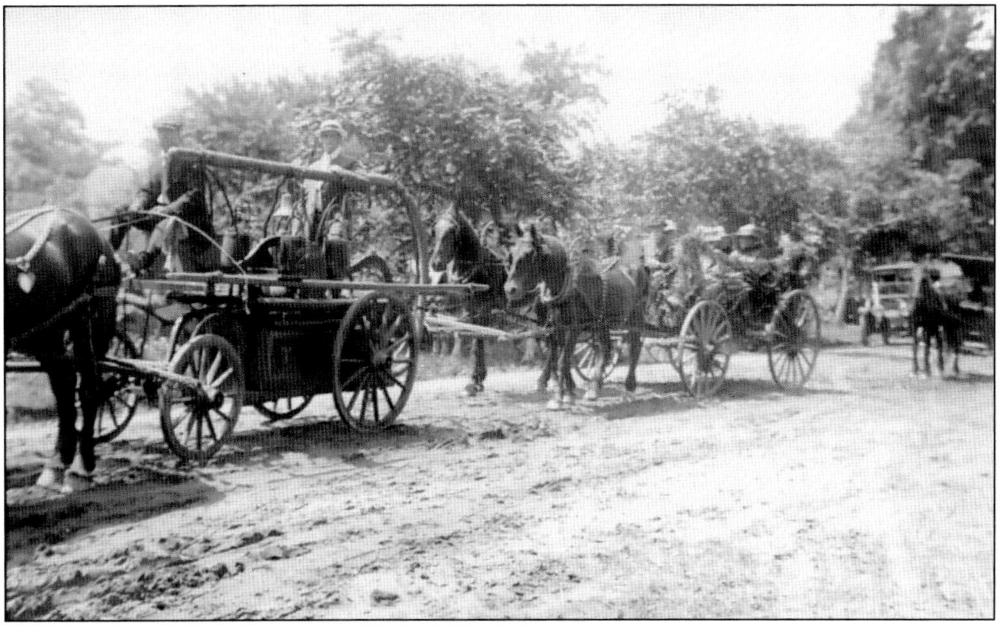

The Tully hand-pumped fire engine appeared in the 1914 parade. It was purchased in 1864. (Clapp and Ingalls.)

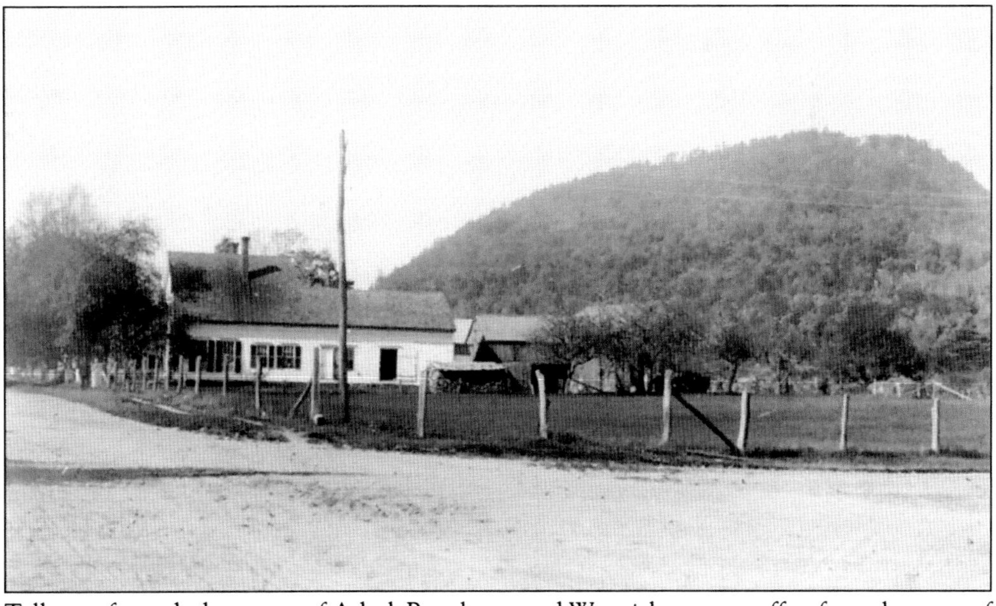

Tully was formed when parts of Athol, Royalston, and Warwick were set off to form the town of Orange in 1783. It was known as the Plains, Furnace Village, and finally Tully around 1904. This view looking north from the intersection of Royalston and Tully Roads shows the area's most prominent feature, "Big" Tully Mountain around 1906.

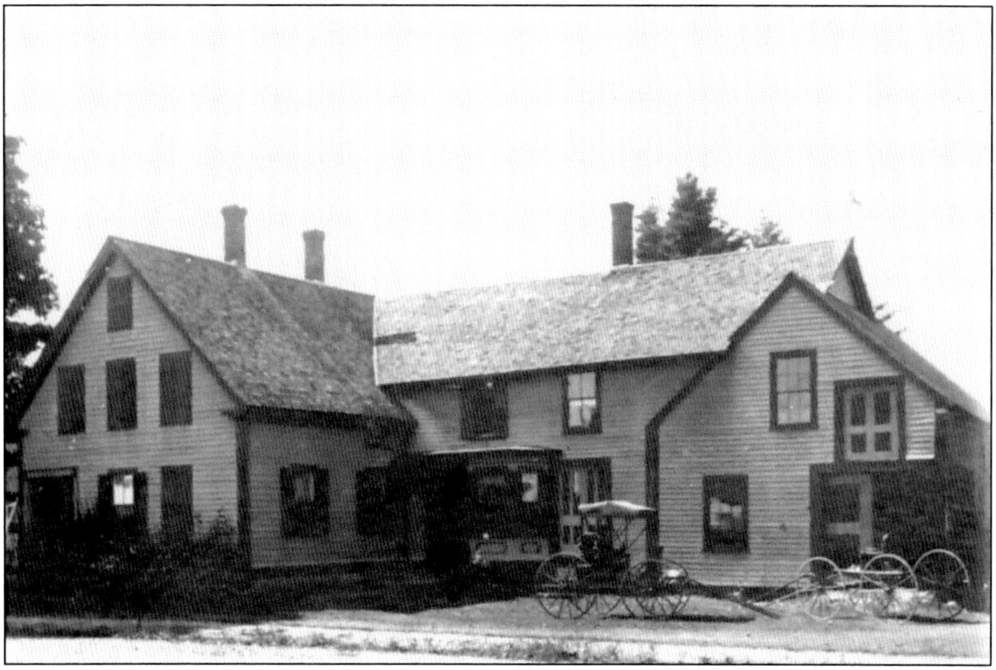

This house at 93 Royalston Road is directly across from the fire station in Tully. It is shown here around 1906.

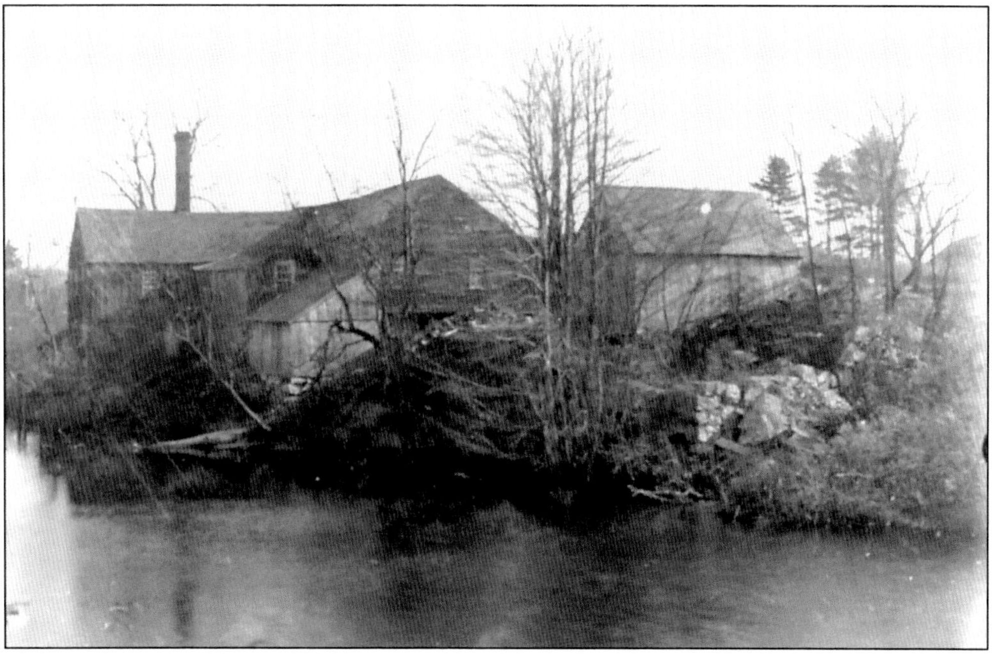

Jesse C. Worrick and Son, Inc. traces its roots in Tully back to 1835. Worrick purchased the furniture business in 1911. The wooden building shown here around 1911, was replaced with a two-story concrete building in 1931. Worrick operated here until 1959. The concrete building was last operated as the Mill Pond Restaurant around 2000.

Six

ATHOL

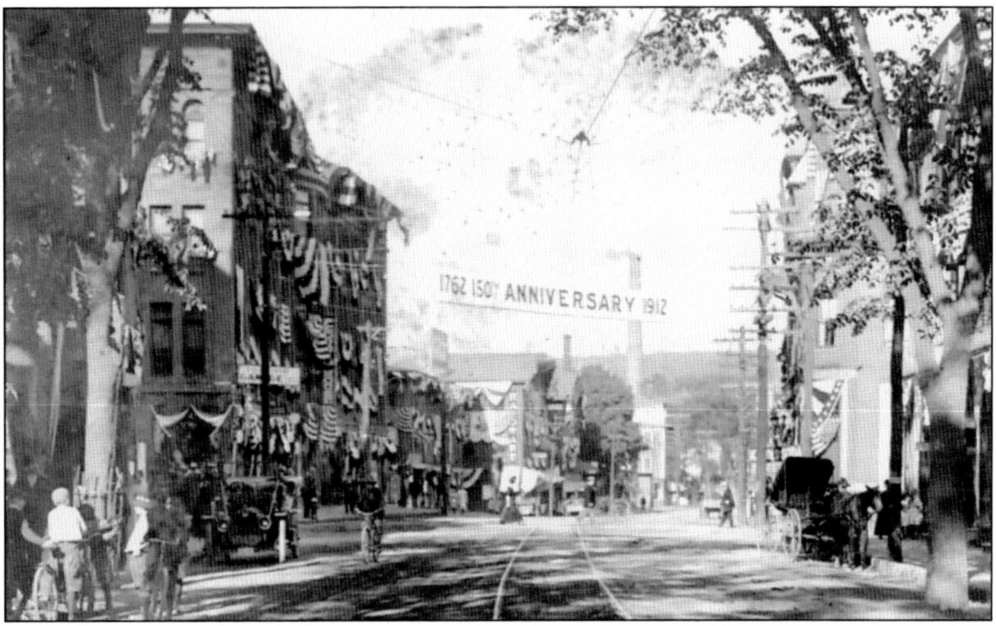

Main Street in Athol is shown here suitably decorated for its 150th anniversary celebration, June 16–18, 1912. This view, looking east at the intersection of Main and Exchange Streets, shows the Pequoig Block on the left. In the distance is the smokestack of the L. S. Starrett Company boiler room at the corner of Main and Crescent Streets.

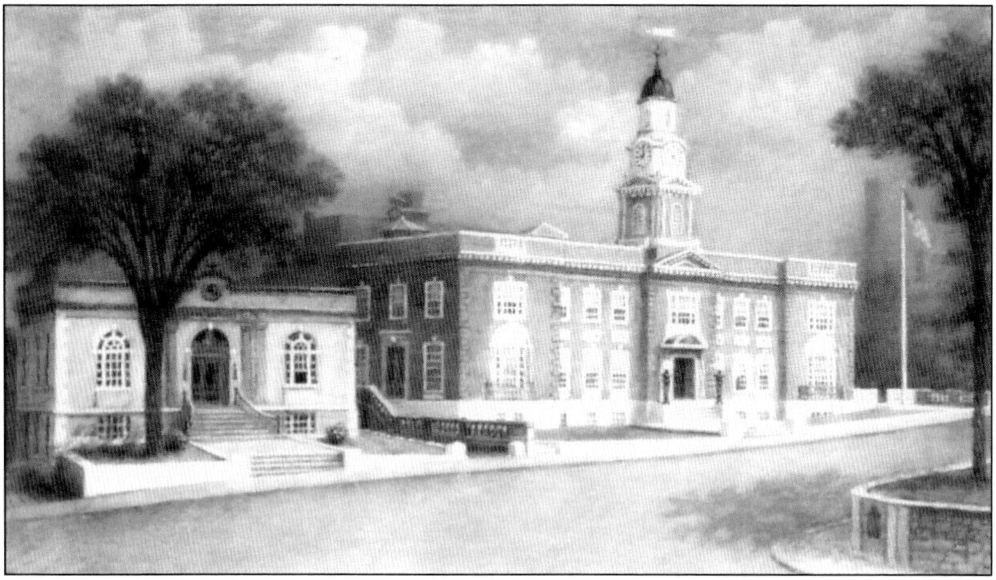

This 1924 painting by J. F. Gilman shows the recently completed Athol Memorial Building at the right and the Athol Public Library at the left. The library opened at this Main Street location in 1918.

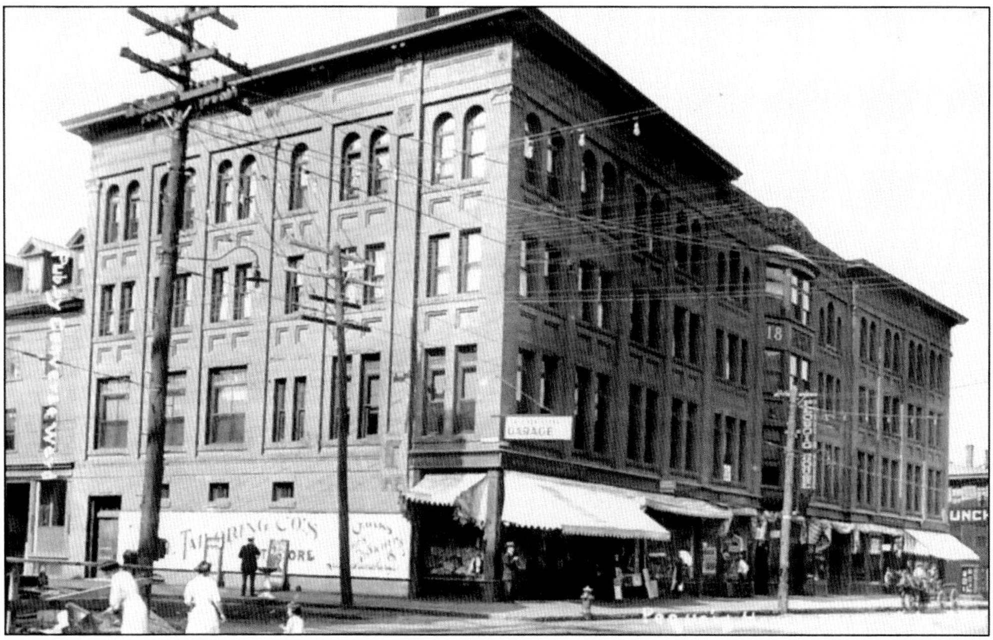

The Pequoig Block at the corner of Main and Exchange Streets was completed in 1895, housing businesses on the ground floor and a hotel known as the Pequoig House on the upper floors. It is now a facility for elders. This image is dated around 1916. (Converse Ward.)

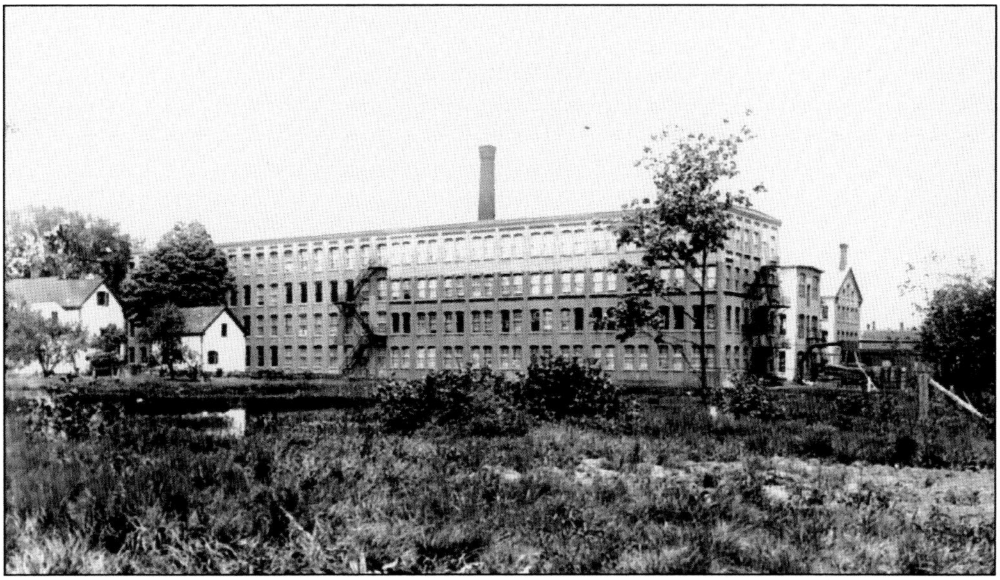

The Lee Brothers Shoe Company began in Athol in 1850 and moved to this location fronting at 349 Main Street in 1858. The brick building pictured here about 1914 was built in 1910. The photograph was taken from the current location of the Ocean State Job Lot store. Lee Brothers Company successively became Ansin Shoe Company, Anwelt Shoe Company, and the J. F. McElwain Shoe Company. (Underwood.)

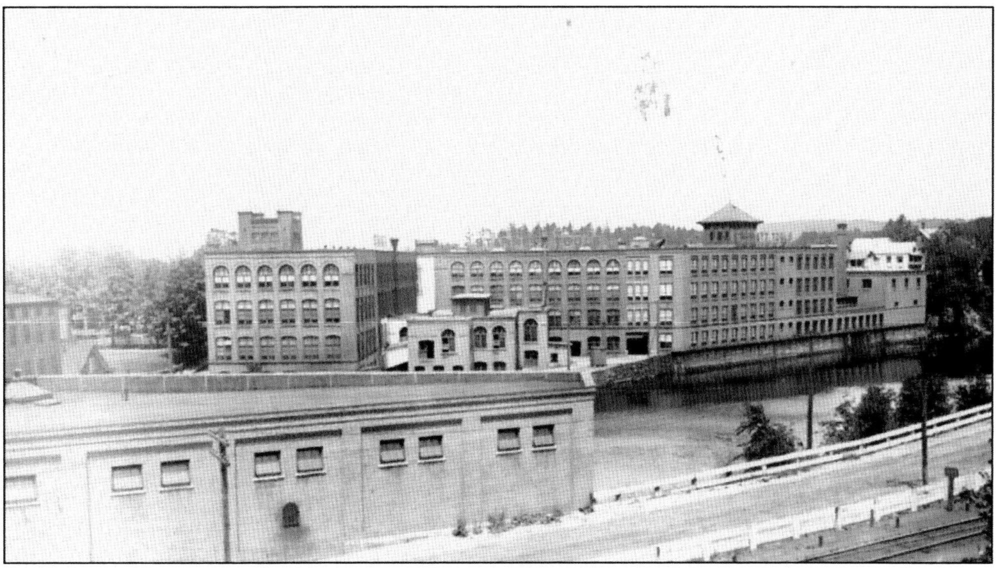

The L. S. Starrett Company at the corner of Main and Crescent Streets is pictured here about 1914. The boiler room in the foreground was completed in 1908. Main Street appears in the foreground with a fence on either side. (Underwood.)

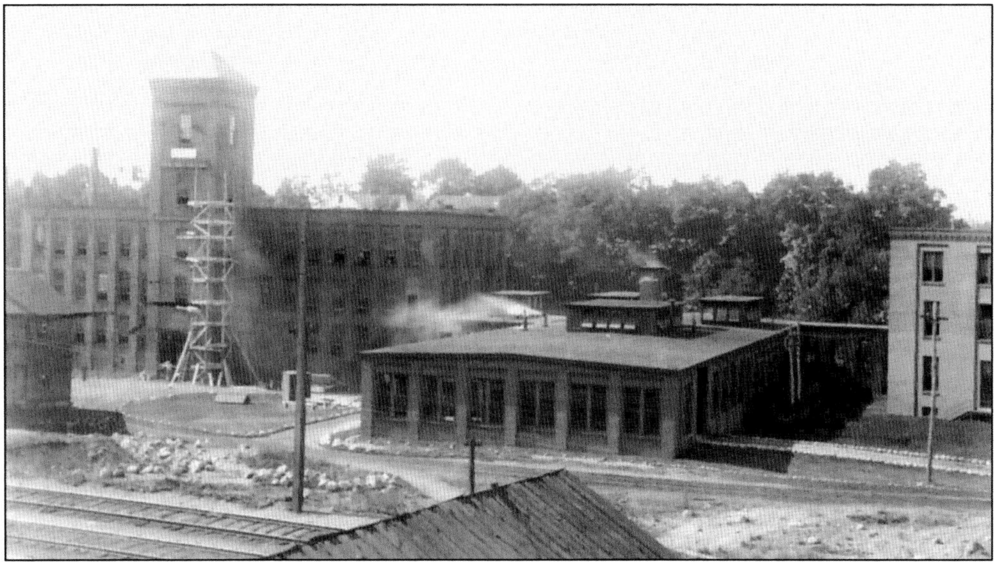

In 1905, a group of businessmen from Providence, Rhode Island, took over the interests of Gay and Ward on the Millers River at Monroe Street. Founded as the Union Twist Drill Company, it manufactured metal cutting tools at this location until the mid-1980s. Today, the L. P. Athol Corporation is located here. This view shows the company around 1911. (Converse Ward.)

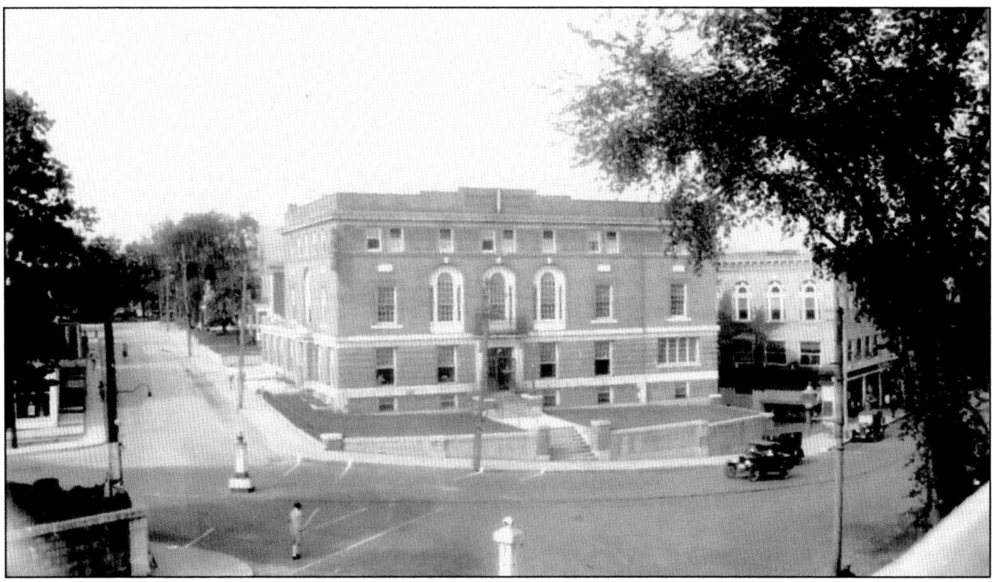

The YMCA building at the corner of Main and Traverse Streets was dedicated on March 15, 1912. The land was donated by Laroy S. Starrett, founder of the L. S. Starrett Company. It is shown here around 1925.

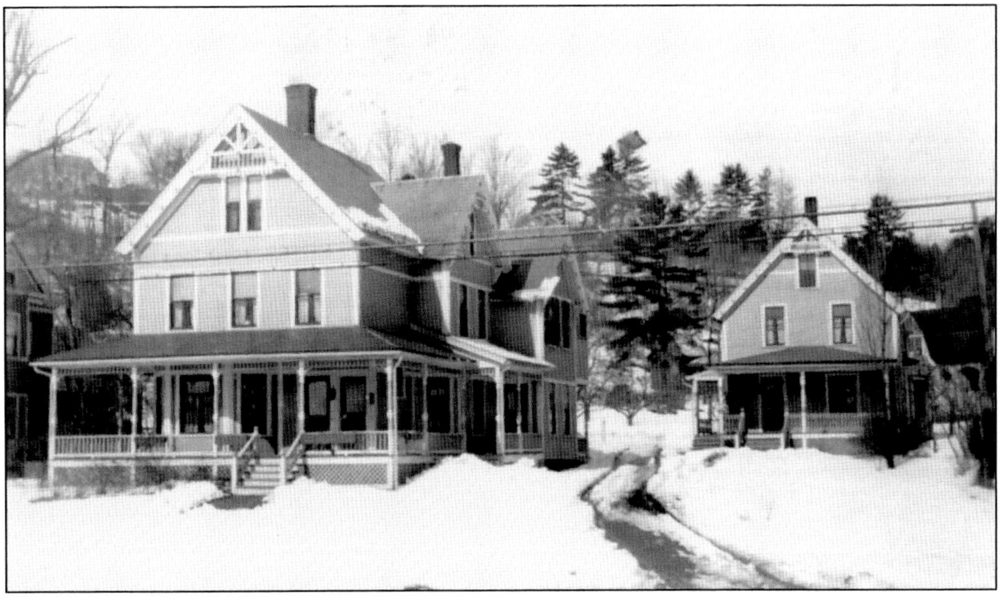

This house at 165 South Main Street is now the home of Athol Orange Community Television. At the time that this image was taken, around 1914, it was the home of Charles L. Johnson, who was a clerk at the M. W. Johnson Meat Market at 605 Main Street. A small handcrafted jewelry shop is now located there.

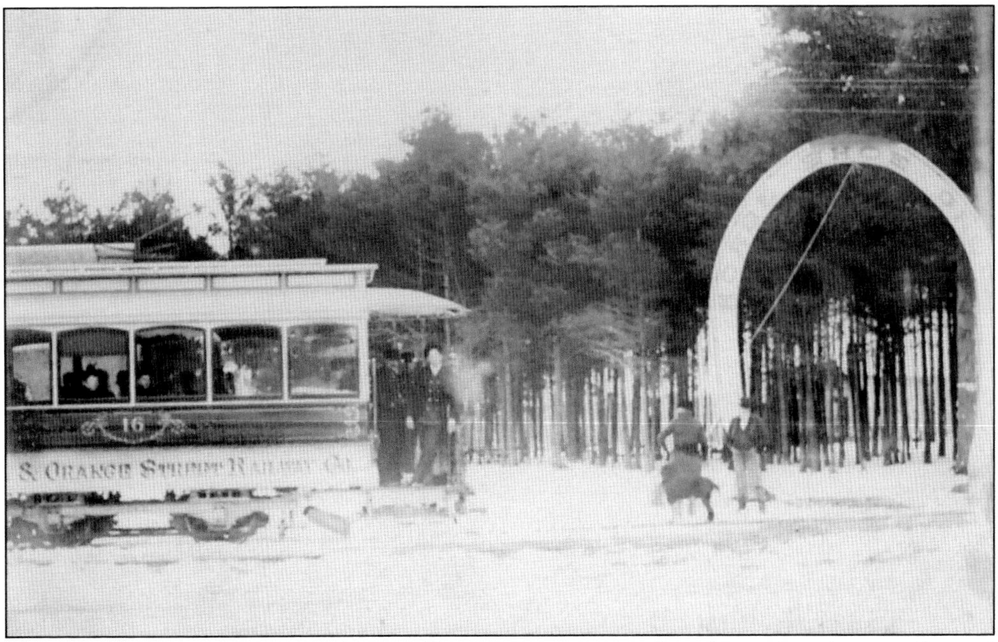

An Athol and Orange Street Railway trolley car is seen approaching Horseshoe Grove at Central Park (as Brookside Park was originally known) on Brookside Road near the Athol-Orange town line around 1895. Athol-Orange trolley service was available from September 19, 1894 until July 4, 1934.

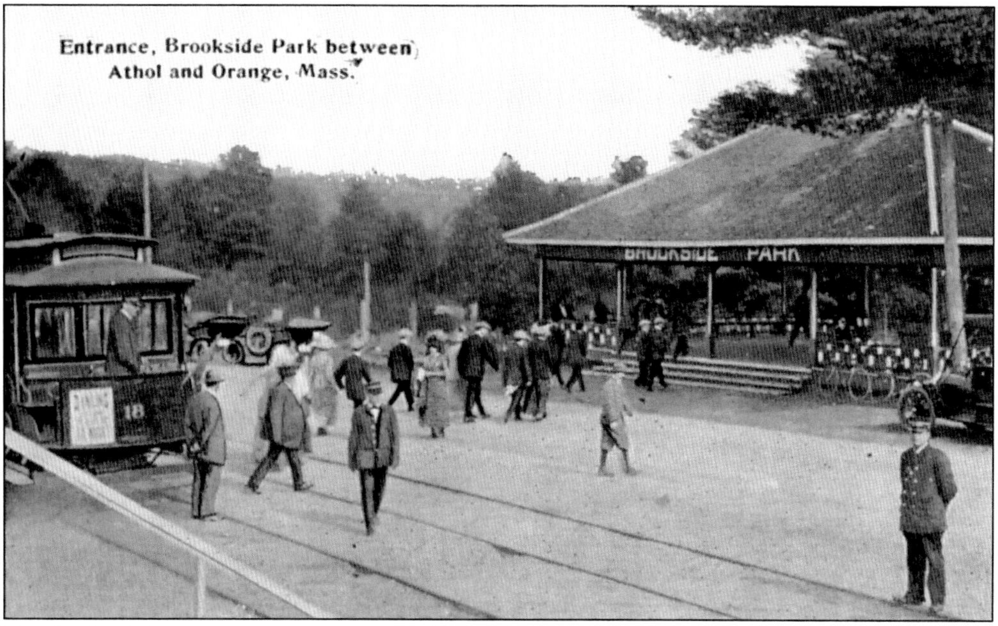

Brookside Park was a recreation center located off Brookside Road near the Athol-Orange town line. It was heavily promoted by the Athol and Orange Street Railway Company as the trolley line traversed Brookside Road. The park offered dancing, entertainment, a ball field, and other recreational activities for local residents. The entrance is shown here about 1912. (G. P. Harrington.)

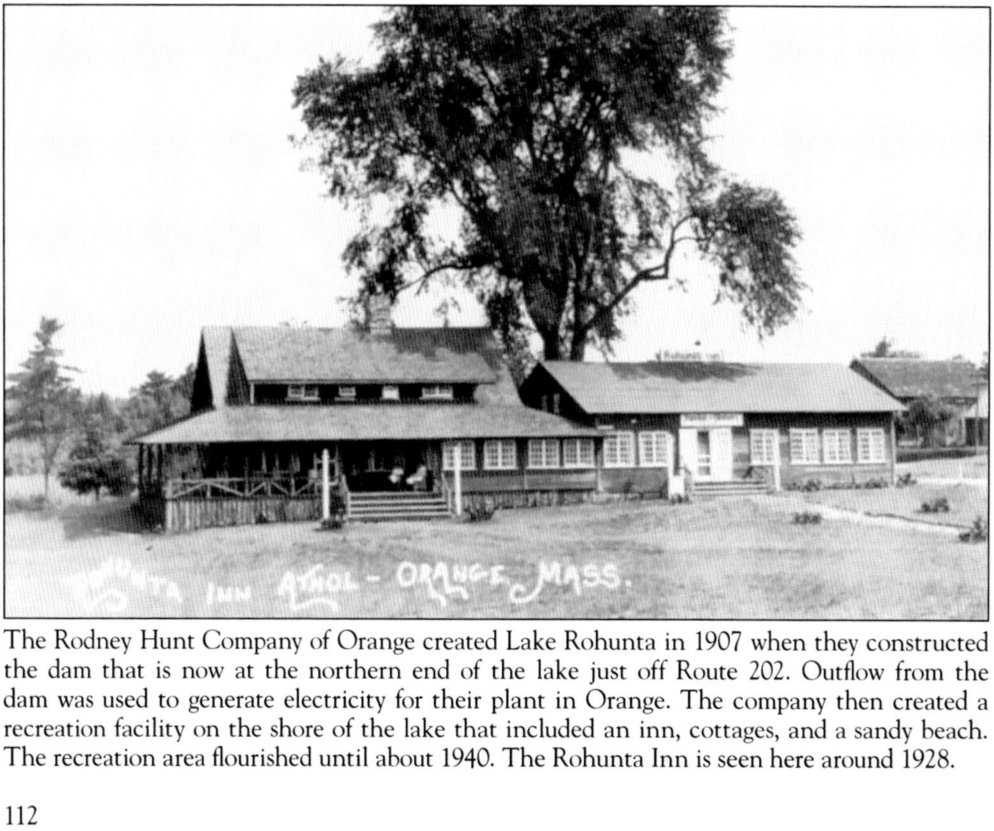

The Rodney Hunt Company of Orange created Lake Rohunta in 1907 when they constructed the dam that is now at the northern end of the lake just off Route 202. Outflow from the dam was used to generate electricity for their plant in Orange. The company then created a recreation facility on the shore of the lake that included an inn, cottages, and a sandy beach. The recreation area flourished until about 1940. The Rohunta Inn is seen here around 1928.

Seven

Erving and Wendell

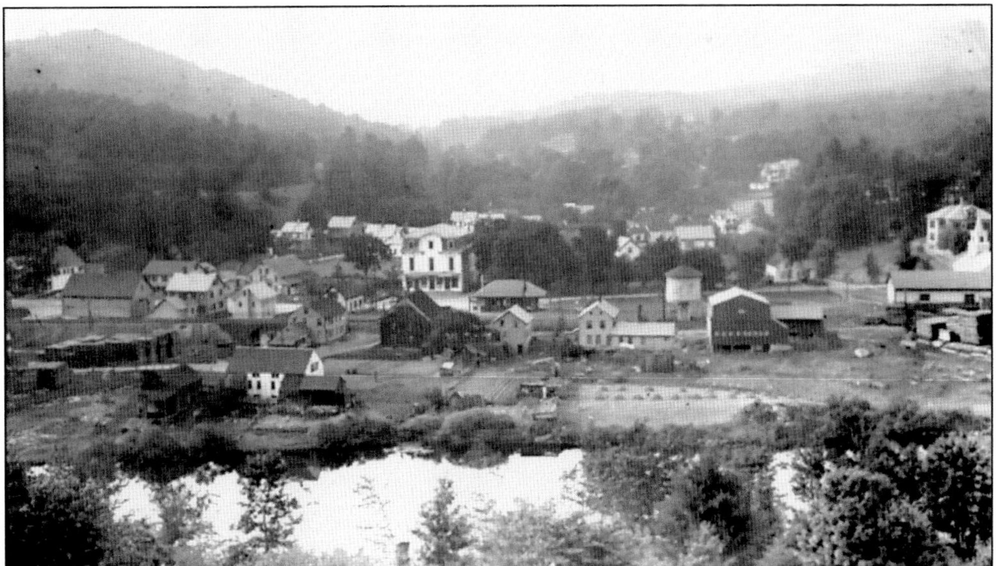

This bird's-eye-view of Erving from about 1912 looks north. The white building in the center is the old town hall. Below the trees to its right is the railroad station. At the far right is the Congregational church with its steeple partially concealing the schoolhouse. Present-day Route 2 passes east-west between the town hall and the railroad station.

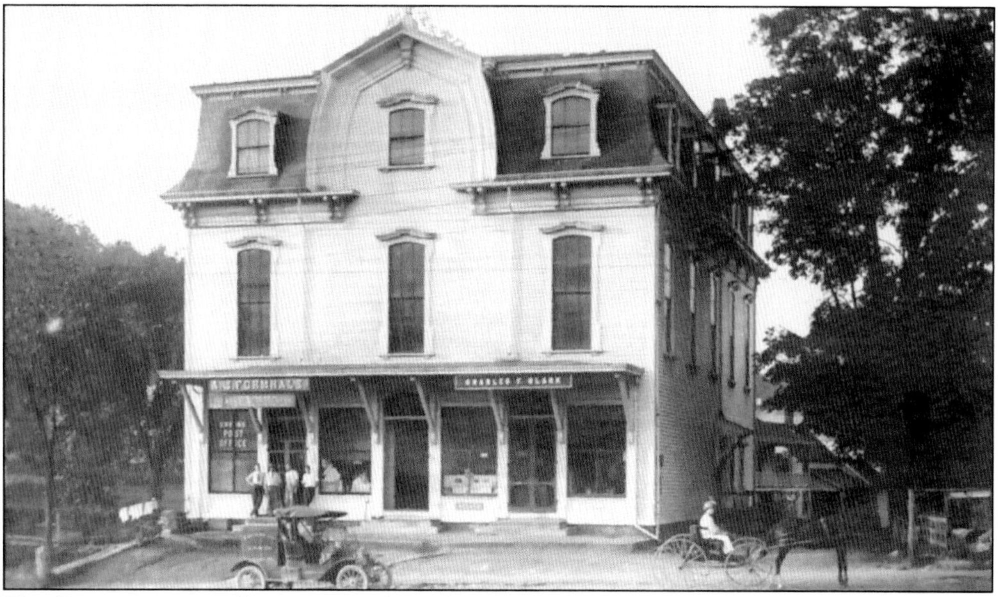

The Erving Town Hall was situated on the north side of Main Street opposite the railroad station. At the time of this c. 1915 photograph, two businesses were housed in the building. On the left was A. J. Formhals, who had a grocery store, soda fountain, and post office. On the right, Charles F. Clark had a grocery store. (Eastern Illustrating.)

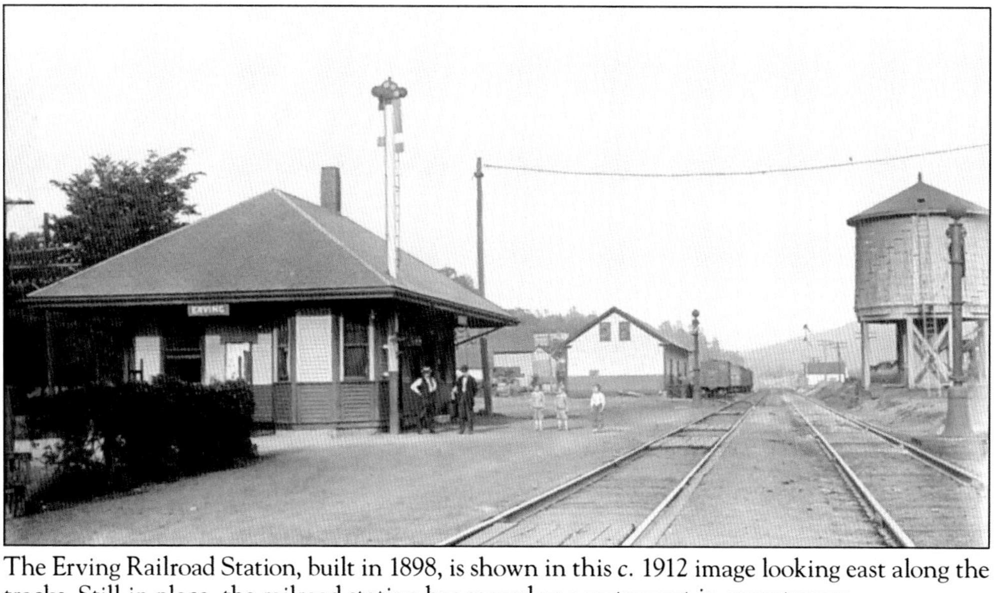

The Erving Railroad Station, built in 1898, is shown in this c. 1912 image looking east along the tracks. Still in place, the railroad station has served as a restaurant in recent years.

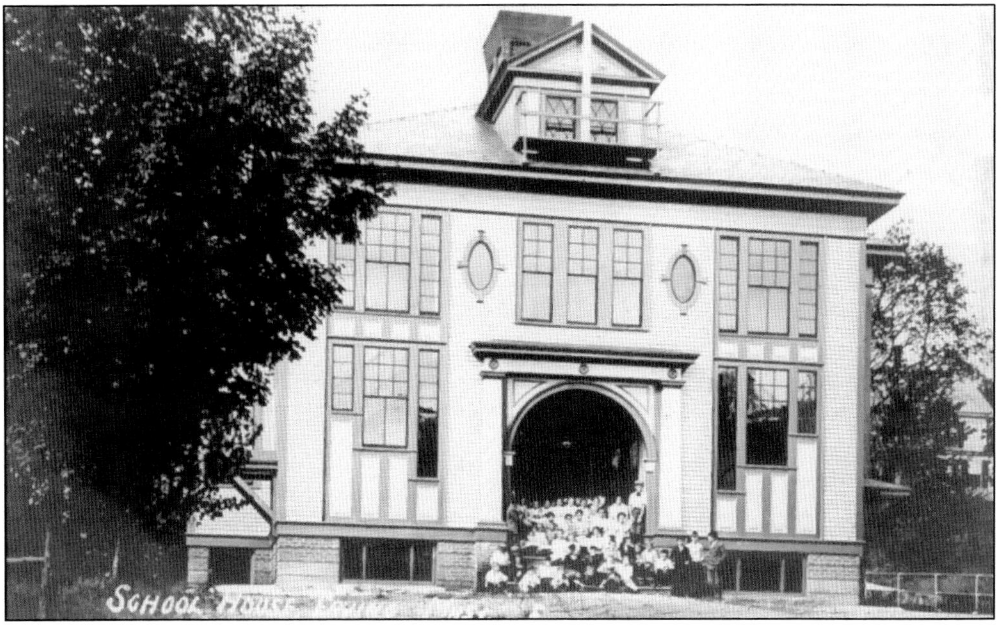

Following the burning of the Center School in early 1901, this new Erving Center School was completed in late 1901 and stood on Main Street. This photograph is from around 1907.

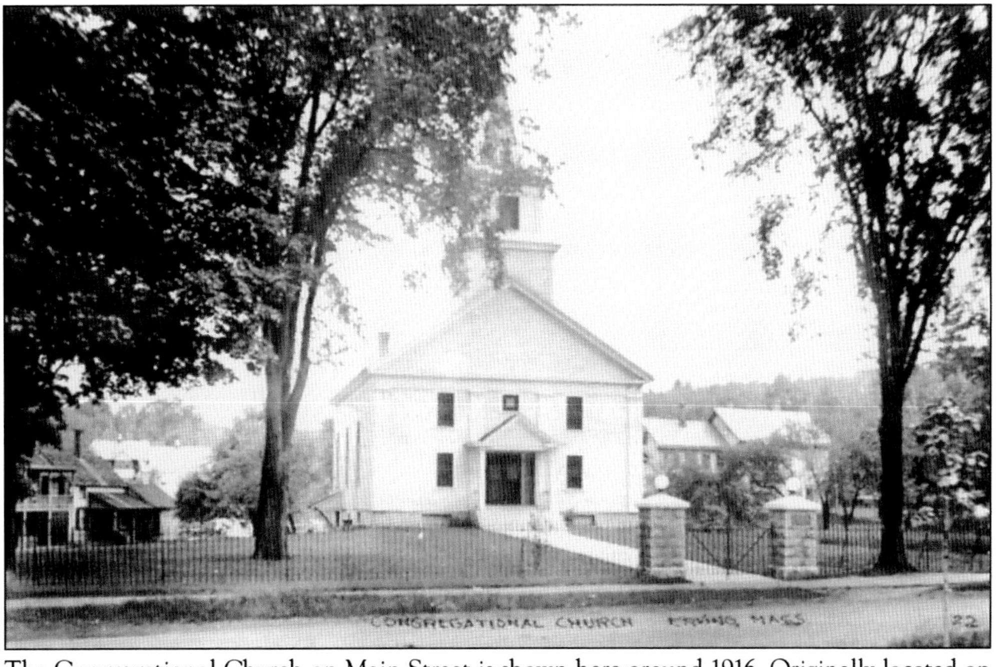

The Congregational Church on Main Street is shown here around 1916. Originally located on the south side of Main Street, the church was moved to its present location on the north side of Main Street in 1913.

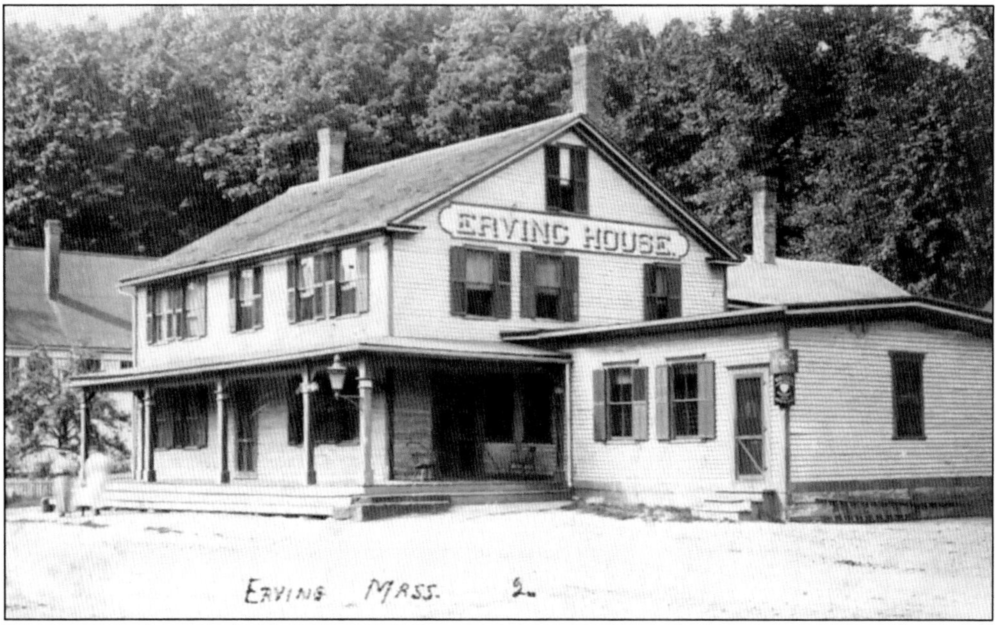

The Erving House on the north side of Main Street served rail and horse travelers well with clean rooms, good food, and a livery stable. It was purchase by A. J. Formhals in 1917. Formhals used the building as a store and post office. It is shown here around 1911. (Eastern Illustrating.)

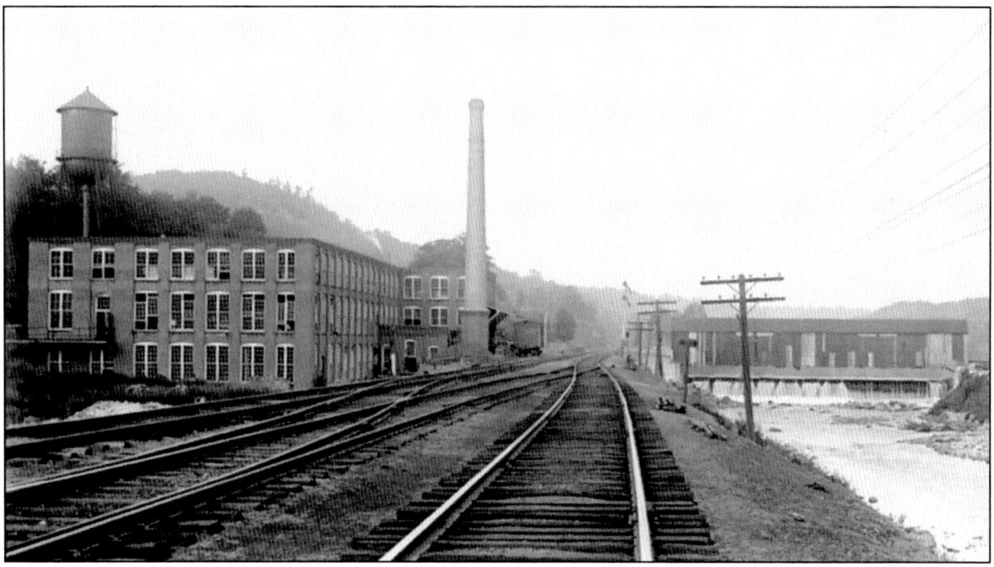
The Erving Paper Mills are shown here looking east along the railroad tracks around 1912. To the right is the old Stoneville covered bridge that spanned the Millers River between Erving and Wendell.

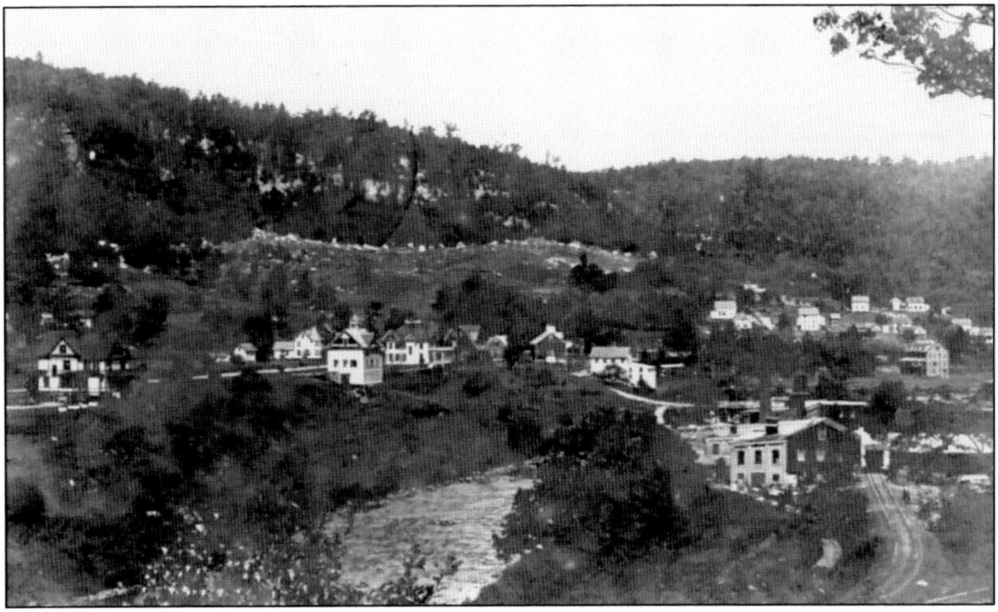

A bit of the village of Farley is shown in this view looking northeast around 1906. Taken from the Wendell side of the Millers River, it shows the Farley Paper Mill to the right on the Wendell side of the river. To the right of the elaborate white barn at left center is the home that would become the Ethel Farley Inn. It is on the Erving side of the river.

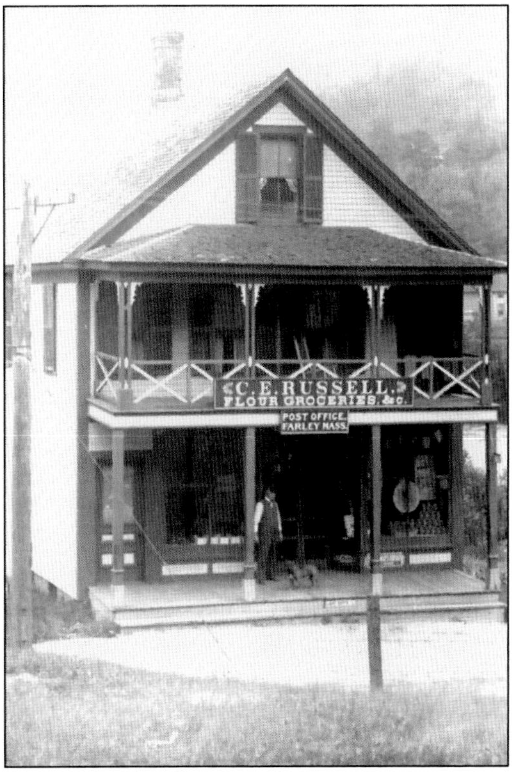

The general store and post office of C. E. Russell was located on Bridge Street. Russell was appointed postmaster in 1891. This image dates to around 1910.

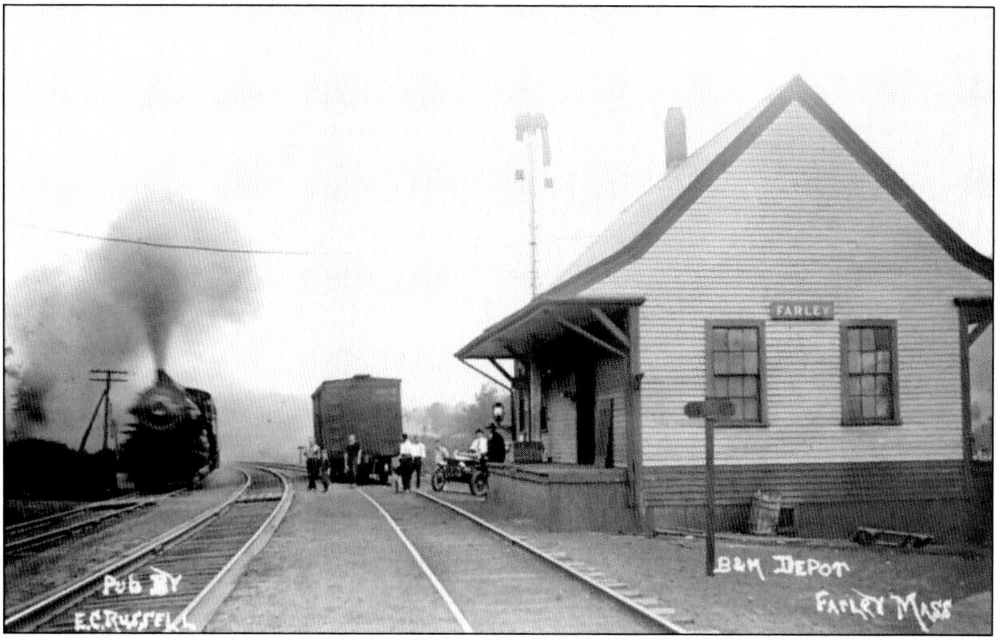

This image shows the long-forgotten railroad station in Farley about 1915. It was located on the Wendell side of the Millers River.

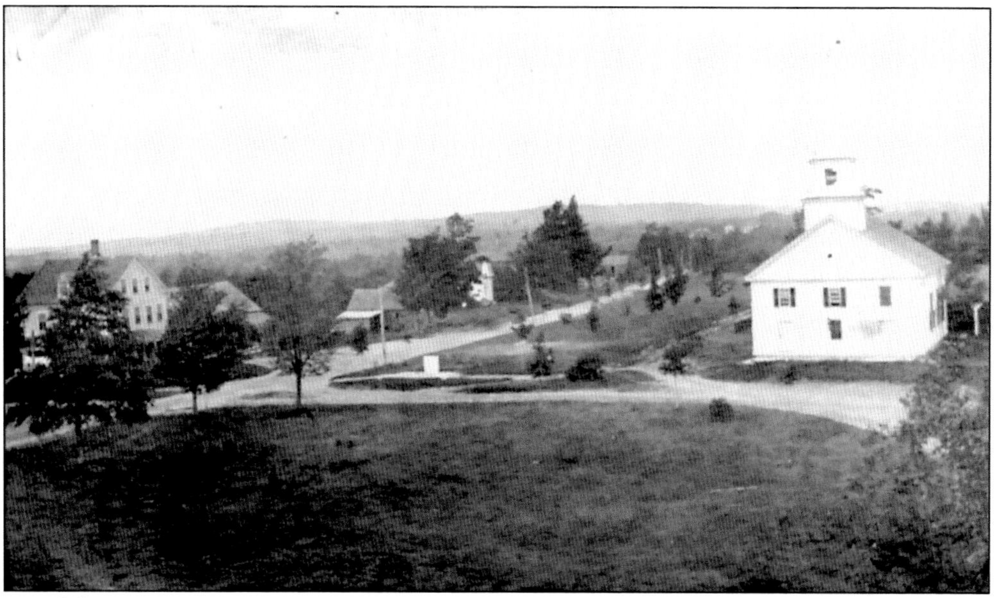
Wendell Center Common around 1907 is shown in this image. The Congregational church at the north end of the common is at the right. At the left, partially hidden by trees, is the general store and post office.

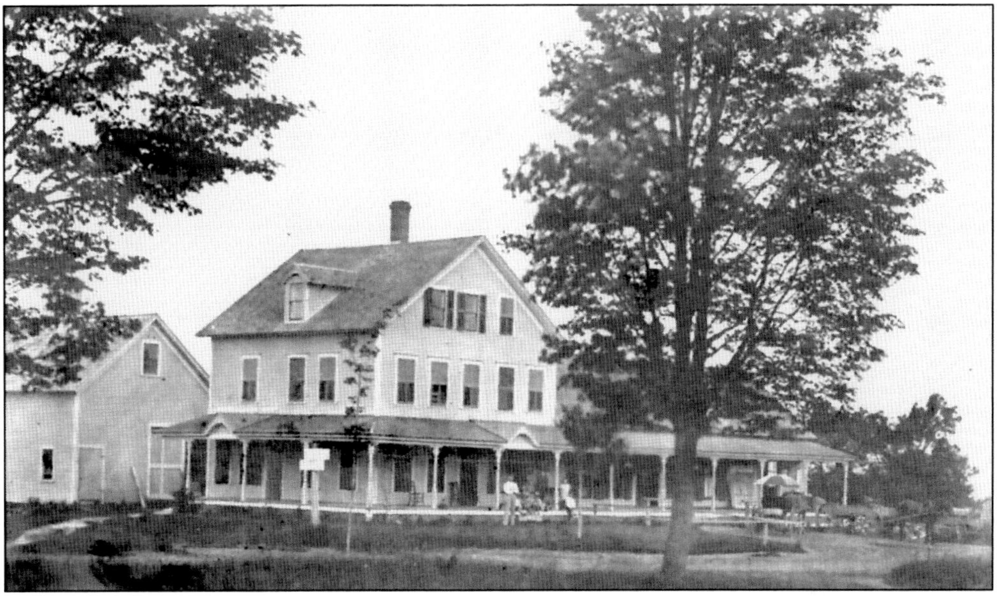

The general store and post office at the corner of Wendell Depot Road and Montague Road at Wendell Center is shown in this photograph from about 1910.

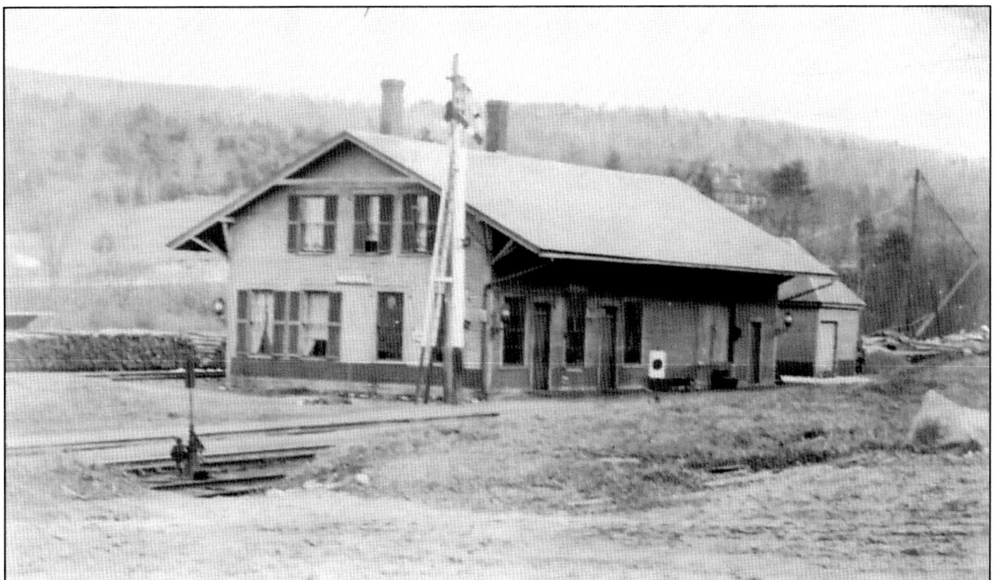

Wendell Depot railroad station is shown in this image from around 1907, looking north from Wendell Depot Road. The station was located between the railroad tracks and the Millers River just off Wendell Depot Road.

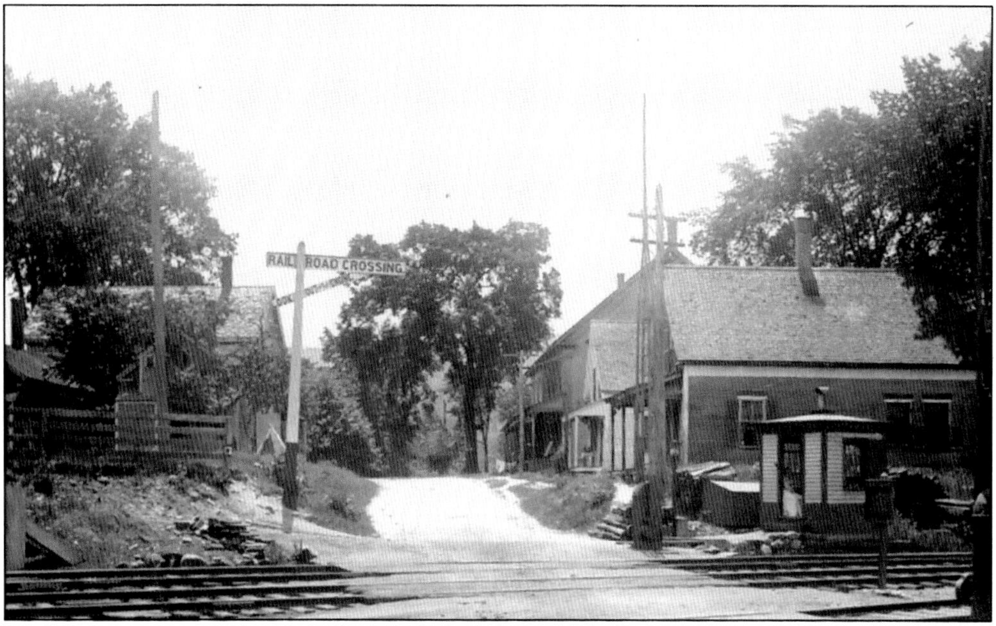

Looking south on Wendell Depot Road from the end of the bridge over the Millers River, around 1907, this photograph shows that Wendell Depot once had several buildings adjacent to the railroad tracks. Just over the tracks, the third building on the right was Putnam's Store and post office. Notice the lady in the small station house waiting for the train.

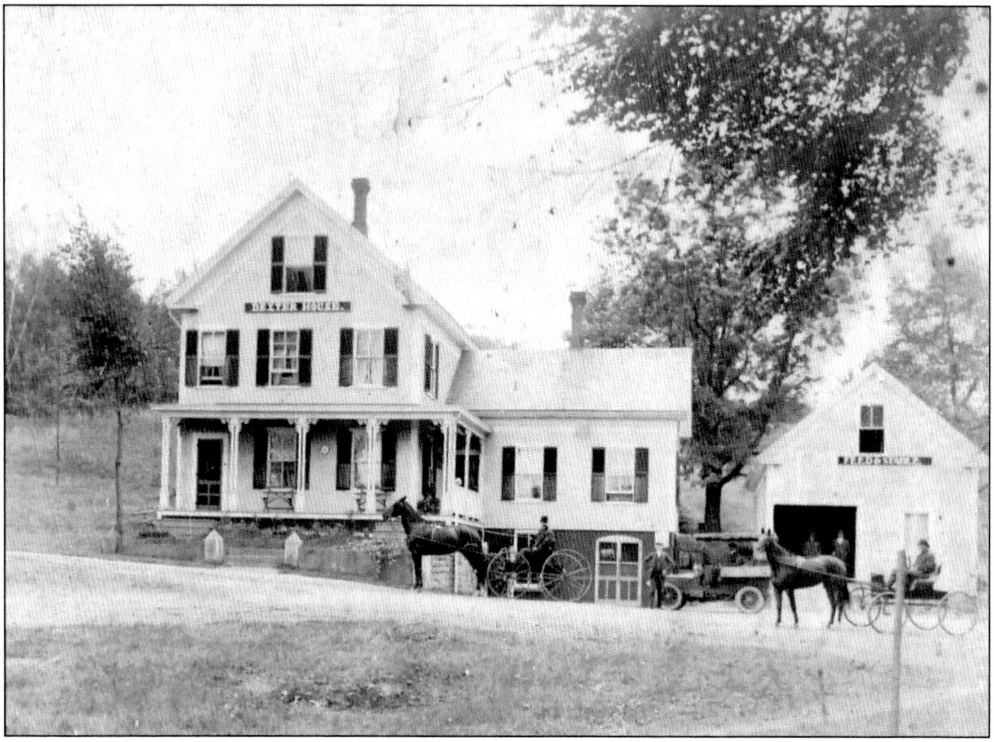

The Dexter House on West Orange Road, opposite the railroad station, once provided shelter and sustenance for the weary traveler. It is shown here around 1915. (Carter.)

Eight

New Salem and Warwick

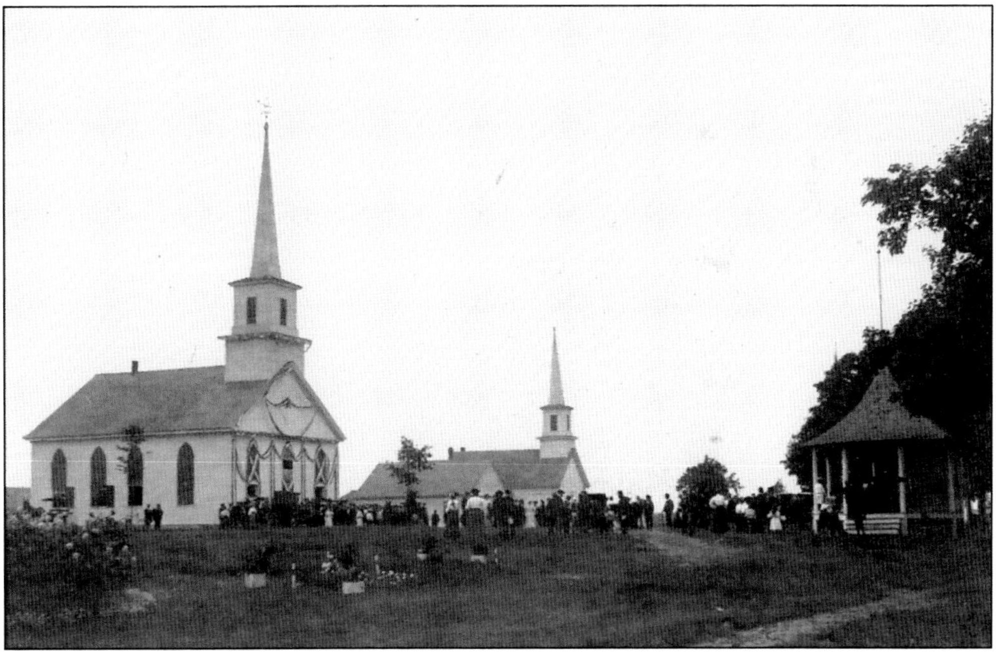

This photograph of New Salem Reunion Day in the early 1900s shows the Unitarian Church, now the 1764 Meeting House, at the left. The small building between the churches was once the town hall and more recently served as the library. Central Congregational Church is in the center of the photograph. At the right is the bandstand located next to the old New Salem Academy building.

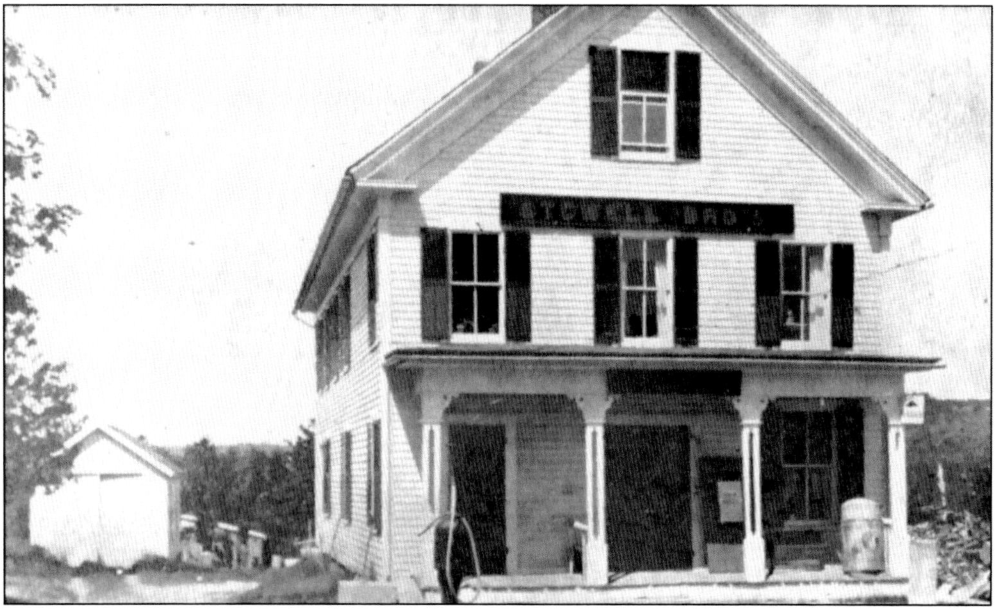

Stowell Brothers store and post office at South Main and West Main streets is shown here around 1925. It was a store until 1935 when the business was moved to Daniel Shays Highway. (Auburn.)

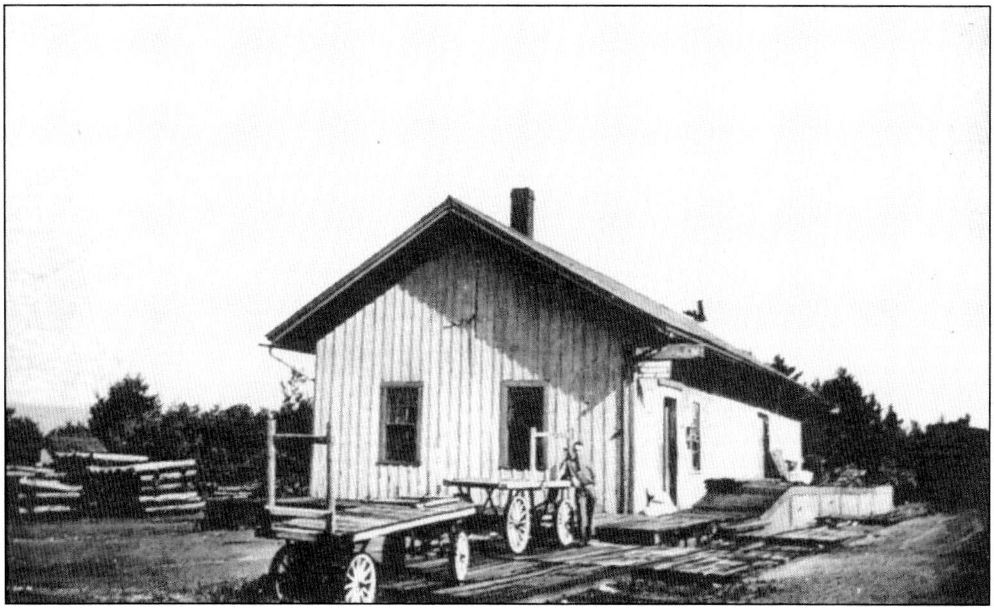

Located a considerable distance southeast of New Salem Center, the New Salem Station was closer to the village of Millington. Serving the Athol-Springfield branch of the Boston and Albany Railroad, this station succumbed to the creation of the Quabbin Reservoir in 1935. The station was dismantled and moved to New Salem Center to be rebuilt as a fire station. (Cosmos.)

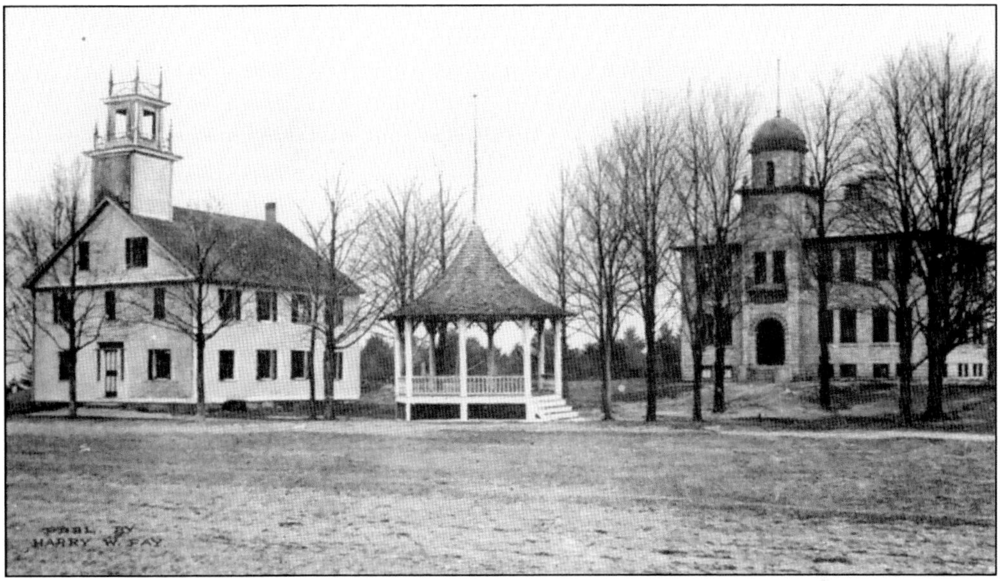

At left in this image from about 1909 is the old New Salem Academy recitation hall. Built in 1838, it served until the completion of the new recitation hall in 1908. A commemorative stone above the front door of the new recitation hall is inscribed "1795-N.S.A.-1908" indicating the year of founding of New Salem Academy and the year of opening of the new building.

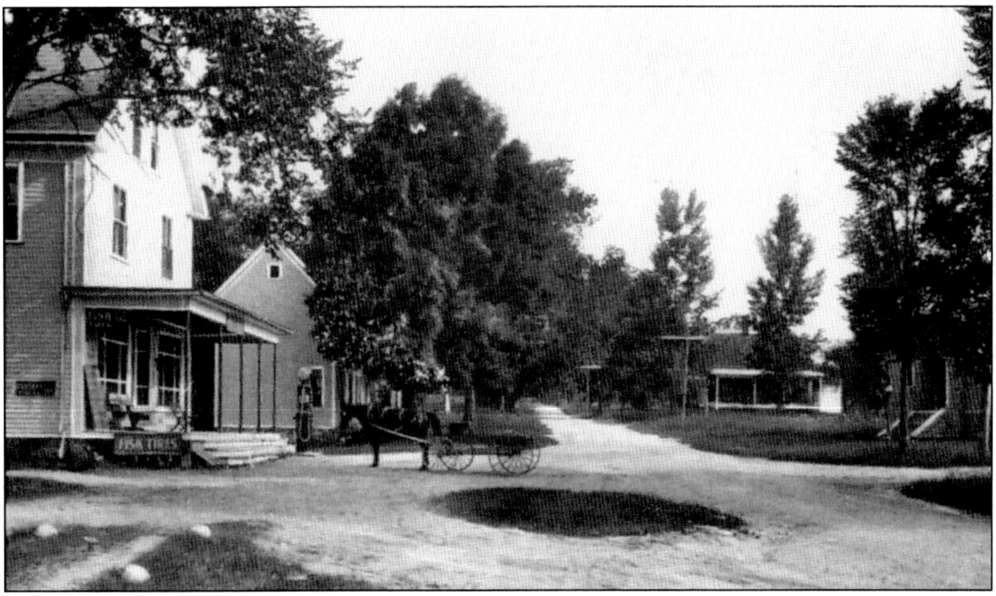

The New Salem contribution to the creation of the Quabbin Reservoir was considerable acreage including the village of Millington shown here around 1920. At the left is the general store and post office. Visible through the trees at the extreme right is the L. E. Moore hall. Moore was a prominent and influential native of Millington. Note the contrast in technology with the horse and wagon next to the gasoline pump in front of the general store.

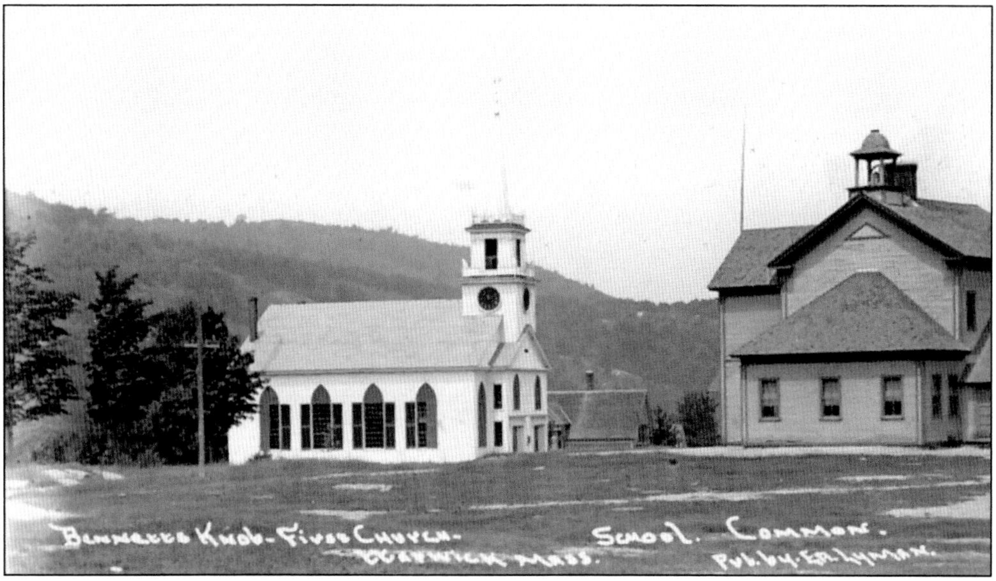

Looking northwest around 1912, this view of Warwick shows the Unitarian Church and the schoolhouse at the right. Today, Route 78 passes between the church and the schoolhouse. (Lyman.)

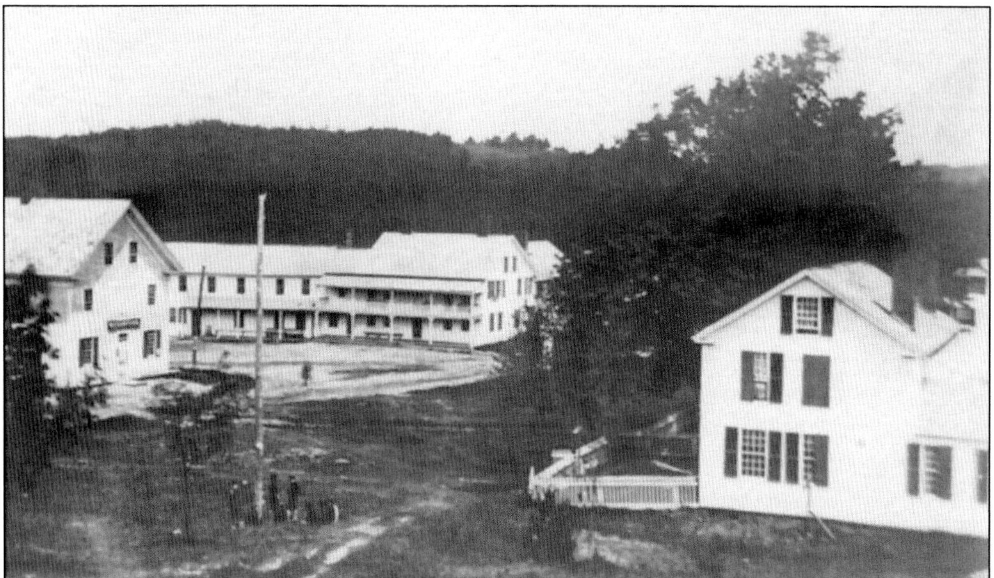

This view in Warwick looking northeast shows the Warwick Inn around 1900. To the left is the Sampson store on the site of the present day town hall. Previously, the Sampson store had been the boot shop of Nahum Jones that closed in 1885.

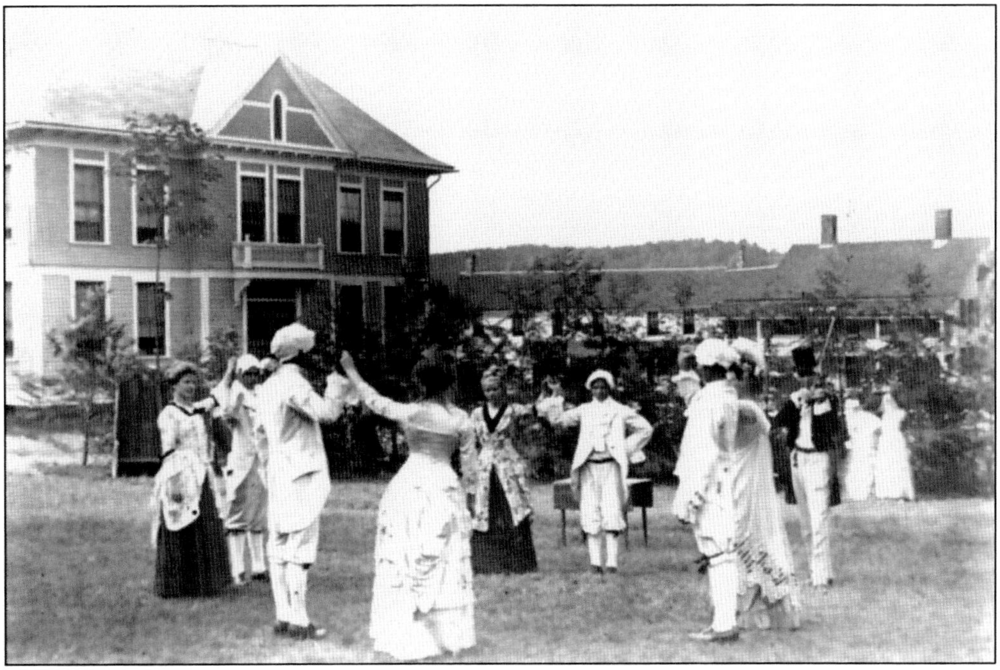

Citizens of Warwick are shown in front of the town hall dressed in period costume during the 150th anniversary celebration of Warwick in 1912. In the rear is the Warwick Inn.

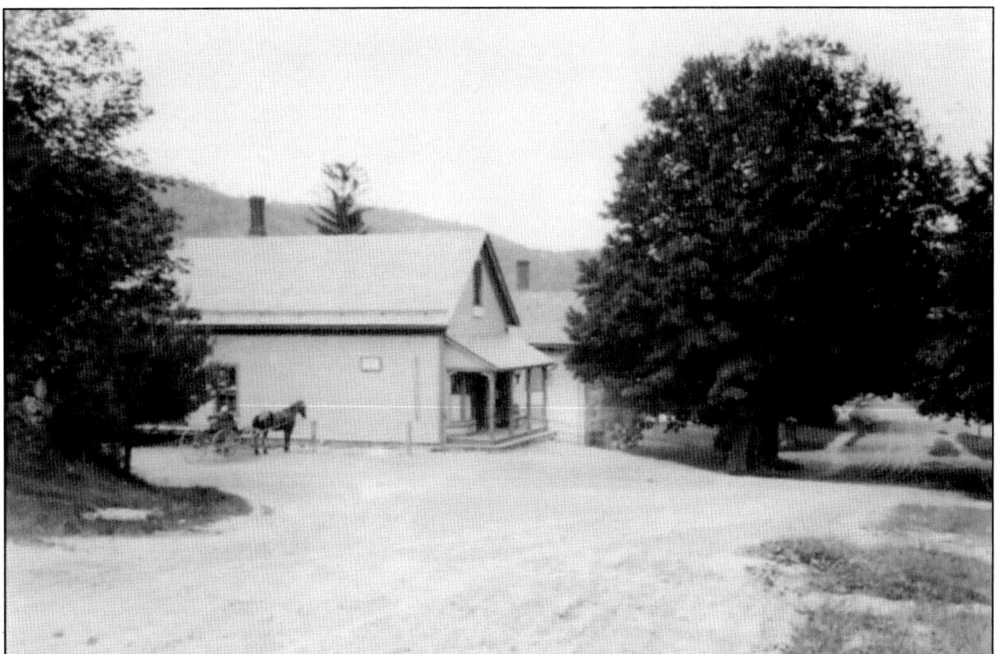

Looking north on what is presently Route 68, the general store is shown around 1910. After several years of vacancy, the store reopened in 2005. (Eastern Illustrating.)

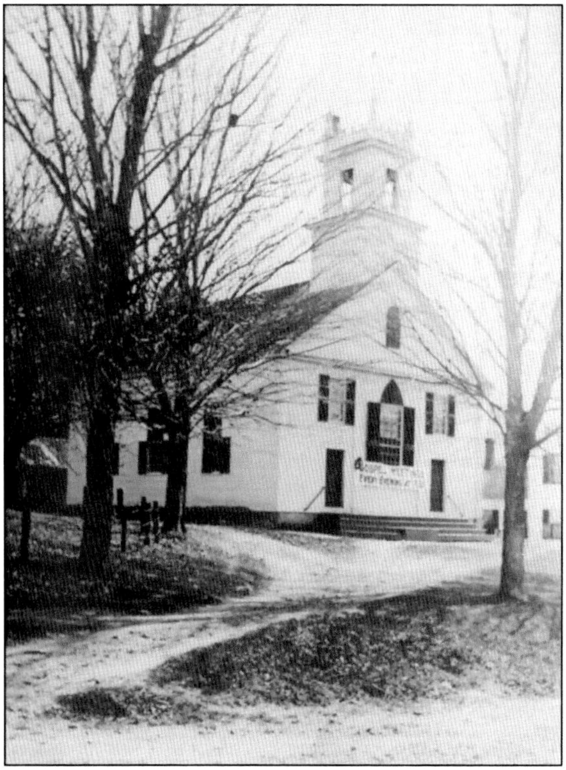

The long-ago removed Congregational church is shown in this image from around 1907. It was located on the east side of present-day Route 68 just south of the Revere Hill Road intersection.

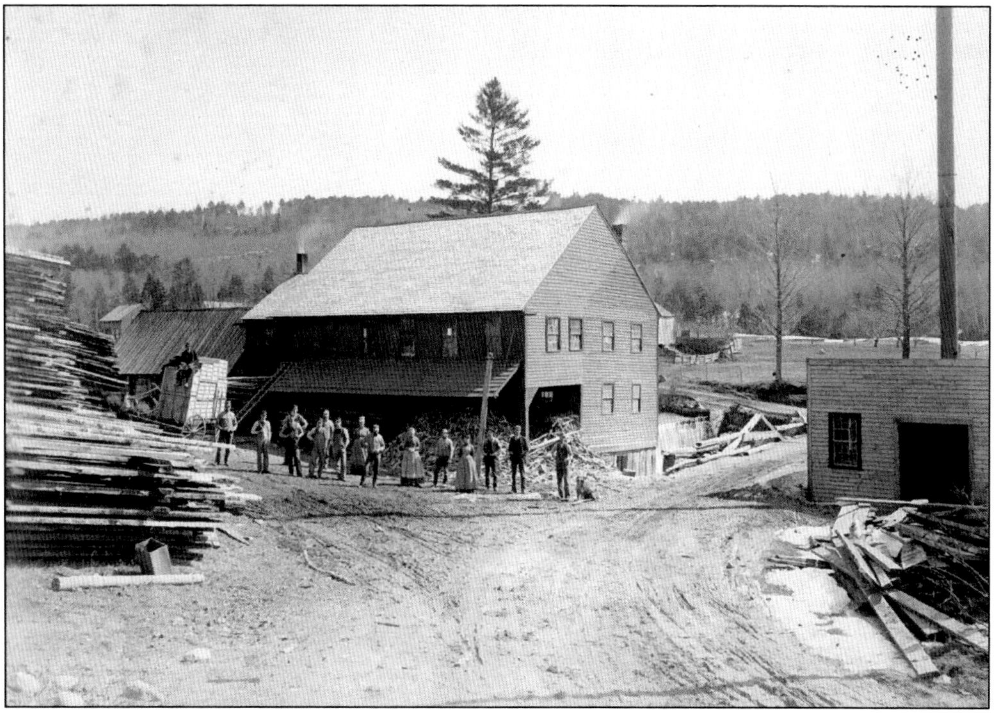

The box shop of George Wheeler, located in Brush Valley, is shown here around 1895. The business continued until it was destroyed by fire in 1920.

BIBLIOGRAPHY

Athol and Orange Directory 1895. New Haven, CT: The Price and Lee Company, 1895.

Athol and Orange Directory 1902. New Haven, CT: The Price and Lee Company, 1902.

Athol and Orange Directory 1914-'15. New Haven, CT: The Price and Lee Company, 1914.

Athol and Orange Directory 1924. New Haven, CT: The Price and Lee Company, 1924.

Athol and Orange Directory 1934. New Haven, CT: The Price and Lee Company, 1934.

Beers, F. W. *Atlas of Franklin Co., Massachusetts*. New York, NY: F. W. Beers and Co., 1871.

Belcher, David B. and Robert Kelly. *Portraits of History*. Orange, MA: The Enterprise and Journal Publishing Company.

Care, Pearl B., et.al. *The History of Erving, Massachusetts*. Turners Falls, MA: Pioneer Litho, Incorporated, 1983.

Cox, Florence Cogswell. *History of New Salem, Massachusetts 1753-1953*. Amherst, MA: Hamilton I. Newell, Incorporated, 1953.

General Views of Orange. Orange, MA: George F. Bacon, 1900.

Millers River District Directory 1885. New Haven, CT: The Price and Lee Company, 1885.

Miner, Beatrice M. *History of Orange 1753-1976*. Orange, MA: Orange Historical Society, 1976.

Morse, Charles A. *Warwick, Massachusetts: Biography of a Town*. Cambridge, MA: Dresser, Chapman and Grimes, 1963.

"Orange 150th Anniversary." Greenfield, MA: *Greenfield Recorder-Gazette*, July 1, 1960, Section O.

Orange Illustrated. Orange, MA: J. S. Whitman.

Orange, Massachusetts 100th Anniversary Celebration July 3-4-5, 1910. Souvenir Booklet.

Discover Thousands of Local History Books Featuring Millions of Vintage Images

Arcadia Publishing, the leading local history publisher in the United States, is committed to making history accessible and meaningful through publishing books that celebrate and preserve the heritage of America's people and places.

Find more books like this at
www.arcadiapublishing.com

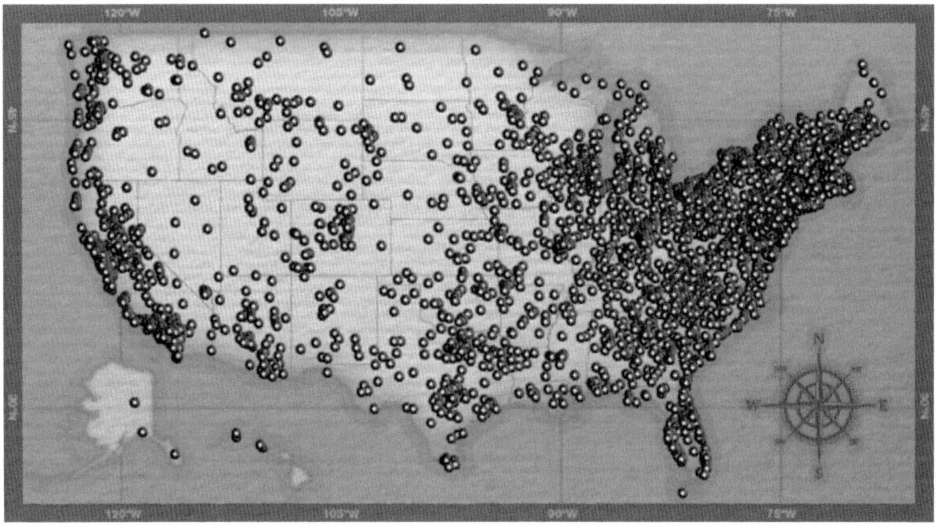

Search for your hometown history, your old stomping grounds, and even your favorite sports team.

Consistent with our mission to preserve history on a local level, this book was printed in South Carolina on American-made paper and manufactured entirely in the United States. Products carrying the accredited Forest Stewardship Council (FSC) label are printed on 100 percent FSC-certified paper.

MADE IN THE USA